Edited by Tony Flannery

Responding to
The Ryan Report

D0104840

the columba press

First published in 2009 by
the columba press
55A Spruce Avenue, Stillorgan Industrial Park,
Blackrock, Co Dublin

Cover by Bill Bolger
Origination by The Columba Press
Printed in Ireland by ColourBooks Ltd, Dublin

ISBN 978-1-85607-673-9

Table of Contents

Introduction

When The Columba Press contacted me, a week or so after the Ryan Report, asking me would I be willing to write a response, I was immediately interested. It is probably fair to say that this Report crept up on all of us. The impending Report on the Archdiocese of Dublin has been hyped for the past year, with stories of the archbishop being sickened by what he had read, and throwing papers across the room in disgust, while warning his priests to be ready for the worst, so our expectations of the horror of it all was such that we hardly considered that another report was coming before it. As a consequence I think most of us were somewhat caught off guard by Ryan, and maybe that added to its impact.

I grew up in the West of Ireland in the nineteen fifties. We would have been aware of the existence of Letterfrack, in particular. We knew it was a place of detention, but I don't think we were particularly interested in knowing much more about it, as long as there was no danger of us being sent there. It was part of life as we lived it. Boarded out children, as they were called, were common enough in our area. One family in my own native village had one. He came to them at the age of three, and stayed there until he grew up and moved on to make a life of his own. I have recently learned that when he was eight the authorities came to take him to Letterfrack. There was no reason for doing so, in that the young lad had settled in with the family, and was being well looked after. As far as I can find out it was the policy at the time that eight year olds would be taken from the foster home and sent to an institution. When the authorities arrived to take him away he ran and hid in the bog, where he could not be found. Eventually his foster mother proposed that if the authorities would allow him to stay she would not look for any further maintenance – which was a negligible sum anyway. They readily agreed to this. The young man stayed for ten more years or so, during which time the state showed no further interest in him, either in terms of supervision or financial support. I have thought of him recently, and how lucky he was to have found a safe bog hole on that fateful day. I have also thought of the warmth and generosity of the woman who cared for him and made him part of her family.

For the first few days, as we digested the contents of the Ryan Report, and were subject to blanket media coverage, I, like probably everyone else, was shocked by what I was hearing. We would have known that corporal punishment was part and parcel of life in Letterfrack and its equivalents, as it was in most schools at the time, including the one I myself was attending, but the seemingly sadistic violence described in some of the accounts was completely unexpected. More than that, the reality and extent of sexual abuse was harder to understand, especially for someone like myself who is a priest and a religious. Of course I knew that there were priests who had abused children. It would have been impossible to live in Ireland since the early nineties without being aware of this fact. The publication of the Ferns Report introduced it to us at a whole new level. I had also read up on the situation in the American church, and had some familiarity with the studies conducted over there, and the efforts to explain how it might have happened. But none of that was preparation for what Ryan revealed. The extent and the brutality of sexual abuse were almost unbelievable. For me it raised many questions – questions about our understanding of God and the Christian faith, questions about Catholic sexual teaching, about religious life, and maybe most fundamental of all, about human nature.

As I was tangling with these questions, and debating them with my friends, I found myself getting more and more irritated by the majority of the media coverage. I thought as the days went on that the level of comment was increasingly unhelpful. Too many of the regular media commentators were clearly not objective, but rather had obvious agendas of their own. I don't blame them for that, and some of them helped greatly in bringing the story out in the open, and for that we owe them a debt of gratitude. I am not here referring to former inmates of the institutions. It was good to hear their stories; they deserved all the airtime they were given, and I certainly would not have expected objective comment from them, no more than any of us are capable of objective comment when we have been the victims of an offence. Their voice was important, but in order to get a very necessary perspective on what had been revealed I felt we needed some really independent, dispassionate voices, people who were genuinely knowledgeable and could help us get our minds around a situation which is deeply complex.

The other absent voice, of course, was that of the religious who lost their nerve and were not willing to go public. They told me they were afraid they would not be listened to and that they would be savaged by more professional and media-savvy spokespeople. Some of them believed that the media were not at all interested in hearing their side of the story and that if they had gone on air to tell it the response would have been 'there they go again'. This may well have been true, but it was a sad comment on all the years of training in communication skills, and all the seminars we attended. Others have spoken about that in this volume, and I agree with them. But the effect of the shortage of genuinely knowledgeable and objective comment was that as the days went on the debate narrowed, and the problem was more and more laid at the door of the church and the religious, until eventually we got to the stage where it was being demanded that the Catholic Church and religious be removed from all involvement with the care of people.

An underlying assumption developed that abuse was a problem almost exclusively associated with priests and religious, and that if they were removed from the scene it would be solved. It was at that point that I decided that, if I was to agree to the request from The Columba Press, what was most needed was something that would broaden the debate, and introduce the sorts of voices that I felt were largely absent. I believed that the issue was of such crucial importance to the future of our society that all attempts at scapegoating had to be contested, and the focus brought back to the extent, the nature, and possible solutions to the problem. So I decided that the best way to respond was to try to get a wide range of people, from different backgrounds and expertise, to address it for me.

I initially approached people with caution, expecting a decided lack of enthusiasm. As one priest friend said to me, we priests and religious are no longer good news, and people might not want to be associated with us. Many were saying that this is not the right time to debate the issues, that it is too soon. But I believed that the church had given way to cowardice too often and that it was worth having a go at asking some people if they would be willing to write, to stick their necks out at this time. I was delighted by the response. Almost all the people I asked were immediately very interested and willingly agreed to write. I am happy that I have achieved what I set out to do. This collection of articles does not cover every aspect of the problem but it does indeed broaden the debate, and challenges many of the assumptions that I believe have been underlying the discussion to date.

Among the assumptions that are challenged in this volume are the following:

- That child abuse can be completely eradicated from society if the proper systems are put in place.
- That any adult who had sexual contact with a minor is a serial paedophile, and cannot be successfully treated.
- That all priests and religious should be living more admirable lives than the rest of the population.
- That a large proportion of priests and religious are child abusers.
- That Catholic Church teaching on sexuality is a true reflection of the teaching of Christ, and is adequate for the present age.

- That the Catholic Church's zero tolerance policy of treating all errant priests and religious in the same fashion is either fair or just.
- That all media outlets deal fairly and adequately with this topic, particularly as it relates to priests and religious.
- That monetary compensation never gives rise to false or exaggerated claims of abuse.
- That the Catholic Church has been seriously damaged by all these revelations.

The trouble with assumptions is that they usually contain some element of truth but may not give a full picture of reality. The contributors to this volume have tried to examine these assumptions and others. Some have verified them and some have challenged them but all have sought to analyse the issue of child abuse within society and the Catholic Church and voiced ideas and opinions that, in my view, have not been sufficiently aired to date.

I wish to thank all those who contributed to this volume for their generosity with their time and knowledge.

Tony Flannery

PART ONE:

THE ORIGINS OF THE PROBLEM

The Abuse and our Bad Theology

Seán Fagan

Ireland was shocked in October 2005 at the publication of the report on clerical sex abuse in the diocese of Ferns, but this almost paled into insignificance when in May 2009 years of investigation culminated in the publication of the Ryan Report. It revealed a cesspool of physical and sexual abuse tolerated by church and state in Ireland for more than 40 years. It named 800 abusers (religious and lay) in 26 institutions. The report made world headlines, but in fact Australia, New Zealand and Canada had already experienced similar scandals. In 2002 the American Bishops' National Review Board spent a year investigating sexual abuse by clergy and reported that since 1950 4,392 priests were accused of engaging in sexual abuse with a minor, which represented four per cent of the country's priests in active ministry. There were approximately 10,667 reported victims of clerical sexual abuse during this time. Shockingly, in very few cases did the diocese or religious order report allegations to the civil authorities, which meant that less than 200 out of a total of 4,392 priests were imprisoned. While numbers may vary, it is clear that the phenomenon is not limited to any one part of the world. It is clear too that the scandal is not limited to members of any particular church. Indeed horrendous cases have been discovered in Britain where abusers belonged to no church. It is a human problem, but the heinousness of it is all the more glaring when found among Christians, who believe that our God is a God of infinite love who created humans in his own image and likeness. The scandal is all the greater when it involves ordained priests and vowed religious.

Books, articles and newspaper correspondents have discussed the causes of this phenomenon around the world, but no single clear-cut suggestion explains all cases. Reputable studies on male rape in US prisons show that it is not a question of sexuality, but of power and control. This is indeed reflected in most cases of physical and sexual abuse, but there were other factors at work. The perfectionism and narrowness of Irish Catholicism itself were also to blame. The formation programmes of priests and religious left much to be desired. In practice, absolute obedience to the rule and the institution often damaged people deeply. They were encouraged to subdue the unruly passions of the body by mortification that often included self-flagellation. The suppression of sexual attitudes and desires at an early age often led to perverted and unhealthy expressions in later life. Today's young Catholics have no idea of what previous generations were forced to accept as 'church teaching' in the area of sexual morality. In fact, it can be claimed that it was the church's own bad theology that was largely responsible for the abuses that are now coming to light.

Cultural conditioning
Official church teaching today seldom acknowledges the harm done by its centuries-long negative understanding of sexuality. It sadly relies on reform by amnesia, quietly and conveniently forgetting the appalling views and attitudes it expressed in so much of its official teaching and practice for most of its history. To recall some of the details of that history can help us to 'relativise some of our false absolutes' with regard to our history and tradition. We too easily forget that all religion is historically and culturally conditioned. There is no word of God in pure unadulterated form, a-temporal and a-cultural. Every word in the Bible comes to us in human words, and every word from the moment when humans first learned to speak is culturally conditioned, reflecting the experience and culture of the speakers. This helps us to understand that the biblical accounts of the creation of the world and the beginnings of the human race are not historical facts, literally true, but stories that teach profound religious truths dressed in the simple thought-patterns of primitive people.

But metaphorical truth is as important as historical and physical truth. The beautiful truth of Genesis is that God created humans in his own image and likeness, that he created them male and female, that they were naked and were not ashamed, and that he was pleased with his creation.

The Israelite understanding of sin developed in keeping with a primitive notion of God. The Jewish people had a special experience of God as a personal being who consecrated them as his chosen ones: 'I am almighty God, obey me and always do what is right and I will make my covenant with you ... I will be your God' (Gen 17). But, just as every adult still carries within him the infant and adolescent he once was, the Israelites down through the centuries continued to be influenced by more primitive notions of an autocratic, enforcing God, a rewarding and punishing God, a God more interested in his own laws and decrees than in people. In spite of the gospels and the teaching of Jesus, much of this attitude carried over into Christian spirituality and church life. Counsellors and spiritual directors today are only too familiar with the fear and scrupulosity this attitude gave rise to in the lives of Catholics.

History is there to show how much the church's teaching has changed through the centuries. A narrow view of the church's teaching role has given the impression that the changes were only minor details, and that on all major points there is an unbroken line of tradition going back to scripture itself or to the early Christian communities. This is simply not the case. So much of church teaching had little or nothing to do with divine revelation. It is too easily forgotten that it was the constant teaching for centuries that intercourse had to be for the purpose of procreation in order to be free of sin, that intercourse during menstruation or pregnancy was a mortal sin, and that any other position apart from the so-called 'natural' one (husband on top) was at least a venial sin. St Augustine taught that intercourse during pregnancy is gravely sinful, indeed a greater sin than fornication, adultery or even incest, provided that these are done with the intention of producing a baby. He set up flawed standards of sexual behaviour which no-one could possibly live out without crippling emotional damage producing failure, shame and guilt. But he was not alone in his views. They were almost universal among Christian theologians for centuries. Catholic spirituality until recent times was deeply influenced by Augustine's negative view of sexuality and his glorification of the celibate state. Although he confessed that for years he could not spend a single night without the company of a woman, he also wrote rhetorically in his book on marriage: 'What Christian men of our time, being free of the marriage bond, having the power to abstain from all sexual intercourse, would not choose to keep virginal or widowed continence, than to endure that tribulation of the flesh without which marriages cannot be?' The culture of Augustine's time idealised intellectual friendship so that he felt free to love and be loved by men in a way that he could not feel free to relate to women. In fact, Augustine would have rejected any affectionate feelings towards women as being sexually motivated.

Anti-feminism

All through the centuries of tradition, reaching back into the Old Testament and beyond, there is a negative attitude to women and all things feminine. In the early centuries all the physical sexual processes of women were associated with corruption. Defloration corrupted the body initially and childbirth even more. Religious rites such as the 'churching' of women did not consecrate childbirth, but cleansed women of the impurity deriving from it. Women's reproductive organs were considered foul and menstruation was perceived not only as ritually impure, but as having magical properties. In spite of the Genesis account of the complementarity of the sexes, and the personal roles played by many women in the Old Testament, women were considered the property of men, with a utilitarian value. In its original context, the sixth commandment of the Decalogue was not concerned about sexual morality as much as with the injustice done to husband or father by the man who has unlawful relations with a girl. Jewish rabbis feared women as a distraction and temptation. They were generally considered greedy, curious, lazy, and jealous. Christian writers took over Aristotle's notion of the female as a half-baked man. Nearly a thousand years later, St Thomas Aquinas (1225-1274) found no reason to differ from this view or even to question it; he accepted it as a fact of nature. With all the arrogance and simplicity of the male, he discussed whether women should have been created at all, and with colossal ignorance (natural enough for his time) he proclaimed that the female is something defective and manqué. Often quoted by church authorities as an oracle on natural law, he maintained that even before original sin, women by nature would have been governed by men for their own good, because the power of rational discernment is by nature stronger in men.

Pessimistic bias
St Paul could compare marriage to the union between Christ and the church and vice versa. But no matter how well the glories of Christian marriage were later sung by the great doctors of the church, their pessimism came through. According to Augustine, only procreation could justify marriage, sex, or even women. Pope St Gregory the Great (540-604) affirmed that it was as impossible to have intercourse without sin as it was to fall into a fire and not burn. Clement of Alexandria (d 215) compared marital intercourse to 'an incurable disease, a minor epilepsy'. The great St Jerome (345-420) held that virginity was the norm in paradise, that marriage came about as a result of sin, and that the only good in marriage is that it can give birth to virgins. St Bernardine of Siena (1380-1444) claimed that of 1000 marriages, 999 are of the devil's making. One wonders how he did the survey. This was in the 'age of faith', when most of the known world was Christian. The same saint, the greatest preacher in Europe in his day, maintained that it was a piggish irreverence and a mortal sin if husband and wife do not abstain from intercourse for several days before receiving holy communion.

From the sixth to the sixteenth century nuns and lay women were forbidden to enter a church or take communion during their periods. The penalty for breaking the law was three days fasting on bread and water. This notion of ritual impurity infiltrated Christian thinking from pagan superstition, according to which terrible things were believed to happen when women touched anything during their periods: crops would dry up, fruit rot on the trees and iron would turn rusty. For centuries women were perceived as intrinsically inferior, passive and dependent, if not the outright possessions of men. As the church became gradually more institutionalised in the early centuries, the power of the clergy depended on their ability to control sexual practices, to impose sexual taboos, and to impose their decrees with sanctions. We have thankfully moved beyond this ignorance and prejudice, but women are still waiting for church leaders to give practical recognition to the equality of the sexes.

Original sin
St Augustine of Hippo (354-430) is regarded as one of the church's greatest theologians, but it is a real tragedy that his teaching on marriage and sexuality has been accepted as the bedrock of official teaching down to the present day. It is taken for granted that his devotion to his slave-girl who was the mother of his son provided him with an experience of marriage, but this is far from the truth. At the age of eighteen when he took an African concubine, he joined the Manichees, a sect which renounced most of the ordinary pleasures of life associated with eating, drinking and sexual expression. When his companion left him after fifteen years to return to Africa, he took another concubine, and then was converted and baptised as a Christian at the age of thirty-three. In spite of the grace of conversion he carried much of the Manichean influence in his thinking for the rest of his life. He had no real understanding of marriage but only his own guilt-ridden experience of long years of sinful fornication. He believed that there was nothing rational, spiritual or sacramental in the act of intercourse. He saw it as intimately

linked to original sin, a distortion that has blighted Catholic theology until the present day, believing that innocent babies are born with original sin (linked to their genitals) needing exorcism in baptism and their mothers needing to be 'churched' to purify them after childbirth. This teaching crucified devout Catholic mothers who suffered up to ten or more still-births and still worry today about the fate of their unborn children in the nonsense teaching about Limbo. Only very recently has the church's theological guess-work on this subject been changed.

It is easy to criticise the views of Augustine on the relations between men and women, but in fairness it must be admitted that his perceptions in this area were cultural, not theological. They reflected the culture of Roman society in the fifth century. Graeco-Roman culture understood marriage as a legal alliance concerned with power, economics and kinship, although during Augustine's life-time a sentimental ideal had been developing which emphasised the desirability of marital concord between spouses. But Augustine had no difficulty with the culture of his time and the status he allotted to women included them in the category of virtual non-persons who could be beaten with impunity. For him married women were not only servile, but unspiritual. He described the sexually active woman in marriage as carnal and unredeemed while her husband shares the same title as Christ, *Dominus*, Lord. Augustine keenly felt that the response of the human body to passion, and specifically the male erection, is beyond the control of the will, and this led him to declare that the inability to control the genital organs becomes a punishment for sin inscribed in the body. As humanity sinned against God, so a man's body rebels against him, and for Augustine this becomes the symbol of the primal or original sin that introduced death into the world. In Augustine's theology the mutual desire between spouses is not a positive aspect of marital relationships, but one which is overshadowed by sin and death. However, in spite of his complex theology of sexual desire as the symbol of death, when it came to sexual relationships in marriage Augustine insisted that both were called to fidelity and chastity. Nevertheless he insisted that carnal desire, namely sexual desire not motivated by the desire for children, is never acceptable, even in marriage, although it may be tolerated and forgiven, because it is an evil which came from original sin. Augustine says quite bluntly that sex is corrupting if it is enjoyed, and in fact a man who loves his wife with passion is an adulterer with his wife. This completely negative, if not abhorrent, view of sexuality is totally incompatible with the Christian mystics who have no hesitation in describing God's love for his people in marital terms, not to mention the bible's beautiful Song of Songs ... It is also far removed from the tradition of Judaism, which holds that intercourse on the Sabbath reflects the divine ideal, and that man is most like God when he makes love with his wife. Augustine's ideal of sexless marriage where intercourse and childbirth are seen as corruption and a loss of integrity should have no place in Christian theology, spirituality or asceticism.

The essence of marriage
Augustine's theology of original sin which was bequeathed to the whole Catholic Church of the West was unknown in the East. Genesis and Jesus describe the essence of marriage as the 'two becoming one flesh', whereas Augustine blasphemously changed those words of Jesus into: 'in intercourse a man becomes all flesh' (Sermons, 62, 2). He also wrote: 'I feel nothing turns the masculine mind from the heights than female blandishments and that contact of bodies without which a wife may not be had.' One tragic result of this is that those beautiful words of Jesus describing the essence of marriage as 'two-in-one-flesh', the intimacy which is the very heart of a couple's relationship, have seldom been used in official church teaching down to the present time. The intimacy of 'two-in-one-flesh' regularly experienced by a married couple is like the co-operation of mating birds lovingly collaborating to build a comfortable nest that will be a home for their family.

Unfortunately the negative legacy of Augustine is still presented as church teaching on sexuality. That sexuality in marriage was marred forever by original sin is clearly stated in the 1994 *Catechism of the Catholic Church*: 'As a break with God, the first sin had for its consequence the rupture of the original communion between man and woman. Their relations were distorted by mutual recriminations, their mutual attraction, the Creator's own gift, changed into a relationship of domination and lust, and the beautiful vocation of man and woman to be fruitful, multiply and subdue the earth was burdened by the pain of childbirth and the toil of work' (n 1607). This is straight out of Augustine, but is it in fact what Catholics feel as they make their marriage vows to each other in the presence of God and of the Christian community? Karol Wojtyla's *Love and Responsibility*, published in Polish in 1960 and in English in 1981 when he was pope, tried to present romantic love in contrast to Augustine's theology, but modern Catholic women are not impressed by much of his thinking. For example, speaking of intercourse he explains that 'it is in the very nature of the act that the man plays the active role and takes the initiative, whilst the woman is a comparatively passive partner, whose function it is to accept and experience. For the purpose of the sexual act it is enough for her to be passive and unresisting, so much so that it can even take place without her volition, while she is a state in which she has no awareness at all of what is happening, for instance when she is asleep or unconscious.' Can this be Catholic Church teaching? It sounds like rape.

St John Chrysostom (347-407), one of the most prestigious of the Doctors of the Church, shared Augustine's view of original sin with his statement that 'only after the banishment from paradise did the question of sex arise. Adam and Eve lost their virginity once they became disobedient. Before that, children were born through God's creative act, since our first parents had the nature of angels.' Almost a thousand years later St Bonaventure (1224-1274), known as the Seraphic Doctor and one of the greatest theologians in the history of the church, distinguished three stages in the sexual act, namely: '(1) the opening of the locked

gate, (2) lust, which is payment for sin, and (3) vile pleasure …
The sex act brings a blush of shame because of the ugliness
associated with it. Originally, the excitement of the genitals
would have only taken place from the action of will and reason.
Adam and Eve would have only copulated at precisely given
times and only for the purpose of reproduction.'

Jansenism
The negative views on sexuality propagated by the church's
most distinguished theologians down through the centuries
provided fertile ground for fear, anxiety and scrupulosity when
associated with the unChristian picture of God as the autocratic,
enforcing God, the rewarding and punishing God who can penetrate the depths of our subconscious to discover our most
shameful thoughts and feelings. This combination gave rise to
the Jansenist movement in France in the 17th and 18th centuries,
which was brought back to Ireland by priests who had studied
in France. Originally the movement had a spirituality with a
special appreciation of the liturgy, emphasising the role of the
laity in church life, with a reverential awe of the holy. But it also
contained a very pessimistic view of the human condition which
quickly became linked with the more severe aspects of Celtic
Christianity. It viewed human nature as totally perverted by
original sin, needing harsh measures to be dominated and controlled. This soon became an integral part of Irish Catholicism,
linking up with the church's own tradition of harsh asceticism
and idealised perfectionism. When seen in the context of the
country's poverty and persecution, it is not surprising that this
combination gave rise to the harshness and cruelty publicised in
the recent reports.

Today's young Irish Catholics have no idea of the Jansenism
of Irish Catholicism in the past, but the older generation still
alive can remember the scrupulosity and fear that accompanied
so much of our religion within living memory. Churches were
crowded for mission-weeks and one of the high points was the
special hell-fire sermons on purity and 'company-keeping.'

These could be titillating and sometimes humorous, but they were also fearsome, and preachers are now embarrassed just to remember them. Those same preachers are now ashamed to think of the morality they were expected to preach. Textbooks of moral theology published up to the 1960s went into great detail explaining the difference between the 'private' and 'semi-private' parts of the human body, and had long lists of 'sins of impurity'. For example, it was taught that 'prolonged and repeated kissing is often a mortal sin; to look at the private parts of a person of the opposite sex is mortally sinful, unless done unexpectedly or superficially, momentarily or from a distance or if it a question of little children, birds or small animals.' It was usually a mortal sin to read bad books, even though they are not entirely immoral, because this excites sexual passion. One of the most appalling principles preached was that 'company-keeping with the intention of early marriage was considered a necessary occasion of sin.' In all of this it must be remembered that mortal sin meant hell for all eternity.

Catholic parents are saddened that so many of their adult children no longer go to church, but church leaders miss the point when they blame only modern culture for this. Materialism, individualism and secularism are part of the modern world, but that is the world we live in, and if our Christian faith cannot cope with it there is something lacking in our religion. That Catholic Ireland could allow the institutionalised physical and sexual abuse that occurred in so many of our institutions for over six decades raises questions about the quality of our Catholicism. We are faced with a huge challenge, but the first step should be to cease the centuries-old policy of *reform by amnesia*. We need to recognise the bad theology that was such a negative feature of our religion, unquestioned for centuries, and face up to the challenge of renewal. We must take seriously the call of Vatican II to return to the gospel and to see that our church, like Jesus, is meant to be a light to the world.

CHAPTER TWO

The Shaping of Irish Religious Life

Brendan McConvery CSsR

In his influential study of religious life, Raymond Hostie advanced two theses that are of particular interest to the story of religious life in Ireland.[1] The first suggested that from its origins in the Egyptian desert in the third century, religious life has tended to develop and flourish on the margins of life, far from the centre. In the second thesis, he suggested that religious groups commonly experience crises at relatively predictable moments in their lives. The first usually comes after about thirty years or so, when the initial excitement has subsided. The second critical moment comes on the death of the founder when identity and memory is threatened. If they survive these two, the history of religious life predicts a further moment of crisis that begins towards the end of the second centenary of their existence. While in many respects religious life in Ireland was little different from elsewhere, there are some distinctions of emphasis that can only be understood by looking at its origins and development. Such is the object of this article.

1. In from the Margins?

By the middle of the eighteenth century, the religious communities that had survived the Reformation and the Penal Laws were at a low ebb. Small communities of friars (Franciscan, Dominican, Augustinian and a smaller number of Carmelites) clung tenaciously to the hinterland of their ancient sites in rural Ireland or functioned discreetly in the towns and cities.[2] Their very survival was threatened by the ban on accepting new candidates into Irish novitiates.[3] The situation of the handful of religious women's communities associated with the friars was even worse. The beginnings of a revival emerged with the introduction of the first community of Ursulines to Cork in 1771. For the rest of that century religious life in mainland Europe was to undergo a cataclysmic change, as the French revolution and the subsequent wars swept many of the convents and monasteries away. It was on the margins of Irish society that religious life was to experience a new impetus.

A woman called Nano Nagle brought a community of Ursulines to Cork to run the free schools for the poor she had established with her own endowment. But she hadn't anticipated the degree to which their observance of the strict rules of monastic enclosure would prove a barrier to the work. Within a few years, she was forced to establish her own Congregation of the Sisters of Charitable Instruction of the Sacred Heart (1776) to undertake the work of education, visitation of the sick and relief of the poor she had in mind. Over the next few decades, there was to be a veritable explosion in the number of native religious congregations. Bishop Daniel Delaney brought together a group of women in 1807 that would prove to be the nucleus of the Sisters of St Brigid. Mary Aikenhead and her first companions made their vows as Irish Sisters of Charity in 1815. Frances Ball formed an Irish branch of the Institute of the Blessed Virgin Mary, known as the Loreto Sisters in 1821. In 1827, Catherine McAuley formed the group of women who had gathered around her 'House of Mercy' in Baggot Street into the nucleus of the Sisters of Mercy. The second half of the century saw the foundation of the Sisters of the Holy Faith (1857) and the Sisters of St John of God (1871).

Men's congregations developed more slowly and remained fewer in number. Edmund Rice and six companions adopted a form of Nano Nagle's rule as the Irish Christian Brothers in 1808. A group which seceded from the main body around 1826 became the Presentation Brothers. The male counterpart of the Brigidine Sisters, the Brothers of St Patrick, was founded in 1808. Two smaller and more localised groups of brothers were also formed about this time. A group following the Carmelite Rule eventually formed two houses in Dublin, while the Franciscan

Brothers founded in Mountbellew, Co Galway in 1818, remained largely confined to the West of Ireland. The number of brothers was increased by the arrival of the De La Salle Brothers, devoted, like the Irish Christian Brothers, to the education of the poor, and the Alexian Brothers and Brothers of St John of God (1880) devoted to nursing work. The Missionary Societies of St Columban (1918) and St Patrick (1932) were the first Irish clerical foundations, apart from an informal group of priests working in the Dublin area during the 1840s which eventually sought entrance into the Congregation of the Missions (Vincentians).

Following the Great Famine, and sometimes in flight from fresh political upheavals on the European continent, new orders of men and women began to arrive in Ireland. They included, in fairly rapid succession, Rosminians (1848), Redemptorists (1853), Passionists (1856) and Oblates of Mary Immaculate (1856). Women's congregations, such as the Faithful Companions of Jesus (1843), Good Shepherd Sisters (1848), St Louis Sisters (1859), Bon Secours (1865) all of which originated in post-Revolutionary France, added a more international character to Irish women's religious life.

At the beginning of the nineteenth century there were six congregations of religious women with a total of eleven convents. By century's end that had grown to 35 congregations with 368 houses, to say nothing of the growing number of men's communities.[4] In terms of membership, religious women in Ireland in 1800 numbered 120. By mid-century, this had grown to 1,500 and in 1901 to 8,000.[5] The phenomenal growth of women's religious life continued into the twentieth century, if at a much slower pace, with the foundation of the Columban Sisters (1924), Medical Missionaries of Mary (1937) and Franciscan Missionaries for Africa (1952). The distinctive feature of the twentieth century foundations is that they were oriented towards the foreign missions as against working for the poor at home.

If the explosion of religious life in late eighteenth and early nineteenth centuries in Ireland confirms Hostie's first thesis, then his second thesis goes some distance to explaining their compar-

atively rapid decline in the past three decades or so. Having survived the death of their founders and undergone sometimes fairly
profound re-orientations of their original vision, the transition to
the third century of their life cycle ushered in a time of upheaval
and decline. Counting two hundred years from Nano Nagle's
initial foundation brings us to the year 1976. The preceding
decade had been a time of unprecedented change. The Second
Vatican Council invited all religious communities to undertake a
radical reappraisal of their way of life (*Perfectae Caritatis: Decree on
the Adaptation and Renewal of Religious Life*, 1965). It was embraced
with enthusiasm by the majority of Irish religious, but it led to a
dramatic level of institutional upheaval. It also coincided with
profound social change in Irish society, so it is little wonder that
these four decades have seen a degree of far-reaching change that
could not have been anticipated at the time.

Social Class – Within and Without

Although religious profess a vow of poverty, one of the most
striking features of the story of Irish religious life is the extent to
which its founders were people of quite considerable personal
wealth or social position. Nano Nagle, Catherine McAuley,
Mary Aikenhead and Teresa Ball all possessed large personal
fortunes which enabled them to endow the first good works undertaken by their congregations. By present reckoning, Edmund
Rice's fortune would probably have made him a millionaire. In
the twentieth century, the founder of the Columban Sisters was
Lady Frances Maloney, widow of the Governor General of
Trinidad. Mary Martin, founder of the Medical Missionaries of
Mary, came from a wealthy Dublin mercantile family.

Maria Luddy has studied the role played by women of
means, both Catholic and Protestant, in philanthropic causes in
the nineteenth century.[6] She notes that while Protestant laywomen continued to support charitable causes throughout this
period, Catholic laywomen became involved with religious
communities.

It was not the founders alone who belonged to a higher social
stratum. Most of the women entering brought with them a sum

of money as a 'dowry'. While the extent of the dowry remains unclear, a study by Clear suggests that they varied in size.[7] The average dowry in the Galway Mercy Convent between 1840 and 1857 was about £375 (c €30,000 in today's value). A wealthy heiress entering Loreto in Rathfarnham brought with her £35,000 (perhaps worth as much as €3million today).

Not all women entering religious life were able to bring a dowry with them, nor did they have the education that would enable them to teach. Although the early founders declared that a dowry was no obstacle to entry and could be compensated with education on the one hand or good will and industry on the other, nevertheless a two tier system of membership began to evolve. The earliest text in western monasticism, the Rule of St Benedict, assumes the existence of a single class of monks who will devote themselves without exception to the same daily round of prayer, reading and manual work. By about the tenth or eleventh century, as monastic estates became larger, monasteries were admitting brothers who would be exempt from the increasingly lengthy Divine Office to devote themselves almost exclusively to manual labour. In time this became the accepted practice in the new orders of friars and female communities. It was also a feature of the newly founded Irish religious congregations. Members were divided into 'choir' (those who were able to read the Divine Office in Latin and who were qualified to teach or nurse) and 'lay' sisters or brothers, exempt from much of the community prayers but responsible for the housekeeping of the convent or monastery and the work of farm or garden. The Christian Brothers for instance, got authorisation from Rome permitting them to receive 'serving brothers' in 1833.[8]

While this division of labour had the advantage of opening religious life to people of more humble origin and with little education, it created a dual form of membership regulated by increasingly water-tight social distinctions. There were, for example, differences of dress. Lay-brothers in Redemptorist communities did not wear the same white collar on the habit as priests, students and choir-novices. Among the Dominicans, lay sisters and brothers wore a black scapular over the white habit instead of the white one of the choir-members. In Mercy communities, the habit of the choir sisters had a train attached like the formal dresses of Victorian ladies, pinned up when not in use but let down to trail along the floor for more solemn occasions such as receiving holy communion. They also wore a white mantel in choir on solemn occasions. The lay-sisters enjoyed none of these: instead, a white apron worn over the habit marked them off as having the more or less same social status as the maids of an upper middle-class household. This up-stairs/down-stairs mentality was manifest in the other aspects of community life. While the Rule might proclaim that all the members were equal and ate at the common table, petty distinctions of status included separate places in chapel or dining-room, shorter periods of recreation for the lay members, and minor irritants such as the prohibition to read newspapers and periodicals. While the majority of the lay entrants had primary education and could read and write, little enough was done to advance their general level of education or culture. As Maria Luddy has remarked, the internal social structure of convents (and houses of men) mirrored the social divisions which existed in society at large. Lay religious probably bore such distinctions in the same spirit of religious fatalism of Frances Alexander's Victorian hymn:

> The rich man in his castle,
> The poor man at his gate,
> God made them high and lowly,
> He ordered their estate.

That it is not to say that the narrowness they imply caused no pain, but they do speak of 'a large gulf that no-one can cross' (cf Luke 16:26) and of possibilities squandered.

Something of the same class distinction is observable in the chosen fields of activity of the congregations. We have seen Nano Nagle's surprise at the reluctance of the first Ursulines to undertake the education of the poor. They devoted themselves instead to the education of the daughters of the well-off. Some congregations soon became identified with a particular segment of society. While the Mercy Sisters and Christian Brothers undertook the education of the working-class, the schools of the Jesuits, Spiritans, Vincentians, and several orders of women, were for the education of the elite. In some instances the curriculum of the particular schools may have been geared to the state in life of the pupils, but this was not universally the case. Asenath Nicholson, a doughty American Evangelical with feminist leanings who travelled throughout the country distributing bible texts in the years immediately prior to the Famine, compares the breadth of the curriculum of the nuns' school in Ventry, Co Kerry with the narrowness of the neighbouring Evangelical Mission school.

> Here there were more than three hundred of the poor taught in the most thorough manner. Their lessons in grammar, geography and history would do honour to any school and their needlework is of the highest order. Their teacher observed: 'Though they are the children of the poor, we do not know what station God may call them to fill. We advance them as far as possible while they are with us.[9]

The needlework taught by the sisters, for example, gave rise to the small industries in Limerick, Carrickmacross and elsewhere.

Maria Luddy has shown that the religious women who ran the houses of refuge for women engaged in prostitution reached out to more women, numerically speaking, than did the lay women who ran the other asylums of this kind.[10] While the management style of these establishments created a strong element of dependency, in that the women were treated as children, the conditions under which they lived, at least as regards diet and clothing, were better than most could hope to aspire to outside the system.[11] Although the nuns preferred to minister to women and children, their impact on every aspect of social care became clearer as their numbers increased. In addition to running schools and engaging in home nursing and relief of the poor, they moved into public hospitals and workhouses, where it was believed that 'they breathe insensibly a higher tone and a different standard'.[12] Also, on occasions, the sisters were capable of responding with courage and imagination to demanding and unforeseen challenges, such as the group of Mercy sisters who went to nurse at the Crimean front in 1854.[13]

Just as the majority of religious would never have dreamed of questioning the unequal social world of their convent or monastery, neither would it have crossed their minds to question the inequalities of the social world of the poor, except where they made a connection between poverty and the tendency to drunkenness, vice or improvidence. That would have to wait for the post-Vatican II generation who would gradually learn the lesson that the 'joys and the hopes, the griefs and the anxieties of the people of this age, especially those who are poor or in any way afflicted, are the joys and hopes, the griefs and anxieties of the followers of Christ. Indeed, nothing genuinely human fails to raise an echo in their hearts' (*Gaudium et Spes* 1). This thinking, emerging in the mid nineteen sixties, gradually led to social analysis, and in some cases social or even political action, which changed the face of religious life.

Who's in charge here?
At the beginnings of monasticism, each house was a self-governing community under an abbot or the female equivalent. With the rise of the Friars in the Middle Ages, authority and decision-making became more centralised under a Superior General, elected by and responsible to the General Chapter which met every three years or so. Many of the religious groups founded after the Reformation adopted the model of government outlined in the Jesuit Constitutions, whereby power lay almost exclusively with the Superior General, often elected for life, and exercised through provincial and local superiors directly appointed by him. Although the General continued to be elected by a Chapter, he was no longer directly answerable to its members, and chap-

ters became relatively occasional affairs (the Redemptorists, for example, held no General Chapter between 1853 and 1896!). These three models of government and authority, sometimes with variations, directed the lives of Irish religious.

It is anomalous that the majority of Irish congregations of sisters founded at the turn of the eighteenth/nineteenth centuries reverted to the older monastic system of independent, nominally self-governing houses. I say 'nominally' because their ultimate superior was the bishop of the diocese. While the superior and her council were elected by the community and followed the guidance of the Rule, Constitutions and Customs of the house, the diocesan bishop was the ultimate court of appeal. It was he who conducted the annual canonical visitation of the community, either in person or through his Vicar. He was the ultimate arbiter of doubtful cases. He determined the apostolate of the school or hospital. He had to be consulted even in many petty details relating to the everyday life of the community, from arrangements for the community holiday to details of the daily timetable. Another drawback in small, independent communities was that two sisters frequently alternated in the office of superior for years on end, like figures emerging from a weather-clock.

While many of these communities were happy family-like places, sometimes including several sets of aunts and cousins, there was a danger that they could become inward-looking. A woman entering was likely to spend the rest of her life in the same community, unless it had a smaller dependent branch house or she was called to be a member of a founding group elsewhere. Religious formation, such as it was, consisted in learning the traditions of the community, studying approved, but mind-numbingly boring, manuals of the spiritual life such as *Practise of Christian and Religious Perfection* by a seventeenth century Spanish Jesuit or the *True Spouse of Jesus Christ*, or the *Nun Sanctified by the Duties of her State in Life* by the eighteenth century Italian St Alphonsus Liguori. There was almost no theology, history or scripture in the wider sense, leading to great intellectual impoverishment of the members. As religious communities became more a part of the landscape, applicants entered at a younger age. While the founders and their first companions were people of mature years (Edmund Rice, for example was a prosperous merchant and widower with a handicapped child), more and more entrants came straight from school, sometimes a preparatory school run by the community. The pattern in the Christian Brothers, for instance, up until the mid-1960s, was particularly unusual: candidates from the brothers' preparatory college entered the novitiate at the earliest age permitted by Canon Law, sixteen years of age, immediately after their Intermediate Certificate and continued their secondary studies after profession.

International congregations were somewhat better off. At least they could refer to a wider world and would be likely to change houses after some years. Their court of appeal was firstly to the higher superiors within their congregation, giving them some independence from the local bishop. Some bishops did not tolerate religious within their diocese looking beyond their authority. Bishop Furlong of Ferns, for instance, insisted that two communities in his diocese break away from their mother stem – a community of Bon Secours became the Sisters of St John of God, and a community of the French congregation of Mary Reparatrice became an independent convent of Perpetual Adoration.

A similar situation in Cork, at a time when Edmund Rice was attempting to centralise the government of his community, led to some members breaking off to form the Presentation Brothers directly under the control of the bishop. After a period as independent communities, they too opted for a more centralised form of government in 1889.[14] It was only in the period of renewal following Vatican II that many of these communities began to restructure. After an intermediate period of diocesan unions, the Mercy Sisters formed the united congregation of Mercy Ireland in 1994. The Presentation Sisters presently form three distinct Irish groups.

From Sisters to Nuns, from Brothers to Monks

Within a little over twenty years of her death in 1784 at the age of 66, Nano Nagle's Sisters of Charitable Instruction of the Sacred Heart had become the Order of the Presentation, bound by solemn vows and monastic enclosure, the very things that had caused her disappointment in the Ursulines she had brought from France. While this imposition of a cloistered style of life was most dramatic in the case of the Presentation sisters, no group was immune from the Roman desire to impose monastic structures on their way of life. Cloister or enclosure implied separation from the world and especially separation from family. In practice, it meant that the inner parts of the convent were reserved for the members of the community and visits home were strictly regulated. In some cases it took on bizarre features. Rules of enclosure often prevented religious from visiting sick parents or family members or even attending their funerals. While admittedly an extreme case, it was not unknown for a sister passing close to her family home on her way to the foreign missions to be allowed visit on condition that she did not enter the house and greeted family members in a car parked outside. Religious who were assigned to a foreign posting, in America, Australia or on the foreign missions, might expect never to return home, though as travel became faster and cheaper, such life-long exile became rarer.

It is difficult to assess the impact of the Gothic Revival on the shaping of religious life in the mid-19th century, but its heritage would endure until Vatican II. The Gothic revival was a child of the late Romantic Movement and sought to retrieve a medieval tradition that was often deficient in its grasp of history. The French Dominican revival is a case in point and it would soon penetrate the rest of the Order, including Ireland. A similar renewal movement would touch the Franciscans later in the century when Leo XIII formed the many disparate congregations into three separate branches (Friars Minor, Capuchin and Conventual) in 1897 and distanced them from the adaptation to local conditions the friars had made during the penal period.[15] This fascination with the Middle Ages was particularly striking in the use of a Gothic style of architecture in convent and church building. The Convent of Mercy, Birr, was founded in 1840, within about thirteen years of the beginning of the congregation. The convent building was designed by A. W. Pugin and would not have been out of place in a medieval English village. Pugin's successors and Irish pupils such as McCarthy and George Ashlin, continued the trend of housing religious in buildings that were markedly medieval, often pleasing to the eye but not particularly practical for those who had to live in them.

Other aspects of the increasing tendency towards monasticism in the new religious orders included the religious habit and the adoption of a religious name. The older orders who had survived the penal period seldom wore a habit, or if they did, it was within the confines of the religious house. Nano Nagle was shocked when her Ursulines proposed to adopt a full religious habit in place of the more discreet 'French nightcaps and black gowns' they had worn at the beginning.[16] Throughout the remainder of the nineteenth century, the dress of woman religious became increasingly monastic and unwieldy in its form. In some cases, what had been at the time of the foundation the ordinary dress of the people, had become stylised into a form that bore little resemblance to what the founders originally had in mind. The most striking case of this is the dress of the Daughters of Charity of St Vincent De Paul with its elaborate starched linen 'butterfly' head-dress that had originally been the formal Sunday dress of French peasant women. While male religious would, with some exceptions, wear a more 'secular' form of clerical dress (dark suit and Roman collar) outside the community, women religious would wear the habit at all times.

Few religious communities permitted members to retain their baptismal names. Although the Christian Brothers were usually known by their surname to their pupils and the world at large, each brother received a religious name for community use. As communities became larger, novice directors were forced to search the martyrology or Butler's *Lives of the Saints* for new names to impose on their charges. In some cases, the name was completed by the addition of a phrase e.g. Sister Mary Berchmans of the Holy Name. The loss of a name brings with it, to some degree at least, the loss of an identity. Theologically speaking, the fundamental Christian identity is that of baptism where one receives a name and status as a child of God. Some theologians conceived (wrongly, it would now be agreed) of religious profession as a 'second baptism' and this was symbolised by the giving of a new name. What were the long-term effects of such a loss of personal and family identity implied in a name change? It gave the person a new patron or model for imitation. But if a woman was given a male saint's name, with its implied negation of feminine identity in favour of a male one, it hardly amounted to a useful model.

Many religious communities also adopted forms of penitential exercises that had become common in the middle ages. Apart from ordinary days of fasting imposed by common church law, most kept additional days according to the traditions of the community. Some also adopted the practice of the discipline, or self-flagellation, and the pointed iron-chain worn on arm, leg or waist, known as the cilice (from the Latin word *cilicium*, hair shirt). Penitential practices like these, it should be observed, were not exclusive to religious. They were commonly practised (and sometimes still are) by lay confraternities, especially in Italy, Spain and its colonies. They have long fallen out of use in religious houses. It is difficult for people today to see their relevance, especially in the light of psychological reservations about their possible sado-masochistic implications. The theory was that religious were inspired by devotion to the Passion of Jesus and wished to experience something of his actual sufferings. Manuals of formation encouraged moderate use of the discipline. The length of time was regulated by the recitation of a prayer (*Miserere* psalm or a number of Our Fathers and Hail Marys). They also warned of the danger of excess, reminding the nun or brother that the real mortification demanded by their way of life was an interior one, the conquest of wrong and unhealthy desires which might be better promoted by the discreet avoidance of some innocent pleasure.

This brings us to the question of formation for the religious vows, especially obedience and celibacy. Formation manuals commonly set the standard of obedience as 'blind obedience', proposing as an ideal that a religious should become like a stick in the hands of a superior. Formation sometimes set simple tasks that seemed to fly in the face of reason but would supposedly train the novice for the time when they would automatically become capable of obeying without hesitation or question. This training in obedience was designed to help the religious to respond generously to what may have been personally unpalatable but was for the good of the community or the church. The primacy of obedience in Catholic life was significantly reinforced by the promulgation of the dogma of Papal Infallibility in 1870. But it received a rude shock during World War II when blind obedience to Hitler permitted the horrors of the death camps. The German Redemptorist theologian Bernard Haring has described the shock to his own religious training when it came in collision with a secular form of the same doctrine during his time as a medical orderly in the German army on the Russian Front.[17] Today's religious would be more in tune with Herbert McCabe's reading of obedience as 'the solidarity of friends with a common task. It is a question of human love founded on a shared purpose but this human love is our life of grace.'[18]

Formation in celibacy was equally complex. Irish Catholic Jansenism, if there ever was such a thing, cannot fully explain the prevailing attitudes. There was also in nineteenth and early twentieth century Ireland a strong element of Victorian social prudery that touched Protestants as well as Catholics. An example of this, I believe, is the reticence of the Christian Brothers about Edmund Rice's status as husband and father until comparatively recent times. The moral theology manuals for the guidance of confessors stated clearly that 'in regard to the sixth and ninth commandments, there is no parvity of matter.' That meant that every transgression of these commandments was potentially a mortal sin endangering salvation unless one could plead a deficiency in the other conditions necessary for committing mortal sin (clear knowledge and full consent). Such a blanket judgement had the potential for creating intense anxiety around something that, especially for young people, already contained enough explosive tension.

Formation for celibacy included not only instruction in what was forbidden by the vow, which included almost anything associated with sexuality. It attempted to promote rigorous emotional self-control by raising the standards of modesty as the remote defence of the virtue of chastity. Especially in women, the habit covered the wearer almost entirely, leaving only the face and hands exposed. It hid most traces of gender distinction whether in bodily shape or hair. Other rules regulated the conduct of religious among themselves and with outsiders to the community. Friendships with persons of the opposite sex, whether in men's or women's communities, were certainly frowned upon. This included social visiting of people in their homes, apart from the strict necessities of the apostolate. Obsession with protecting the modesty of sisters working in hospitals meant that they were forbidden to take up night duty or to nurse maternity cases or male patients.[19] Indeed, it was only in the 1920s that the Holy See removed the prohibition on religious sisters practising midwifery. In many communities, sisters never left the convent alone: apostolic work was undertaken in pairs, with one sister acting as chaperone to the other.[20] Convent rules and spiritual manuals were particularly hard on the formation of 'particular friendships': all sisters in the community were to be treated alike, with no place for deeper friendships based on shared interests. While it would be wrong to describe the resulting atmosphere in religious houses as uniformly bleak,[21] such a narrow view of chastity surely had the potential to contribute to a lack of development and maturity at the emotional level and, in some cases, to a very tense and anxious outlook on the world. Although it is a deeply personal realm, the individual's self-understanding as a sexual person has a social aspect. It contributes to their construction of the world, whether benign, affirmative, inclusive on the one hand, or anxious, deeply flawed and loveless on the other. As educators they run the risk of passing on these attitudes to the coming generation. There may well be something profoundly self-hating latent in some of the accounts of violent sexual abuse of children and minors outlined in the Ryan Report that can be traced back to an inadequate view of sexuality.

The process of renewal set in train by the Second Vatican Council was not an easy one. The new thinking and questioning started by World War II, which led to the Council, had passed Ireland by, cocooned as it was in its neutrality. Like most members of the Irish church, religious were not well prepared for what lay in store for them, but they soon rose enthusiastically to the challenge. One of the most important aspects of that renewal process has been termed a 'return to the charism of the founder'. A slow and sometime painful sifting of history led to a clearer vision of what the founder and the early followers had in mind. Some aspects of their history that had been forgotten, or conveniently ignored, came once more to the surface, sometimes challenging them to set out on a new direction. It also permitted religious to clear out monastic elements of their way of life that had never been part of the founding vision but had slowly crept in over time. Areas like authority and sexuality proved more difficult to get a handle on, because they had to look beyond theology and church teaching to include the newer sciences of psychology and sociology.

Conclusion
A sad effect of the recent disclosure of horrible and unpardonable abuse in religious-run institutions in Ireland has been the devaluing of the contribution of countless religious women and men to society over the two hundred years covered briefly in this article. It would be impossible to measure the contribution they have made through education, health-care, relief of poverty

or development work in the Third World. Include with that their extra-curricular nurturing of the GAA and other sports organisations, choirs, drama groups and the general raising of a level of culture and sensibility, especially in working class and rural Ireland. The late John McGahern wrote: 'For a novelist there has almost to be an agreed notion of society. In that sense, I often think that you could never find Jane Austen writing poems or short stories. And it's through the church that I first came to know all I'd know of manners, of ceremony, of sacrament, of grace.' Many of those religious helped forge this 'agreed notion of society,' making those in their charge aware of its manners, ceremony and grace.

In this article I have tried to show that the phenomenal growth of the religious life we have been familiar with in Ireland was a complex process. It was inspired initially by a generous and unselfish vision of men and women of talent and imagination that subsequent generations carried on for the most part, allowing for human frailty, with conviction and enthusiasm. If, as Hostie's first thesis suggests, religious life renews itself on the margins, we must acknowledge that in this age, the margin has shifted both to the new churches of the Third World and to the churches of Eastern Europe re-emerging from a dark time not altogether unlike that of Ireland in the late 18th century. In an often quoted remark, Leon Tolstoy says 'happy families are all alike; every unhappy family is unhappy in its own way'. As Irish religious life evolved, history and place imposed common features on it both in terms of the work they did and the forms of life they developed. Unhappy families have a tendency to conceal their inner unhappiness from the world at large. There may be a secret story of unhappiness still to be written but, for truth's sake, it will need to be part of a larger story. Individual religious families may not always have been best served by some in authority in the Irish church, who occasionally attempted to control the lives of religious in ways that went beyond their remit or with an eye only to local conditions. A way of life that takes the gospels and a critical reading of the Christian story as its inspiration can only be healthy to the extent that it is constantly renewed from the living sources of that tradition. It is commonly accepted that the theology in vogue for much of this period was not up to the task of doing this. It was too marked by legalism and a narrow fundamentalism, and Irish religious life had invested too little, I think, in the theological formation of its members to benefit fully from the renewal of theology when at last it came. Lamenting the state of the Ireland he had left, James Joyce wrote with a degree of sarcasm:

> Oh, Ireland my first and only love
> Where Christ and Caesar are hand and glove!
> (*Gas from the Burner*)

The contribution of Irish religious to the public life of the nation, especially through education and health-care, has been a noble one. It may be that, precisely because they were good at what they did, the state left them to it and asked no questions. Being hand in glove implies both dependency and control, but there is always a price to be paid for being hand in glove with Caesar. Sadly, it is a price that seems to be exacted from the present generation.

Notes:
1. *Vie et Mort des Ordres Religieux: Approches Psycho-sociologiqes*, Paris 1972 (E.T. *Life and Death of Religious Orders : A psycho-sociological Approach*, Washington 1983)
2. The Franciscan Church of the Immaculate Conception, for instance, take its better known name of Adam and Eve's from an inn behind which it stood in the eighteenth century.
3. See Hugh Fenning, *The Undoing of the Friars in Ireland. A Study of the Noviciate Question in the 18th century*, (Leuven, 1972).
4. Caitriona Clear, *Nuns in Nineteenth Century Ireland,* (Dublin, 1987), page 36.
5. Maria Luddy, *Women and Philanthropy in Nineteenth Century Ireland*, (Cambridge, 1995), page 23
6. *Women and Philanthropy.*
7. Clear, *Nuns*, page 87.
8. M. C. Normoyle, *A Tree is Planted*, 2nd edition (Dublin 1976): 'these made the ordinary vows of the Congregation, except that of gratuitous instruction. Their training was minimal: they worked in the kitchen or

garden and attended the religious exercises as far as their other duties permitted,' page 468.

9. Asenath Nicholson, *Ireland's Welcome to the Stranger*, 1847, page 372, (reissued, Dublin: Lilliput Press 2004)

10. *Women and Philanthropy*, p 174.

11. See for example *Women and Philanthropy*, Table 4.13: 'The maintenance of penitents in the Magdalene asylum, Donnybrook, 1840', page 130, which provides details of the women's weekly diet, clothing and bedding.

12. Lord Mounteagle, quoted in *Women and Philanthropy*, page 51.

13. For a full length study, see Evelyn Bolster, *The Sisters of Mercy in the Crimea* (Cork: 1964). Also Maria Luddy (ed), *The Crimea Journals of the Sisters of Mercy 1854-1856*, (Dublin, 2004)

14. *Edmund Ignatius Rice and the Irish Christian Brothers*, (Dublin, 1926), page 177.

15. On nineteenth century attempts to reform the Irish Franciscans, see Patrick Conlon, *Franciscan Ireland* (Cork, 1978), especially chapter 8: 'A Period of Searching for a Way of Life (1830-1899)', pages 49-58.

16. T. J. Walsh, *Nano Nagle and the Presentation Sisters* (Dublin, 1959), page 85.

17. Bernard Haring, *Free and Faithful: My Life in the Catholic Church* (Liguori, 1998).

18. Herbert McCabe. *God Matters* (London, 2005), page 233.

19. Clear, *Nuns*, page 127.

20. This too was a social convention of the time.

21. One has only to read some of the writings of Kate O'Brien, such as *Presentation Parlour* or *Land of Spices* for a view of two Limerick communities of the Presentation and Faithful Companions of Jesus for a contrary view.

Searching for Reasons:
A former Sister of Mercy looks back

Margaret Lee

Some years ago my sister gave me a present of a nun doll for Christmas. The doll was dressed in full nun's habit and the card read 'Look back in Anger?' Unlike John Osborne, I think that I look back more in regret than in anger.

In 1961, I entered a Mercy Novitiate. I was 17 years old. I wanted to make the ultimate sacrifice of my life, give it to God, do the idealistic thing, or so I told myself. In retrospect I see things differently and I have to acknowledge that I had a whole other set of motivations that were mostly, if not all, unconscious. 1961 was the Patrician Year. It was a time in Ireland when nuns, priests and brothers were held in the highest esteem, were looked up to and greatly admired, even revered. The status accorded to members of religious congregations showed itself in many and varied ways. A simple example I remember is that we were not charged on the buses. In schools, older lay members of staff stood aside to allow even the youngest slip of a novice pass by on the corridor. It was a world where one had merely to wear a veil and deference was given. So it is quite possible that when I consciously thought I was giving all to God, I was instead unconsciously seeking to occupy a position of rank in society.

In the late sixties I got the opportunity of attending university to study sociology. I can recall two experiences from those years that had a particular significance for me, and that came to mind again when the Ryan Report was published. I studied Erving Goffman's book *Asylums* in which he analyses the characteristics of what he terms 'total institutions'. By that he means institutions where people sleep, work and play in the company of the same other people and under the same authority figures. Goffman describes this as 'batch living' that does not allow for any degree of individuality and where everyone is required to do the same things at the same time. Such institutions operate according to a rigid schedule where the entire day is devoted to a prearranged sequence of activities. There is no freedom of choice because the schedule is dictated and imposed, either by formal rulings or by a body of officials, and the overall purpose is to fulfil the aims of the institution. In short, the individual is subservient to the institution. The big revelation for me, a young religious sister, was that when Goffman listed his examples of total institutions, he included not only orphanages, but also convents and monasteries. I was very taken aback, but had to admit that religious life fitted the bill even if at that time things were beginning to change in the wake of the Second Vatican Council. Authority was centralised in the person of the superior; we followed a fairly rigid daily programme, we did everything at the same time and we wore a common uniform. More important than all of this, we were discouraged from thinking for ourselves, and because we lived in a closed society (Goffman's *total institution*) the collective mindset was hardly ever challenged. When I applied Goffman's characteristics to the orphanage attached to the convent where I lived I had to acknowledge that, for the most part, it was run like a mini convent.

In this communal outlook two beliefs subconsciously underpinned our value system— the social class system was the way things should be and the Catholic Church had the answers to every possible moral and social dilemma. Looking back, I think that it was this structure, and these beliefs that were underpinning it, that led to the abuse of children in the industrial schools and orphanages.

The membership of the congregation that I entered was predominantly middle class, and the children who were placed in the orphanage were seen as coming from the lower strata of society and therefore as unequal to us and less deserving. There was a significant contradiction between our religious beliefs and our secular beliefs and sadly, when it came to our treatment of the poorer classes, it was our secular beliefs that defined our behaviour. Religious life was meant to be a sign of the kingdom of God, a kingdom where a person's dignity was based on their humanity, and our faith told us that as baptised Christians we were all children of God and part of the Body of Christ, but we failed to apply this to the orphans. Even the word 'orphans' by which we referred to them was inaccurate, as many of them had parents.

A further result of our allegiance to the prevailing class system was the way in which the resources of the community, both in terms of money and personnel, were deployed. Professional training was largely confined to two areas, teaching and nursing, and the sisters who were lucky enough to receive such training were assigned to the schools and hospitals. These were the favoured apostolates. The secondary schools in particular were highly valued because these schools provided an education for the middle class section of society from which our own roots had sprung and were also the recruiting ground for new members to the congregation. Through the forties and fifties secondary schools were growing in most towns in the state and it is a tribute to the nuns and brothers that such a vibrant system of second level education spread throughout Ireland. Parents were delighted that their children could receive an education at a relatively low cost, an education that would give their children an opportunity to get a job, to have greater earning power, to have a more comfortable lifestyle than they themselves had. These parents did not question what happened to the children who could not afford secondary education, and they certainly did not question what was happening to the children in the orphanages or industrial schools – because they, like ourselves, saw these children as being of lesser social importance. (As an aside, it must be noted that if any children in an industrial school showed any academic promise, they were more likely to receive a secondary education than their counterparts in society whose parents lacked the wherewithal to purchase such opportunity. I have been informed of the existence of a letter from one well publicised victim in which she thanks the sister in charge of the industrial school for the opportunities afforded her). However, in general, the tragedy was that we, the religious, adopted the prevailing belief system rather than bearing witness to the gospel values which would have made us a counter-cultural force in society. To ensure that the secondary schools advanced and that the pupils got good examination results and made a name for the particular school, the brightest and most talented sisters were assigned to the secondary school system. In contrast, untrained personnel were often deployed to the care of the children in the orphanage, reflecting the scant regard in which both the carer and those cared for were held.

The orphanage attached to the convent in which I spent my postulancy and novitiate remained open until 1963. I recall the children getting up for the seven o'clock Mass. They did not attend every morning but probably came to the transept of the convent chapel at least three mornings each week. I remember thinking that there was something wrong about getting the young children up so early on cold winter mornings but I never said this to anyone nor do I remember anyone else commenting on it. During that time two young children from a rural background came to the orphanage. They must have been very lonely and upset to find themselves in such strange surroundings but mostly what comes to my mind was their initial spontaneity. At first, they used to stand inside the railings that separated the orphanage from the convent grounds and ask us questions, like if we bought our clothes in a shop and if our heads were shaved. As I look back, I recall that their artlessness faded quickly and they must have learned that nuns and orphans did not mix, and so they withdrew into their institution. Two institutions, side by side, but separate. We as religious were institutionalised and in turn imposed institutionalisation on the children who lived in our orphanages and industrial schools.

At the time I thought all this was normal and in accordance with the natural order. It was similar to the old dog Fly telling

Babe, in the film of that name, that he could not come into the house because 'it is the way things are'. When I think back to the two vulnerable and helpless children, I do so from the standpoint of all the child development theory that we have learned in the intervening years. In that religious world that we inhabited in the early sixties our knowledge derived from religious books and church teaching. We knew nothing about the work of John Bowbly, British psychiatrist and psychoanalyst, who was writing in the nineteen fifties. He stressed the idea that children needed a warm, intimate and continuous relationship with their mother or with their primary care-giver and that to be deprived of this would have an adverse effect on the mental and emotional health of the child. He contended that mother (or care giver) and child should find mutual joy and satisfaction in this relationship. I believe that it would have been well nigh impossible for a religious sister of that era to provide a child with this kind of relationship, because the obsession with chastity and bodily purity would have precluded the kind of physical intimacy that the child needed. Furthermore, as religious women, we would not have been able to accommodate Bowbly's theories in our mindset because they would prompt us to question how we related to the children, and this, like so much else in our lives, was dictated by the collective way of thinking that was set out for us by the rule and the superiors. It wasn't that we rejected the ideas of people like Bowlby, it was rather that such ideas could not find a way into the type of total institution in which we lived. It was only in the mid to late sixties that this system of *una duce, una voce* began to break down. One of Bowlby's foremost theories is that children mourn and become depressed when separated from their mother. We certainly did not recognise that the children in our orphanage were grieving in this way. How could we, given that we were not supposed to be attached to our own parents or families? It must be admitted that there were some sisters who seemed to be able to disregard the rules, but they did so quietly so as not to draw attention to themselves.

Because of how we lived in our convents, and the common

mindset that we developed, as I have described above, I can see now that we were not able to equip the children who were placed in the orphanage with the skills necessary to negotiate the various stages of human development. Eric Erickson, a psychologist and psychoanalyst writing in the post war era, lists eight such stages, and he sees each stage as a challenge between two opposing forces, the outcome depending on which force gains supremacy. He identifies the first stage as that of negotiating trust versus mistrust. According to Ericson, the successful achievement of this stage can only come about if the infant is cared for lovingly by someone with whom it has a lot of visual contact and, more significantly, someone who touches it with warmth and tenderness. We had absolutely no understanding of the infant's need to form such a bond with one person in whom they could put their trust and the upshot of this must have been that the children did not have a basic foundation for their emotional lives and presumably had great difficulty in trusting the external world or living with a sense of hope that the world was a safe place. I am not aware that Irish society at the time ever questioned the ability or appropriateness of celibate men and women caring for children. It is possible that this arrangement was never queried because of people's unwavering confidence in church figures, but it is equally possible that the issue was not raised because people were not interested in what happened to the children consigned to the orphanage and industrial school system.

The fact that the convent and the orphanage were both *total institutions* led to a further problem. Goffman categorises his total institutions according to their overall aim. The aim of the orphanage was to provide for persons who (due to their age) were not able to care for themselves. The aim of the convent at that time was the sanctification of its members, in other words to provide the environment in which the members could ensure the salvation of their souls. The convent's aim, being of its nature eternal, took precedence over that of the orphanage, and as the convent system worked (or thought it worked) toward its goal it lost sight of the needs of the children. The incongruity of celibate men and women, who lived such a common, regulated life, caring for children only came home to me, or began to come home to me, in my second year at university. In the sociology class we had a lecturer who was pushing back the frontiers of discussion and often questioned the role of the Catholic Church in society. I could feel myself becoming defensive but was too shy and awkward to confront him in the presence of the other students, because in many ways the convent system had rendered many of us voiceless once we stepped outside its protective structure. Learning to assert oneself in a system where all power was concentrated in the superior and where a culture of fear reigned was not easy. At some point this lecturer's name was listed as one of the signatories to a letter to the editor of the *Irish Times* calling for a change in the management of the industrial schools. The letter appeared shortly after the publication of the 1970 *Kennedy Report on Industrial and Reformatory Schools*. It suggested that group homes should be set up for the children and that these group homes would not be managed by religious but by house parents of both genders. I happened to meet the lecturer on the corridor and, feeling safer in a one to one situation, I asked him why he wanted to take the management of childcare away from religious. He courteously explained to me that such children needed a family type atmosphere and that single sex celibate management could not provide this. The fact that this was the first time that the anomaly of celibates caring for small children occurred to me shows how totally myself and my contemporaries in religious life adhered to the notion that the Catholic Church was best placed to provide this service.

While I freely acknowledge our collective, and more honestly, my own individual failure to live by the gospel teaching that demanded that we treat the children as we ourselves would like to be treated, I have considerable sympathy for the religious who are now being condemned on all sides. I have already mentioned how pervasive the concept of social class was in religious life. It was also prevalent among the different religious congregations. To put it bluntly, there were posh orders and plebeian orders and it was the latter that were charged with providing education for the poor and caring for the children who were truly dispossessed. Sadly, as I have already said, we gave most of our attention to educating the middle and lower middle classes and this was because we mostly came from this sector of society ourselves. However, it is a bit galling to hear the more upper class orders now condemning congregations such as the Sisters of Mercy and the Christian Brothers and saying how really positive it is that 'all this has come out into the open'. It might be more fitting if they and some of their past pupils spent a bit more time pondering how they have upheld the very unequal, socially segregated society that we had, and continue to have, in Ireland.

It would not be appropriate to respond to the Ryan Report without addressing the level of abuse and cruelty that it depicts. The obvious question is how did men and women who prayed and read books about the love that God has for each one of us, lash out at the children in their care, children who were very, very vulnerable? It is a hard question to answer. One possible reason is that these people were voiceless and without any great status in their congregations and, consequently, within themselves were simmering with anger, frustration and dissatisfaction with life. I believe that they were often alienated from their inner selves. In the religious communities they were powerless but in the world of the orphanage they had absolute power. Put with this the fact that they could be fairly certain that that any violence or rough treatment, indeed any punishment of the children, would go unchallenged, and we may be coming to some explanation for it all. Even if some parents did challenge what was occurring they were unlikely to get a hearing from any authority figure in church or state, due to the commonly held perception that they were not worthy of a hearing.

So where are we now? How are we to view the religious, how are we to view the adults who as children were placed in industrial schools? We have heard the outcries, the classification of the religious as monsters, the calls for the primary school system to be taken out of church management. I will return to Erickson and his stages of human development. The final task of human development, he says, is to negotiate integration versus despair. By this he means that towards the culmination of our lives we must be able to consider all the things that have happened to us and integrate them, accepting them as part of the whole. When I apply this to Irish society, I think that we are still very young and immature. We are not able to look at life in the round and we are not able to hold good things and bad things in our consciousness at the same time. We want to simplify people, life, and its myriad events into dichotomies – good/bad, success/failure, brave/cowardly. When the Ryan Report was published, the religious were called monsters by one politician who, in my opinion, has contributed very little to society other than getting himself elected to the Dáil. One journalist said that no one should sit in a room with any Christian Brother. No interviewer in our Irish media challenged this language; indeed, if anything, the interviewers seemed to encourage more hyperbole. No one referred to what these religious had contributed to Irish society despite all the flaws, all the petty snobbery, all the failure to live by Christ's law of love. We cannot deny the abuse and harsh treatment of children in industrial schools. Neither can we deny that it is largely thanks to Sisters of Mercy, Christian Brothers and Presentation Sisters that substantial sections of society were educated at little cost to the taxpayer, because these men and women did not receive any personal financial remuneration. The religious women managed to run clean, efficient hospitals (where a patient could go to be cleared of an infection, not to acquire one); again at much less cost to the taxpayer than the price tag that comes with our present public service bureaucracy. But because we cannot integrate two sides of a situation, our current view of religious is unable to see the good that they have done. As time passes, this may change.

Not all children who were placed in industrial schools were abused or suffered torture. Recently I heard yet another journalist asking a politician if it was right to be promoting a united Ireland, given that it was asking the population of Northern Ireland to come into a state where 'children were tortured'. This is surely a distortion of the full picture. Following the publication of the Kennedy report – the one to which my lecturer friend was responding – the religious who managed the industrial schools did begin to implement its recommendations. I know of at least one institution where, despite the limitations of the building, the sister in charge divided the children into small groups and paid very particular attention to ensuring that siblings were in the same group. This congregation immediately availed of the training that was made available for its personnel in 1970 and housed the children in family type homes, known as 'group homes' in housing estates.

One of the sisters who spearheaded these developments spoke to me following the publication of the Ryan Report. She said 'you have only be a nun' to be pilloried and maligned in the current climate. She spoke of her sense of betrayal when she received a communication from the state redress board which stated that she had physically and emotionally abused a child who had been in her care. The sister was taken aback to hear that she had not allowed the claimant to attend the secondary school of her choice and that the young person had been forced to leave the care system and school at the age of 16 despite her academic potential. The reality was very different. The sister in question had begged and pleaded with that claimant to continue in education past the junior certificate but met with a blank refusal. Furthermore, that same sister had provided a high quality aftercare to the claimant and even allowed her back to the group home on a number of occasions when life got difficult; supported her through her wedding and the birth of her children. She had never physically abused or slapped the girl; she had not neglected her in any way. The sister was not claiming any credit for this as she saw it all as part of her duty of care. She told me that she wrote a letter to the redress board denying the charges but the person in question was awarded significant money. She added, 'I could have gone and defended myself in person but what is the point, as claimants are getting compensation anyway?' For her, there was no forum to establish the truth and her real sadness about the redress board was that it fractured permanently the relationships that many of the claimants had previously had with their erstwhile carers.

I believe that many other religious feel as this woman did, which begs the question as to why they have not defended themselves in public. It is because they are now fearful of being devoured by the media that, in their view, is not really interested in finding out the truth. Not only are the religious frightened of the media, they are equally fearful of the adults who were placed in the industrial schools as children. They see themselves as being turned on viciously by them and I think that if I were in their position, I would be equally terrified. No one has challenged the accounts of those who term themselves survivors. They have been given an iconic status by the popular media and press. In accordance with our inability to embrace two sides of a situation, all that is good, brave, honest, truthful is being attributed to them – in short, we have idealised them. This is what we did to the religious in the middle of the last century and it was surely counter productive. I have the temerity to suggest that we begin to adjust both our rose-tinted and foul-tinted spectacles. We need to see the different groupings, the religious and the people who were placed in industrial schools, as human beings, who are a mixture of good and bad, who are capable of great generosity and capable of mean spiritedness, capable of giving a service to society and capable of bending the truth. I believe that the story of the industrial schools is much more complex than presented to date.

In summary, my view is that the religious who managed the industrial schools until the late sixties failed to treat the children with due dignity because these same religious were trapped within the social class structure, and the gospel values did not penetrate the secular value system. I contend that Irish society or its political leaders were not capable of giving justice to the children because they too adhered firmly to the class system. In the recent debate, religious have not been given a fair hearing and the views of the adults who, as children were placed in industrial schools, have not been challenged, leaving us with a very one-sided picture.

Letterfrack: Peter Tyrrell and the Ryan Report

Dáire Keogh

Peter Tyrrell, a former resident of Letterfrack industrial school (1924-32), committed suicide by setting fire to himself on Hampstead Heath in 1967. His badly charred body was identified only by a postcard found next to it, upon which the words 'Skeffington' and 'Dublin' were visible. The story of this poor soul might have ended there, were it not for the discovery of his manuscript memoir among the papers of Owen Sheehy Skeffington in the National Library of Ireland. Carefully edited, together with a thoughtful introduction, the memoir was published as *Founded on Fear* by Diarmuid Whelan in 2006.[1] Forty years after it was written this compelling narrative emerged in a very different Ireland: what was intended as a warning cry appeared as confirmation of the scenario described at the *Commission to inquire into Child Abuse* (CICA).

I

The publication of *Founded on Fear* produced an immediate response. For Dermot Keogh, the Cork historian, it was a 'text which cries out to heaven ... a mirror to official Ireland, the Irish State and the Catholic Church'.[2] Bruce Arnold compared its 'compelling strength' to Solzhenitsyn's *One Day in the Life of Ivan Denisovich* (1962), except that for Tyrrell the day stretched into years.[3] Mary Raftery drew parallels between Tyrrell's tragic cause and that of Primo Levi, whose harrowing holocaust memoir, *If This is a Man* (1947), became an undisputed classic of twentieth century literature.[4] The Christian Brothers, too, were stirred by Tyrrell's 'moving perspective on his troubled life'; 'saddened and ashamed', they apologised unreservedly 'to all

who had suffered similar hurt' while in their care.[5] Commentators were struck by the candour of their statement which Mary
Raftery, a long-time critic of the Congregation, described as their
'most generous public utterance to date'.[6] Moreover, the
Brothers acknowledged the even-handedness of the narrative,
and, despite its description of the 'intolerable behaviour' of
some of their confrères, they recognised 'a generosity of spirit
that enhances the memoir'. Peter Tyrrell, the statement concluded,
'was clearly a sensitive and generous man'.[7]

There are difficulties with the memoir genre. In the context of
the Irish Industrial Schools these were discussed in a seminal
essay by Michael Molino.[8] Yet while *Founded on Fear* was the latest memoir to be published, it predated and largely affirms the
narratives of Mannix Flynn (1983), Paddy Doyle (1988), and
Patrick Touher's (1991) experience of Irish industrial schools.[9] If
there were doubts about the veracity of the shocking circumstances described by Peter Tyrrell, these have been dispelled by
the recent publication of the findings of the Commission of
Inquiry, which characterised Letterfrack as an institution where
'physical punishment was severe, excessive and pervasive ...
[and where] sexual abuse was a chronic problem'.[10]

Leaders of church and state have struggled towards an adequate response to such conclusions. The Taoiseach characterised
the abuse as the 'source of the deepest shame on us all', but that
failed to capture the universal revulsion unleashed by the report.[11] Surprisingly, the general public was unprepared for the
findings of the Commission despite the publication of a succession of memoirs, high profile television documentaries and the
publication of the *Ferns Report* (2005). Thirteen years had passed
since the broadcast of Louis Lentin's *Dear Daughter* (1996),
which exposed the abuse of Christine Buckley at Goldenbridge,
while Eoin O'Sullivan and Mary Raftery's *Suffer the Little
Children* (2001) had largely anticipated the findings of the Ryan
Report.[12] 'It should not have taken another decade for that truth
to fully enter our collective consciousnesses', an *Irish Times* editorial concluded, but the eventual wake-up was 'a tribute to the

work of the Ryan Commission – and to the value of official in-quiry'.[13]

The scale of the abuse described, and the failure of the au-thorities and society at large to respond, shattered complacency and blew away the fig-leaf of denial. 'This could not be worse', wrote Madeline Bunting in the *Guardian*, 'the Ryan Report is the stuff of nightmares. It's the adjectives which chill: systematic, pervasive, excessive, arbitrary, [and] endemic.'[14] CORI, which represents 138 religious congregations in Ireland, conceded that 'no excuses can be offered for what has happened', for the 'hor-rendous' emotional, physical and sexual abuse 'suffered by so many children on such a vast scale'.[15] Batt O'Keeffe, the Minister for Education, accepted that 'the Department failed to protect these children for whom it had a duty of care'.[16]

Some journalists and bloggers described the scandal as Ireland's equivalent to the Holocaust, but such analogies can blind us to the personal stories of the thousands of children who were resident in the fifty institutions examined by the Commission. In one of the most poignant moments of 'Schindler's List', the protagonist is struck by the presence of a girl in a red coat amongst the monochrome masses of the Krakow Ghetto. Spielberg used this potent image, and the moment of Schindler's conversion, not simply to focus on the human misery of this global scandal, but to expose the failure of the Allied powers to react once they had become aware of the Holocaust. In seeking to understand the implications of the Ryan Report, it is perhaps instructive to rescue the individual voice from the anonymity of the Commission's findings. In this sense, Peter Tyrrell, whose memoir expresses a boy's betrayal and the failure of society to respond when abuses were exposed, can become for us the child in the red coat.

The Ryan Report is difficult to fathom.[17] Its 2,600 pages pre-sent a damning judgement on the Industrial School system. It does not purport to present a holistic impression of the regime, and the positive experience of former residents is treated in fewer than ten pages.[18] Each of the five volumes focuses upon specific aspects of the Committee's remit. Structurally, it lacks an overall coherence, and contains no index. It offers no quantitative analysis of the incidence of abuse; it is repetitive and poorly edited.[19] The lack of uniformity in the treatment of institutions makes cross-referencing difficult, while the Commission's decision to employ pseudonyms frustrates comparisons between the report and what is already in the public domain. Volume one and two contain fifteen hundred pages relating to the institutions named in the Institutional Redress Bill. Four hundred pages of the third volume deal with the work of the Confidential Committee, and its conclusions are presented on a thematic, rather than personal or institutional, basis. The fourth volume assesses the role of the Department of Education, Finance, and the development of childcare policy in Ireland since 1970. The final volume of 'Additional Material' is the least focused, containing a discussion of the ISPCC, details of the Commission personnel and legislation. It also contains a number of expert reports, including a reflective essay by Diarmaid Ferriter which sets out the historical context of the events discussed at the public hearings. Commissioned by a firm of solicitors representing a large number of complainants, it is crudely scanned into the Report; its pagination is out of sequence, and it is difficult to read both online and on the CD rom. As a consequence, the implications of this important historical perspective are lost on the entire report.

A reading of Tyrrell's narrative affords an invaluable perspective in this regard. It is not simply, as Caitriona Crowe has observed, 'that these memoirs run like a parallel stream of information alongside the official documentary record':

> but they complement it with their personal immediacy and vibrancy … it is the fact that we are hearing these stories from the inside … that give these books their value as human testimony.[20]

Moreover, *Founded on Fear* has a coherence and scope, which, by definition, is lacking in the Ryan Report, and it provides a vital

narrative of the world of Peter Tyrrell and the children institutionalised by the Irish state.

II

Tyrrell's memoir makes for disturbing reading. Currently re-
searching a commissioned history of the Christian Brothers, I
attended the public sessions of the Commission and have studied
a wide range of documentary sources, but none presents the
child's perception of industrial schools as Peter Tyrrell (1916-67)
does. From the outset, we are introduced to the appalling poverty
of his childhood in Ahascragh, County Galway, his 'lazy and
irresponsible' father and the heroic efforts of his mother to raise
10 children in a converted stable, by 'begging and borrowing',
while the children scavenged in neighbours' fields for 'potatoes,
turnips … or anything which [would] keep [them] alive for one
more day'. Circumstances deteriorated when his father lost his
job, breaking stones on the roads. From that point, the children
couldn't go to school because they had literally no clothes to
wear. On one occasion, Peter wore his sister's coat and when the
teacher asked him to remove it, the children laughed because he
had nothing underneath.[21] The family was eventually taken into
care in 1924, an odyssey which began with the father's pathetic
prayer that God would be 'merciful and kind to his children in
their new Catholic home'.[22]

The description of the journey to Connemara and his recep-
tion at St Joseph's is beautifully written, but the tenor of the institution is quickly established when, 'all at once, a Christian
Brother [appeared] … chasing the young children with a very
long stick, and beating them on the legs'.[23] This dispelled any
illusions Peter may have had about his new school and he
became 'frightened and struck with horror'. These emotions remained with him throughout his time in Letterfrack, where, he
believed, 'children were beaten and tortured for no other reason
but lustful pleasure'.[24] *Founded on Fear* illustrates the anachronistic nature of the industrial schools, Dickensian institutions
which survived in Ireland into the late 20th century. Indeed, the

parallel with Dickens is uncanny. In *Nicholas Nickleby* (1838) he describes the boys of Dotheboys Hall with 'pale and haggard faces ... children with the countenances of old men', while Tyrrell's companions were 'terribly pale, and their faces are drawn and haggard ... the children of Letterfrack are like old men'.

This is an extremely complex world which is depicted in an even-handed and credible way. There was a community of ten Brothers in Letterfrack which could accommodate 190 boys. Several of the Brothers were twisted, but others were kind and one is described as a 'saint'. The tyrants, both Brothers and laymen, preyed not merely on the boys, but upon each other; boys suffered peer abuse while the local population combined in a conspiracy of self-interested silence. Letterfrack's remote setting made it an entirely unsuited location for an industrial school, and educating children there has been likened by Bishop Willie Walsh to the historic transportation of convicts to Van Diemen's Land.[25] Isolation accentuated the desire to abscond; it militated against the provision of adequate staffing and presented difficulties which 'haunted the school ... and eventually contributed to its closure in 1974'.[26] Described in the Report as an 'inhospitable, bleak and isolated institution', contact between the boys and home was limited.[27] There was provision for families to stay at the school, but few received visits in Tyrrell's time. Just one boy had a regular annual visit, but for most families, including his own, poverty kept them away.[28] Indeed, while most boys were committed on account of poverty, few would admit it. Attempting to avoid this stigma, the narrative recalls a Dubliner boasting that he was there 'for robbing and not because [his] parents were paupers'.[29] Visits from home, however, betrayed their origins, and boys fearful of being exposed by their 'ragged and badly dressed parents' would hide in the toilets.[30] Correspondence, too, appears to have been censored. Complainants at the Commission recalled that 'every letter ... had to be a good letter', but Tyrrell was sadly relieved that this was so, for fear that the truth would shatter his parents confidence that their 'boys [were] well looked after by the good kind Christian Brothers'.[31]

For the Brothers, too, the isolation of Letterfrack compounded what was already a difficult station. Indeed, it is to be regretted that none of the Brothers who served at the school has left a memoir of his experience which might inform our perception of the Brothers' role in such schools.[32] This is one of the challenging questions posed by Ryan, attempting to comprehend the Brothers' Christian vocation and what they believed they were achieving in the industrial schools. In the absence of memoirs or contemporary correspondence, some insights may be gleaned from the proceedings of the Inquiry. Br *Ruffe* told the Commission that he had 'shed bitter tears' on receiving his appointment and Br *Anatole*, described it as 'a tough job, a tough station, something you would not particularly choose, on account of ... its isolation'.[33] A succession of respondents noted that many of the children were difficult; several had psychological problems and others were violent. For Br *Sorel*, Letterfrack was 'a harsh place' in the 1940s, where he was advised never to let his guard down:

> One of the Brothers said to me, 'Whatever you do don't smile, walk along with a very serious face', and I was shivering. Nobody knew that I was shivering in my boots. Quite a number of the lads there were big strong lads ... huge guys there, I was shivering in my shoes because I never had this experience.[34]

Such sentiments echo Patrick Touher's sense that the Brothers were themselves victims of the system. 'The Brothers were doing their best', he argued, 'within limited circumstances, in hard times and with frightening numbers. They had no luxury [and] nothing to look forward to except more of the same.'[35] Unfortunately, this frustration took its toll on some of them, but while the Commission acknowledged the stresses and challenges facing 'untrained and inexperienced' young men, it offered no mitigation for their 'shameful' behaviour towards the children in their care.[36]

Tyrrell's perceptive narrative describes the hostile environment at Letterfrack, and the pervasive physical violence which undermined any positive ends the Christian Brothers hoped to achieve at the school. Significantly, this brutality affected all, adults and children alike. Br Keegan flogged boys for 'improper acts', but the 'cunning and cruel' Br Walsh, beat a lay teacher and reduced him to tears before the boys.[37] Br Fahy, a 'conceited ... arrogant bully', intimidated not only children, but Brothers and masters.[38] And of the lay teachers, Ackle, a former resident of the school, 'carried an ash plant and often flogged the very young children during meal times'.[39] The bandmaster, too, was 'a cruel bully', while the night watchman beat children for bedwetting.[40] Such arbitrary and public punishments created a nightmare for Tyrrell. In one pathetic passage, describing the peaceful face of a boy killed in a motor accident, he confessed, 'for just a moment a sinful thought came to my mind. I too would like to be dead.'[41]

Of all the staff, none compared to the predatory tyrant Br Vale [Veale, aka Br *Perryn*], who returned to the school in 1926. At the outset, the narrator is intrigued by this new arrival. Enquiring his age from the laundry girl, Annie Aspel, she replied, 'he is about forty five ... the age when they all go strange'.[42] Vale was clearly disturbed and his presence blighted Tyrell's years in Letterfrack. The narrative is peppered with detail of his wanton cruelty. Children were flogged during meals, beaten as they showered, and leathered with a rubber car-tyre for failing to polish the floors to his exacting standard. During this latter humiliation, the smaller children 'trembled and twitched' and it was not uncommon for them to soil themselves.[43] Such demonstrations were particularly traumatic for witnesses, but the exposure to terror appears to have been an instrument in the Brothers' armoury to 'engender fear and ensure control'.[44] Children were horrified by the abuse meted to their siblings, and Tyrrell recounts an episode where his younger brother was knocked unconscious by Vale, whom he had enraged by allowing 'Nigger', his black cat, escape.[45] There are no explicit references to sexual abuse in Tyrrell's account, although there are allusions. In conversation with the Tuairim group (a liberal circle founded in 1954 to promote reform), however, he claimed to have been sodomised by a Brother, presumably Vale.[46]

III

This issue of supervision, or lack of it, is at the heart of Tyrrell's narrative and formed a central strand in the deliberations and recommendations of the Commission on Child Abuse. The state was gravely negligent in its duty of care to the children. The staffing of the inspectorate was totally inadequate; there was just one medical officer employed to monitor up to 60 institutions and some schools were not inspected for years on end. Brigid McManus, Secretary General of the Department of Education, conceded before Justice Ryan that her department 'was not effective in ensuring a satisfactory level of care, indeed the very need to establish a commission of inquiry testified to this'.[47] Similarly, Batt O'Keeffe accepted that if 'the Department had done its job properly, thousands of children would not have suffered the way they did'.[48]

The leadership of the Christian Brothers, too, failed to exercise proactive supervision of industrial schools, which were in breach of the Order's own guidelines and the regulations of the Department of Education with regard to physical punishment. Successive General Chapters and circulars from religious superiors had sought in vain to eradicate excessive punishment, which, in 1940, the Superior General condemned as contrary to the law of the Congregation and abhorrent to humanity.[49] Yet, the failure of the school to maintain a Punishment Book, the basic requirement of the law, meant that incidents remained unrecorded and unchecked.

Tyrrell's narrative highlights the human consequences of this failure, but illustrates the operation of informal, though inadequate, disciplinary mechanisms. He lampoons Dr Lavelle, the medical officer at Letterfrack, as an ineffectual character in plus-fours, who visited the school each month, but did little more than walk the yard with his dog.[50] Yet elsewhere, there are accounts in *Founded on Fear* which suggest more frequent visits, and while no formal complaints from him about the beatings received by boys survive, one episode suggests his critical intervention. On that occasion Tyrrell was laid up with a broken arm, sustained resisting a ritualistic beating from the sadistic Br Walsh. As instructed, the boy told the doctor that the injury was the result of a fall, but an examination revealed marks on his back. Lavelle left the infirmary with the superior, and while the narrator makes no connection, we learn subsequently that Walsh, a temporary professed Brother, would 'soon be leaving … that was good news as I now was no longer afraid'.[51]

Unlike the Department of Education, however, the Christian Brothers conducted annual visitations of the institution and maintained extensive records. These were preserved in the so-called 'Roman Files' which were discovered to the Commission in 2004. This was not, in fact, Roman material, but rather the archives of the Superior General who was resident in Dublin until the late 1960s. At that point the archive was transferred, when the generalate moved to Rome in the aftermath of the Second Vatican Council. The Commission considered the visitation reports as 'the single most valuable source of documentary evidence' about the institutions.[52] They record a lot that was very positive in the schools; they illustrate the perennial problem of insufficient funds and chart the gradual attempt to transform Victorian institutions into care facilities. They also reveal incidents of abuse and document the response of the congregational authorities when these were exposed. Ultimately it was these files, rather than the statements of former residents before the Confidential Committee, which informed the Commission's judgement of the Christian Brothers' management of the schools.

It is instructive, too, to compare the Visitation reports with the records of the Department of Education. The former, the Commission concluded, were 'more in-depth and thorough, whereas the latter tended to be … cursory'.[53] In its discussion of the Brothers' school in Salthill, for instance, the Commissioners described the Visitor's criticisms 'as much more severe than any corresponding comments by Dr McCabe', the Medical Inspector.[54] With regard to Glin, too, it noted that the Visitation report of 1948 'was very negative about the standard of education', while the Department Inspector 'made a favourable report on the school and did not pick up on the criticisms of the Visitors'.[55] Where such contradictions existed the Commission accepted the negative commentary of the Visitation Reports, as 'a more reliable source of information about conditions in the school'.[56] This raises significant methodological questions about the workings of the Commission and the weighting of evidence. One could infer that the leadership of the Christian Brothers had higher expectations of the schools than the state, but the Report suggests that the Inspectors were negligent, insincere, or coerced, and that consequently the Archives of the Department of Education are of limited historical value.

However, while the Visitation system could identify problems, it did not provide a mechanism for their resolution. The leadership of the Christian Brothers did not have the resources, expertise or imagination to solve habitual problems, but it failed hopelessly in the face of serious revelations. The dynamics and shortcomings of the system were graphically illustrated in the case of Tyrrell's tormentor, Br Vale. His case was beyond the time-span of the Ryan Commission, but it was considered because Peter Tyrrell had informed the Brothers of his abuse in 1953 which was within the relevant period.[57] Vale [Br *Perryn*] had been in Letterfrack for six years from 1913. During that first term, the Sub-Superior wrote to the Provincial, in April 1917, complaining of his 'notorious' severity towards the boys:

> Last Autumn I complained of Br [*Perryn*'s] harsh and cruel treatment, and now he still continues along the same lines. About a month ago he took a boy out of bed at near 10 o'clock at night and punished him in the lavatory in his night-shirt, and that because the boy took a pinch of salt … About a week after he did the same to another boy who took a potato … and on last Thursday night … he did the same to

another boy for calling him names! In each case he acted on the report of another boy ... I stood and counted 27 slaps given in the space of about five minutes to some juniors in the knitting room. He uses a rod also and strikes them on the legs and ... uses it wildly and wantonly as if for sport some-times ... His severity in the knitting room is notorious – and the more so to be deplored as many of the young children are delicate and their hands are sore, chilblains being prevalent among them.[58]

No action was taken and Vale remained in the school for two more years, until removed to Baldoyle following the interven-tion of a Visitor who considered that 'a change to a non-residen-tial school would be very desirable'.[59]

Despite his record of violence, Vale returned to Letterfrack in 1927 and remained there until 1941. At the Commission, the Brothers described his reappointment as 'most unfortunate', but attributed the neglect of the 'early warning signs' to administra-tive changes within the Congregation which deprived the Provincial Council of the institutional knowledge and detail of Vale's record of abuse.[60] During the Visitation of 1941, however, the visitor was made aware of allegations of sexual abuse against the Brother:

> Accusations have been made against [Br *Perryn*] ... and my investigations seem to confirm the charges. I have got state-ments from the boys with whom he is alleged to have had immoral relations. They are so shockingly obscene, revolting and abominable that it is hard to believe them. I have sent him to the O'Brien [Institute, in Marino] on the plea of ill health as I could not conscientiously leave him in charge of the boys until the matter is dealt with ... Boys whom I inter-viewed told me that they were afraid to reveal the malprac-tices through fear of Br *Perryn*. It is alleged that he beats them, kicks them, catches them by the throat etc and uses them for immoral ends.[61]

This report prompted decisive action. A trial was arranged at

Marino to hear the case, but this proved unnecessary when Vale applied for and received a dispensation. This crime was not communicated to the civil authorities. There was, of course, no legal obligation to do so, and in their defence the Christian Brothers have consistently stressed the view that sexual abuse was seen historically as 'a moral failure rather than a crime'.[62] Certainly, contemporary Visitation reports referred to such acts in terms of 'immorality', but the leadership was cognisant of the scandal and potential prosecution which would result from such revelations.

Vale's abuse, and the Congregation's inept reaction, demonstrates this and the failure of communication within Letterfrack. A Brother in the community had been informed of the abuse by one of Vale's victims, but he had not communicated this to his superior, claiming subsequently that he would not have been believed. He chose, instead, to wait and disclose the accusations at the next provincial Visitation. In consequence, the children remained exposed to danger.[63] That the Superior was oblivious to such abuse may be difficult to comprehend, but Tyrrell was emphatic that the previous superior, Br Kelly, 'did not know what was going on' with regard to severe punishment in the school and would have stopped it if he did.[64] Elsewhere, he claimed never to have seen one Brother beat children in the presence of another.[65] In its assessment of the Vale case, the Ryan Report underlined this breakdown of communications and its implication for other cases. The Congregation did not address the issue of the Brother's failure to report the matter to his superior. Indeed, the Brother was criticised for his indiscretion in mentioning the matter to another Brother in the school, a criticism which the Commission concluded, reflected the leadership's priorities, which were to avoid scandal and protect the reputation of the institution.[66]

If a Brother could not communicate with his superior, it was little wonder that boys could not speak up. A culture of fear and silence amongst the boys contributed to abusers' avoidance of detection. Indeed, the Visitation of 1941 had identified this, but no corrective measures were taken. There was a reticence amongst the boys to talk about sexual abuse. One complainant spoke of his exploitation by Br *Dax* [Maurice Tobin] who was convicted in 2003, on 25 sample cases of sexual assault and the rape at Letterfrack.[67] Not only was he too embarrassed to tell the superior about this, but 'none of us lads ever spoke about these things'.[68] In Tyrrell's time, too, 'the most terrible law in Letterfrack was that we must not complain'.[69] Redemptorist Missioners reinforced this imperative at annual retreats: 'the more we suffer on earth, the greater will be our reward in the next ... It is sinful in the eyes of God to complain.'[70] Tyrrell revealed to the Tuairim group that he had been rebuked by a confessor when he complained of the sexual abuse.[71] Significantly, Br *Dax* confessed to the Commission that while his abusive activity spanned nearly the entirety of his period in the school, it had been interrupted for two years when his Confessor, 'made it clear to him the sinfulness of his conduct'.[72] Such revelations raise important questions about the role of chaplains in the institutions, the extent of their knowledge of abuse and their obligation to report it, irrespective of the limitations imposed by the seal of confession.[73] Several complainants, however, reported that the intervention of confessors, in instances of physical abuse, could result in additional punishment.

Abuse may also have been concealed by the fact that, as a 'lay' or non-teaching brother, Vale lived apart from the community. The boys considered him different, and Tyrrell described him as 'a very lonely man with no real friends'; he didn't mix with the other Brothers, but spent most of his time in the kitchen or pantry.[74] These perceptions were confirmed by the 1941 Visitation report which described him as a 'dirty, untidy, almost repulsive' character who rarely attended community exercises.[75] In the kitchen and on the farm, lay brothers enjoyed unsupervised access to boys; there were greater opportunities for abuse, and the possibility of detection was reduced. This was the case with Br *Dax*, a cook at the school in two periods from the 1950s until 1974, whose record mirrors that of Vale.[76] None of the respondents, Brothers or former Brothers, who had worked along-side Br *Dax* suspected that he was an abuser.[77] When asked by the Commission how he avoided detection, he attributed it to the fact that he worked alone in the kitchen and was isolated from other members of the community. By virtue of the fact that he cooked for the boys, he never attended a community meal in the 15 years he spent in Letterfrack.[78] Cruelly, this responsibility for the kitchen drew victims to him. Boys selected to work in the kitchen thought they were 'on the pig's back' because it gave them access to extra food and warmth.

IV

There is a dualism about Tyrrell's Letterfrack. In addition to the terror, he describes normal schoolboy diversions which resonate with the Brothers' opening statement to the Commission, but are absent from the Report. There were sports and operettas; the band (the 'second best in the country'), football, and the trips to Tully Strand. There are curious asides: Brothers with girlfriends, gambling on games of handball, and boys giving a shilling to a former teacher to buy a drink.[79] There were the annual Missions, too, when Redemptorists would descend upon the school and prepare the boys for the joy of Christmas with the fear of hell. There was the couple who sinned and were found dead together; the boy who roasted in the flames of hell, or the Missioner, in 1929, who had computed the depth of Satan's dominion and the three seconds it took for the damned soul to reach there.[80] There are details of the regime and the regular diet, too:

> Dinner was at 1 pm. On Sunday, Tuesday and Thursday it was boiled or roast beef with two or three potatoes and cabbage, peas or turnips. On other days, except Fridays, we had a bowl of soup with half a slice of bread and boiled potatoes. On Friday we had fish, usually mackerel, or rice boiled with raisins, and on some Fridays rhubarb and rice was served. Supper, which was at seven, consisted of one slice of bread and dripping and a mug of cocoa.[81]

But for each positive depiction, there is one which disturbs our ease, as when he describes the pig feed 'as lovely, … much better than our own'.[82]

There were dramatic seasonal interruptions, too. At Christmas, the Brothers would 'play games, laugh and joke', and even Vale, who 'would stay up half the night to prepare a meal', contributed to the 'lovely atmosphere of kindness and friendship'.[83]

> Christmas Day is a big occasion and there are few restric-
> tions. After Mass we have breakfast without having to parade
> and be marched to the refectory. In addition to the usual
> bread and margarine, we have corn loaf and extra tea if re-
> quired. During the day we can talk anywhere without per-
> mission and we may leave the yard or go to the village or the
> shops. About half the lads get a parcel or letter at Christmas.
> We get a cake and a half a crown. With the money we go to
> the village and spend it all on sweets and chocolate. It is the
> practice to share everything with the children who have no
> presents or those who do not hear from home.
>
> Dinner is very good. We have roast meat, gravy and peas,
> followed by Christmas pudding. Very few are able to eat the
> pudding, so it is kept for the next day. For the evening meal
> there is cake, bread and jam and tea as required. … The
> Christmas spirit lasts until the New Year.[84]

The summer holidays, too, brought a reprieve; not only was 'life was good', but it was 'the only time worth living' at Letterfrack.[85] And when the usual staff was withdrawn, justice was meted out to the Brothers' spies and 'pets would be beaten up by the other lads'.[86] Tyrrell does not mention this, but it was the usual prac-tice to bring in a relief staff from the congregation's day schools. These 'Summer Brothers' were clearly different, and this raises questions about the staffing of the institutions. Industrial schools were a tough station, and the perception seems to have been that only good disciplinarians, or 'institutions men', would make it. Moreover, if Brothers proved themselves as such, they often remained in residential schools, as is reflected in the rotation of staff between Letterfrack, Artane and the other industrial schools. The ostentatious Br Fahy of Tyrrell's narrative had been in the Dublin school, and there appears to have been a rumour mill in which boys transferred between schools would carry news. In evidence before the Commission, Br David Gibson, leader of St Mary's Province, implied that a more frequent change of personnel would have been beneficial, not only for the institutions, but for the Brothers' wider ministry, since the experience of Letterfrack would help them 'in their normal work in schools'.[87]

The 'Summer Brothers' were different, but not all in the regular community were alike. Certainly there were 'evil creatures' who turned the school into a 'terrible prison', but there were others, like Br Scully 'who got more out of boys by singing a song'.[88] And of all the Brothers, Kelly was Tyrrell's favourite: 'a good and religious man, he was most kind to everyone.'[89] 'Genuinely humble and sincere', he was Tyrrell's 'interpretation of a saint'.[90] There were tensions between the Brothers, too, and conflicts were manifest in public clashes between them described in the narrative. Indeed, in Justice Ryan's opinion, it was often the existence of such cleavages which prompted the reporting of abuses.[91]

Many of Tyrrell's cast were openly critical of the system. Brother Murphy attributed the illiteracy of many boys to the fact that 'too much time is spent on learning Irish and beating the lads'.[92] The schools' inspector, too, challenged the misguided patriotism which was the consensus, adding that 'many of our own people have done more harm to Ireland than ever the British'.[93] And Annie Aspel, Tyrell's heroine, confessed that she had not been there 'with her eyes shut'; she knew what was going on:

> I don't have to ask questions. I can see in your face what I have seen in the faces of hundreds of children for many years. No one will ever take the place of your mother.[94]

Yet, if the laundry girl was unable to challenge the system, one of the community was vocal in his radical condemnation of it. Rejecting the 'stickology' of his peers, Br Byrne echoed the sentiments of Fr Edward Flanagan, founder of Boystown and pioneer of juvenile care, who ironically lavished praise on 'the great work being done' by the Brothers in Artane.[95]

> Brother Byrne's lectures were most educational in preparing children for life outside the school. He said on several occasions that 'children who were brought up in industrial schools, were generally failures' ... He went on to say that children brought up in schools and convents were starved of love and affection which was the very foundation of a healthy and happy life. 'Children with memories of an unhappy early life, very often become a serious problem to themselves and society.'[96]

In time, Brother Byrne's sentiments became Tyrrell's own campaign cry, but he was haunted by the implicit prediction of his own failure.

V

The challenges of discharge and the shortcomings of 'aftercare' were identified by Ryan. Tyrrell's peers had a variety of destinations: some were 'none the worse for their years at Letterfrack', several were employed in the school, others worked on farms and business, while one left for France to work at a convent in Marseilles.[97] Of the Tyrrells, Paddy was a mechanic at Ahascragh; another was ordained in the United States while a sister entered a convent. Peter Tyrrell, who left Letterfrack in 1932, was less successful. His attempts to reintegrate into society proved almost impossible on account of the universal contempt for industrial school boys in an Ireland obsessed with respectability. They were mocked and ridiculed, and considered low class, within the same category as paupers or prisoners.[98] Joe Dunne, in his otherwise positive memoir of life in Carriglea

Industrial School, recalls being assailed as 'a jailbird' and 'a bastard' in the streets of Dublin.[99] The trade union movement, too, conspired in the exclusion of former-residents and refused entry to boys who had learned some trades in the industrial schools. Irish society appalled Tyrell, particularly its pervasive violence, manifest in the abuse of animals, and the physical assaults on patients at the mental hospital at Ballinasloe.[100] There was drunkenness, too: the dirt of the people, the exploitation of women within marriage and what he perceived as an oppressive subservience to the Catholic Church which had kept the Irish 'unhappy and the most backward race in Europe'.[101]

'There was no future in this country for an industrial school lad', one of his mates remarked, but neither did emigration offer respite from the stigma. Amongst the Irish in London, 'it was the most awful disgrace to be identified as a boy from the Christian Brothers'.[102] In the end, like so many former residents of the institutions, Tyrrell found a secure refuge within the ranks of the British army. He served in India and Palestine with the King's Own Scottish Borders regiment, and was redeployed to the Western Front in 1944. He was imprisoned by the Germans in 1945, and while he described the four months internment at Fallingsbostel as 'hard and unpleasant', it was 'heaven on earth in comparison to life in school'.[103]

On his return to civilian life Tyrrell became involved with the Secular Society in London. In time he launched a crusade which he hoped would not merely draw attention to the 'criminal brutality' in the institutions, but would lead to the withdrawal of religious from education.[104] Letters to President De Valera, government ministers, the media, bishops, and Brothers were largely ignored, while the limited responses followed a similar pattern. Fr Derek Worlock, future Archbishop of Liverpool and secretary to Cardinal Wiseman, explained that the matter was outside the Archbishop of Westminster's jurisdiction.[105] The editor of the *News of the World* accused Tyrrell of 'dangerous' generalisations and 'assuming that what may have happened to you must have happened to everyone similarly placed'.[106] Amongst his Irish correspondents, however, the prominent Jesuit Fr Robert Nash did him the service of communicating the complaints to the Superior General of the Christian Brothers. Writing to Br Ferdinand Clancy, in 1965, he explained, 'I need hardly assure you that I do not accept the statements at their face value, but it is right at the same time that you should know what this man is saying.'[107]

The correspondence came almost a year after Tyrrell had published an account of Letterfrack in *Hibernia*, but unknown to the Jesuit, Tyrrell had been in communication with the provincial of the Christian Brothers for almost a decade. In the first exchange, described by Counsel for the Commission as 'a discriminating' letter, Tyrrell informed the provincial of the circumstances and the abuse which he later developed in the narrative.[108] 'Some of the Brothers were good and kind to the boys', he told the Provincial, 'but three [named individuals] were a disgrace to the Christian Brothers.'[109] In a second letter, two days later, he expressed a desire to see his abusers brought to justice, an end to such brutality and the closure of the school.[110] The Commission believed that neither of these letters received an acknowledgement, although the leadership of the Christian Brothers was fully aware of the veracity of the charges.[111]

A meeting took place between Tyrrell and Br Adrian Mulholland, the Brother Provincial, in March 1957, during which he revealed his plan to 'launch a great campaign against the torture of children in Catholic schools'.[112] The Brothers became defensive in the face of this threat and referred Tyrrell to their solicitors, Maxwell Weldon and Darley:

> This evening I had a 'gentleman' named Tyrrell ex-British army to see me. He said he was an ex-pupil of our industrial school in Letterfrack and that the doctors had said that all his troubles were due to the hardship he got whilst in Letterfrack. I took it that he was working on the blackmail ticket and after listening to him for some time I gave him your name and address as our solicitor. I know you will know how to deal with him if he approaches.[113]

Seeking to explicate the Congregation's response, Br David Gibson offered explanations of ignorance and disbelief, but conceded that this response was 'totally inadequate'.[114]

The Commission rejected Br Gibson's interpretation, and seized upon the episode as indicative of a systematic failure to respond to allegations of child abuse and the marginalisation of victims, 'gentlemen' like Tyrrell. In a sense, the Commission's reflections on this case represent a cogent summary of its conclusions with regard to the eighteen congregations which had responsibility for industrial schools. The Commission concluded:

> The Congregation's refusal to respond to *Noah Kitterick*'s [Tyrrell] complaints was indicative of an organisation that chose not to investigate criticism or admit failings.
>
> The Congregation sought to protect itself from the allegations rather than seeking to ascertain the truth.
>
> The Christian Brothers' records contained potential corroborative material, and the complaints warranted full investigation.
>
> The Congregation's current position [2009] is that allegations of abuse, both physical and sexual, came as a shock to the Congregation, but such allegations had been dealt with for many years.

Significantly, in this instance, too, the Christian Brothers were damned by their own records discovered to the Commission, rather than the statements of complainants, or the sparse records of the Department of Education.

Tyrrell was frustrated by such stonewalling by the authorities, but was greatly encouraged by the interest expressed in his case by Owen Sheehy Skeffington, a champion of education reform in the Irish Senate. The senator encouraged him to write an account of his time at the school, which might achieve reforms similar to those which followed Walter Mahon Smith's *I Did Penal Servitude* (Dublin, 1945).[115] In the interim, Joy Rudd (his former student) secured the publication of an article in *Hibernia*.[116] It was through her, too, that he made contact with the Tuairim group. Tyrrell was excited to be involved with this circle, particularly as the London group had taken up the cause of residential care of the poor. At one meeting in the Irish Club, following the publication of the *Hibernia* piece, Tyrrell spoke about Letterfrack. Greatly enthused, he informed the senator: 'the meeting was a great success … our aim now must be for secular schools. Education should be in the hands of educated people who have been trained for that work.'[117]

The subsequent Tuairim report, *Some of Our Children* (1966), however, not merely failed to incorporate his critique of the industrial schools, but lauded the progress made at Letterfrack.[118] It acknowledged informants 'alleging excessive corporal punishment in the past', but concluded that these were from an age when 'the belief that beating was good for boys appears to have been widespread in Ireland'. Moreover, in stark contrast to Tyrrell's conviction that such institutions should be closed, Tuairim was:

> particularly impressed by the appearance of the boys. They seemed to be well cared for and neatly dressed in bright, casual clothes, coloured and floral shirts, blazers and sports jackets. They were cheerful and talkative and, except that some of them had very small physiques, had not the appearance of being deprived or depressed.[119]

Neither was there progress towards the publication of his memoir, the length of which appears to have presented difficulties for the Senator. Prone to depression since his youth, and crushed by the apparent failure of his crusade, Tyrrell took his life on Hampstead Heath. In Dermot Bolger's estimation, it was this final rejection – not by the state or the church, but by the middle class Irish intelligentsia – which proved the final straw, and led him to make his final protest, when, echoing the Vietnam protesters, he set himself alight.[120]

It took a year to identify Peter Tyrrell's charred remains, while the narrative which was his legacy lay undiscovered for a further four decades. *Founded on Fear* transcends simplistic representations of Industrial Schools, and the cold analysis of the Ryan Report. Institutional care was the legacy of a failed Victorian experiment in childcare, which even without abuse, tended to compound rather than alleviate the misery of its charges. Br Byrne had impressed this on Tyrrell's class, and a succession of reports by Cussen (1936) and Kennedy (1970) confirmed it. *Founded on Fear* demonstrates the tragic human consequence of the state's failure to accept what was obvious. Moreover, while the Commission of Inquiry exposed what happened in the institutions, Tyrrell's narrative reveals what it felt like for children to suffer incarceration and rejection in later life. Like the Ryan Report, it is a stinging indictment of an entire society, which was content, with the essential collaboration of a supine judiciary, to institutionalise children of the poor and to damn them on their release.

Notes:

1. Diarmuid Whelan (ed), Peter Tyrrell, *Founded on Fear: Letterfrack Industrial School, War and Exile* (Dublin, 2006).
2. Dermot Keogh, jacket notes, *Founded on Fear* (Dublin, 2006).
3. Bruce Arnold, *Irish Independent*, 19 November 2006.
4. Mary Raftery, *Irish Times*, 19 October 2006.
5. The Christian Brothers in Ireland, Media Statement, October 2006.
6. Mary Raftery, *Irish Times*, 19 October 2006.
7 The Christian Brothers in Ireland, Media Statement, October 2006.
8. Michael R. Molino, '"The House of a Hundred Windows": Industrial Schools in Irish Writing', *New Hibernian Review*, 5.1 (2001), pp 33-52.
9. Mannix Flynn, *Nothing to Say* (Dublin, 1983); Paddy Doyle, *The God Squad* (Dublin, 1988); Patrick Touher, *Fear of the Collar: Artane Industrial School* (Dublin, 1991). Joe Dunne's, *The Stolen Child* (Dublin, 2003) presents a contrasting memoir of Carriglea Park Industrial school which characterises the Brothers there as kind and humane.
10. *The Commission of Enquiry into Child Abuse* (CICA), (Dublin, 2009), Executive Summary, p 4.
11. *Irish Times*, 11 June 2009.
12. Eoin O'Sullivan and Mary Raftery, *Suffer the Little Children: the inside story of Ireland's Industrial Schools* (Dublin, 2001).
13. *Irish Times*, 30 May 2009.
14. *Guardian*, 21 May 2009.
15. Statement from CORI on the Ryan Report, 25 May 2009.
16. *Irish Times*, 12 June 2009.

17. For a critique of the Report see Bruce Arnold, *The Irish Gulag: how the state betrayed innocent children* (Dublin, 2009), pp 297-305.

18. CICA, Vol 3, pp 199-206.

19. David Quinn, *Irish Independent*, 5 June 2009.

20. Caitriona Crowe, *Sunday Tribune*, 15 June 2000.

21. Peter Tyrrell, 'Early Days in Letterfrack', *Hibernia*, (June, 1964), p 9.

22. *Founded on Fear*, p 8.

23. *Founded on Fear*, p 12.

24. *Founded on Fear*, p 157.

25. *Irish Independent*, 8 November 2002.

26. CICA, Vol 1, p 287.

27. CICA, Executive Summary, p 4.

28. *Founded on Fear*, p 37.

29. *Founded on Fear*, p 37.

30. Peter Tyrrell, 'Early Days in Letterfrack', p 9.

31. CICA, Vol 1, p 386; *Founded on Fear*, p 42.

32. There are several autobiographical accounts of Irish Christian Brothers. See Kevin O'Malley, *Inside* (Trafford Press, British Columbia, 2004); Patrick C. Power, *Once a Brother: an Irish Christian Brother's Story* (Appletree Press, Belfast, 2008). Tom Dunne, author of *Rebellions* (Dublin, 2003), gave evidence before the Commission on Child Abuse. See Tom Dunne, 'Seven Years in the Brothers', *Dublin Review*, 6, (Spring, 2002).

33. These are pseudonyms, CICA, Vol 1, p 386.

34. Br Sorel, CICA, Vol 1, p 305.

35. Touher, *Fear of the Collar*, p 173; see Ferriter Report, CICA, Vol 5, pp 28-29.

36. CICA, Vol 1, p 305.

37. *Founded on Fear*, p 59.

38. *Founded on Fear*, pp 60-61.

39. *Founded on Fear*, p 15.

40. *Founded on Fear*, pp 15, 31.

41. *Founded on Fear*, p 72.

42. *Founded on Fear*, p 35.

43. *Founded on Fear*, pp 46, 51.

44. CICA, Executive Summary, p 4; CICA, Vol 3, pp 104-05.

45. *Founded on Fear*, pp 44-45.

46. Mavis Arnold and Heather Laskey, *Children of the Poor Clares; the story of an Irish orphanage* (Belfast, 1986), pp 129-30.

47. *Irish Independent*, 13 June 2006.

48. *Irish Times*, 12 June 2009.

49. Br Pius Noonan, CICA, Vol 1, p 294.

50. *Founded on Fear*, p 86.

51. *Founded on Fear*, p 40.

52. CICA, Vol 1, p 76.

53. CICA, Vol 1, p 521.

54. CICA, Vol 1, p 553.
55. CICA, Vol 1, p 521.
56. CICA, Vol 1, p 521.
57. CICA, Vol 1, p 296.
58. CICA, Vol 1, p 297.
59. Visitation Report, 1919, CICA, Vol 1, p 332.
60. CICA, Vol 1, p 332.
61. Visitation Report, 1941, CICA, Vol 1, p 331.
62. CICA, Public Hearings, 16 June 2005.
63. CICA, Vol 1, p 332.
64. *Founded on Fear*, p 97.
65. *Founded on Fear*, p 96.
66. CICA, Vol 1, p 333.
67. *Irish Times*, 29 November 2003.
68. CICA, Vol 1, p 345.
69. *Founded on Fear*, p 97.
70. *Founded on Fear*, p 42.
71. Mavis Arnold and Heather Laskey, *Children of the Poor Clares*, p 129.
72. CICA, Vol 1, p 337.
73. Disclosure to Confessors are discussed in CICA, Vol 3, pp 113-15.
74. *Founded on Fear*, p 60.
75. CICA, Vol 1, p 330.
76. *Irish Times*, 29 November 2003.
77. CICA, Vol 1, p 345.
78. CICA, Vol 1, p 340.
79. *Founded on Fear*, pp 41, 87.
80. *Founded on Fear*, pp 74, 85.
81. Tyrrell, 'Early days in Letterfrack', p 8; see 'Submission of the Christian Brothers on St Joseph's Industrial School, Letterfrack', CICA, 2005.
82. *Founded on Fear*, p 93.
83. *Founded on Fear*, p 48.
84. *Founded on Fear*, p 26.
85. *Founded on Fear*, p 84.
86. *Founded on Fear*, p 15.
87. Br David Gibson, Public Session, 16 June 2006; see Robbie Gilligan, 'The "Public Child" and the Reluctant State?', in *Éire Ireland*, 44:1 & 2, Summer 2009, p 272.
88. *Founded on Fear*, pp 58, 99.
89. *Founded on Fear*, p 61.
90. *Founded on Fear*, p 71.
91. CICA, Vol 1, p 294.
92. *Founded on Fear*, p 85.
93. *Founded on Fear*, p 96.
94. *Founded on Fear*, p 32.
95. *Irish Independent*, 24 June 1946.

96. *Founded on Fear*, p 61.

97. *Founded on Fear*, p 95.

98. *Founded on Fear*, p 101.

99. Joe Dunne, *The Stolen Child*, p 219.

100. *Founded on Fear*, p 103.

101. *Founded on Fear*, p 170.

102. *Founded on Fear*, p 163.

103. *Founded on Fear*, p 157.

104. *Founded on Fear*, p. 1.

105. Fr Derek Warlock to P. Tyrrell, 3 March 1958, NLI, Sheehy Skeffington Papers.

106. John Hilton to Peter Tyrrell, 21 April 1958, NLI, Sheehy Skeffington Papers.

107. Robert Nash to Br Ferdinand Clancy, 13 April 1965, CICA, public hearings, 16 June 2005, p 124.

108. Brian McGovern SC, Public Hearings, 16 June 2005.

109. Tyrrell to Br ..., 16 August 1953, CICA, public hearings, 16 June 2005, p 124.

110. Tyrrell to Br ..., 18 August 1953, CICA, public hearings, 16 June 2005, p 124.

111. CICA, Vol 1, pp 302-3.

112. Tyrrell to Owen Sheehy Skeffington, 1964, NLI Sheehy-Skeffington Papers, MS 40,543/13 cited in Diarmuid Whelan (ed), *Founded on Fear*, p xxiv.

113. Br Mulholland to Maxwell Weldon, 27 March 1957, CICA, public hearings, 16 June 2005.

114. Br David Gibson, CICA, public hearings, 16 June 2005.

115. It was this book which informed Fr Edward Flanagan's criticism of Irish penal institutions during his visit of 1946. See Dáire Keogh, 'There's No Such Thing as a Bad Boy', *History Ireland* (12), 1, 29-32; Shane Kilcommins, *Crime, punishment and the search for order in Ireland* (Dublin, 2004), p 57.

116. Peter Tyrrell, 'Early Days in Letterfrack', *Hibernia*, June 1964, p 9.

117. Tyrrell to Owen Sheehy Skeffington, 7 November 1964, NLI Sheehy-Skeffington Papers, MS 40,543/12 cited in Diarmuid Whelan (ed), *Founded on Fear*, p xxxii.

118. *Some of Our Children: a report on the residential care of the deprived child in Ireland by a London Branch Study Group* (Tuairim, 1966), p 22.

119. *Some of Our Children*, p 22.

120. Dermot Bolger, *Sunday Tribune*, 26 November 2006.

PART TWO

THE REPORT, AND REACTION

Bricks on the Road to Hell

Terry Prone

They were punished because they were an easily-identified minority. They were punished because a generation projected evil on to them. They were punished because, in the punishing, Ireland could convince itself that it was righteous, fearless and dedicated to the greater good.

History repeated itself, these last few years, except that instead of innocent children damaged by religious in whom their care had been vested, the victims, this time around, were innocent elderly nuns and priests and brothers and the attackers were the state, the media, the general public – and their own.

Never before has a single, formerly powerful and highly regarded sector of Irish society turned, within little more than a decade, into a focus for almost universal contempt and condemnation. Admittedly, the church isn't alone in this quantum shift in public perception. Bankers are up there, too, and the generality of the odium applied to them parallels what has happened to churchmen and women, as front-line staff who were and are innocent of any culpability in past or present decisions, are spat upon in public.

But bankers never enjoyed the level of public appreciation and influence on societal thinking enjoyed for generations by the church.

The reversal has been total. Satisfactorily total, from the point of view of those who suffered at the hands of the church in the past, and from the point of view of media professionals who exposed the fact that vile individuals empowered and concealed by clerical garb de-humanised the children placed in their care by categorising them as criminal, intrinsically evil, misbegotten or abandoned and therefore the living definition of 'bad seed,' to be used for perverted pleasure or disciplined with inhuman rigour.

For the past few years, the same process was applied to their successors, who were lumped together as, if not collectively committed to perversion, brutality and money-making, at least culpable by association and shared culture. They all got it in the neck from media. In a general way. But some of them got it personally, as well. The nuns who don't wear uniforms slid under the wire, unidentified. The ones in the veils and the long gowns didn't. One had her veil yanked off her in public. Another, bumping into a young woman on a pedestrian crossing, was treated to a theatrical shudder, as if she stank or was infectious. (Neither of the two was a member of an order accused of anything, or involved in any way in childcare.) Several sisters in their eighties were publicly spat upon. Guilt was assumed to be uniform and homogeneous.

This kind of consensus is without precedent, leading, not just to stereotyping and caricature, but to a set of assumptions so widely held as to silence and taint any attempt to understand the mechanisms which led to what happened: They must have known. They're all the same. They didn't apologise. If they did, it was too little, too late. Anyway, they were just using apology to get out of paying. They fooled the government. They are money-grubbing, uncaring, recalcitrant, arrogant recidivists.

One of the key contextual factors contributing to this meltdown is a failure of the church unrelated to the institutional abuse issue: the abandonment, throughout the latter half of the twentieth century, of the communications imperative by the institutional church and the congregations alike.

From the beginning, Christianity placed huge emphasis on communication, and demonstrated both innovation and skill at making the most of the possibilities provided by each century's emerging media.

The preaching of Christ, according to the gospels, demonstrated all of the key principles of good communication. It was:

Interesting
Understandable
Memorable

It was interesting, because Jesus started where his listeners were. He didn't batter them with abstruse concepts. He told stories.

A sower went out to sow his seed ...

A father had two sons ...

What made the stories interesting and understandable to the people who heard them was that they were rooted in their own experience. What made them memorable was that they were told in a way which allowed the listeners to imagine for themselves what was happening. When you force an audience to visualise what you're talking about, as opposed to presenting them with ready-made pictures of what you're talking about, examination of brain-wave patterns indicates that they become much more involved and are much more likely to remember the point you've made to them.

Because Christ talked simply, vividly, sequentially and visually, it was easy for his illiterate listeners to soak up what was said and repeat it to others. The great oral tradition of the church started there – and was built upon by each layer of people hearing the message, so that, for example, a strong folk tradition grew up which held that Lazarus had a miserable time after his resurrection. According to this legend, he lived in awful anxiety and depression, knowing he would have to re-enter the gates of death.

Great stories attract secondary storytellers, who may never have encountered the charismatic initiator of the narrative, but who, once engaged with it, tend to live, elaborate and interpret it for their generation. In the early church, that secondary storyteller was St Paul. He took the first wave of information and elucidated it using a different medium to that of the originator of the narrative. Paul used the written word, as opposed to the spoken word.

That was the pattern of church communication through the ages. Constant adoption of new media to convey the message to a new generation. Relentless concentration, not just on the message, but on finding and enforcing the best method of delivering the message.

So the Council of Mayence in 813 established that it was the duty of a priest, when preaching, to use simple language that would be immediately understood by common people.

As the great cathedrals were built, they incorporated rose windows, so that church teachers could use long pointers to focus the listeners on the visual representation of some saint or biblical figure while they were being talked about.

The illuminated manuscripts, many of them coming out of Ireland, brought together the written word and the use of visuals in a uniquely effective package.

The saints were 'branded' in the way we now brand products and corporate entities. They had a name, a logo and a Unique Selling Proposition. St Hubert was the patron saint of hunters and was the one whose help was to be sought if you were bitten by a wild animal and believed you might have contracted rabies. Other saints came with dragons or crowns of thorns or other identifiers, and were seen as having special efficacy in different situations.

Whichever way you look at it, the history of Catholicism is a history of great communication used by brilliant and reflective communicators. Nor were the listeners, down through the centuries, necessarily in a state of passive acceptance. In the Middle Ages, sermons frequently met with applause, whistling, or other expressions of either agreement or contempt, and now and again the preacher had to face being quizzed on how well he knew his topic. As a result, church communicators had to study them closely in order to get through to them and keep their attention.

By the beginning of the twentieth century, the church had an unequalled track record of either inventing, adapting or co-opt-ing every possible means of communication available at any given time: music, colour, ritual, repetition.

When radio came along, it quickly became part of the church armoury, although, in some cases, when churchmen made themselves superb at its use, it wasn't always a good thing. Before World War II., the lamentable Fr Coughlan reached radio audiences comparable with Oprah's current TV ratings.

After WWII, a few churchmen showed an extraordinary appreciation of what television could do for the church, most notably, in the US, Bishop Fulton Sheen, a native speaker of television, DVDs of whose televised sermons are still steady sellers.

In Ireland, the churchman who spotted what mass media could do for the church was Fr Joe Dunn, who, with two others, Fr Peter Lemass and Fr Desmond Forristal, hammered home to the hierarchy of the time the imperative of coming to terms with mass media; of training priests, nuns, brothers and activists to represent the church on radio and television; of using this fantastic technology the way the church had previously used each emerging communications technology.

Surrendering to the imperative, the hierarchy set up the Communications Centre with a mission to train religious, not just in homiletics, but also in the skills to broadcast and write for newspapers and magazines. The sense of excitement around the old Communications Centre was fantastic. Bunny Carr, one of the most popular TV personalities in what was then one-channel Ireland, became the Director.

A generation of media-competent religious emerged from the Communications Centre, as did some great television programming. The Radharc documentary series for TV pioneered independent TV production and allowed Irish viewers to examine social and religious issues worldwide. Figures trained there became columnists in newspapers and magazines.

It was a time of optimism and ideas, openness and enthusiasm, in the best traditions of Catholicism and media.

And it was woefully brief.

One of the problems was that the role and potential of mass

media was too narrowly understood. Intellectuals within the church regarded TV as a space best ceded to come-all-ye singing bishops and publicity-seeking priests hankering after an entertainment career. They failed to see electronic media as the 'agora', the marketplace in which the church had to be, as it had always been present in the place where people learned the news and views. In that failure to value a singular opportunity lay the seeds of the meltdown of recent years.

Scott FitzGerald, asked how he had gone broke, said 'Slowly at first, and then very quickly.' It was much the same with Catholicism and media in Ireland. One decade, the most interesting thinkers, the most influential talkers, the most passionate advocates on radio and television were prominent Catholics, particularly churchmen and women. Fast forward to the eighties and you find comedy on television dominated by caricatures like Fr Trendy and Fr Jack. You find the most interesting thinkers, the most influential talkers, the most passionate advocates on radio and television are environmentalists, journalists, economists and people with problems or causes. You find an almost total absence of church figures on TV programmes discussing the major issues of the day. You find the church portrayed through papal visits or primatial pronouncements.

When the TV programmes about the Magdalene laundries and the sexual abuse of children by clerics were broadcast, they were broadcast into a desert of media skill on the side of the church, best exemplified by Cardinal Desmond Connell, an academic whose language and episcopal garb lethally distanced him from TV viewers. TV and radio programmes hunting for church representatives had no contact book on their computers, filled with the names and mobile phone numbers of bishops, priests, nuns or brothers known to be good TV/radio communicators. In consequence, on several high profile current affairs programmes following up exposé packages, the church was represented by media virgins: men and women who had never sat in a studio in their lives. Everybody else headed for the hills and prayed they wouldn't be doorstepped. Absolutely absent was the cohort of credible, known personalities which should have been available to address the emerging horrors.

Media responses by congregational umbrella groups came late and in print. Spokespeople eventually offered were incompetent due to inexperience. The wrong language was used in the beginning, and then the fear of in some way attacking abuse survivors robbed church people of any but the blandest and least acceptable words. Lawyers attended meetings to warn of the legal dangers of saying anything of any interest to anybody. And, astonishingly in an organisation which claims to be a one-church entity, non-congregational figures within the church turned publicly on congregations.

The end results were many, varied and uniformly disastrous. Survivors provided media with heart-rending personal stories and with moments of historic drama including Michael O'Brien's contribution to one of the last editions of *Questions & Answers*. Colm O'Gorman, one of the most impelling communicators to emerge in this country in the last quarter century, was a devastating presence, most notably destroying an American Catholic who protested the generalising of the term 'abuse' to cover what he regarded as deprivation not untypical of that afflicting the poor in the thirties and forties, when it should, he proposed, be more specifically applied. Broadcasters and journalists became one with the public attitude which had developed, and which regarded any kind of wider discussion of the issue as a) further victimising the victims, b) trying to excuse the inexcusable and c) a device for squirreling out of financial compensation.

The most frightening aspect of the discussion of the Ryan Report was the belief that to examine any of the context was in some way an attempt to ameliorate the crimes committed by the religious involved. But to understand is not to excuse, and to refuse to understand the totality of what happened is in itself a version of the coercive stereotyping that leads to a lumping together of guilty and innocent, thereby empowering newer forms of injustice.

Humanity always seeks to site evil within a discrete group which is visibly different to the majority. That's what leads to anti-semitism, racism and what led to the witch craze of the fourteenth and fifteenth centuries.

The reality is, as Solzhenitsyn observed in the aftermath of thirty years incarceration in the Gulag, that 'the line separating good and evil passes not through states, nor between classes, nor between political parties either – but right through every human heart – and through all human hearts.'

That complex implication has gone unaddressed because of the satisfactory consensus that the congregations should pay up to the point of bankruptcy. But that consensus is predicated on two unexamined beliefs. The first is the conviction that the congregations are all rotten with money. The second is that the money will help the healing of survivors.

The first will be tested by the 'Three Wise Men' (or, hopefully, women) appointed by the Taoiseach to examine the statements of assets and liabilities presented by the congregations in the summer of 2009.

The second has yet to be fully explored, possibly because of the assumption that increased spend on counselling, into which some sixteen million euro has gone thus far, will be of major benefit to survivors.

Little, if any, objective data supports the value of counselling, despite its current unquestioned value in public perception. Instead of making the self-comforting assumption that the millions spent in this area will in some way lead to healing, wholeness, greater life competence or that chimera, 'closure,' it would be more honest to admit that – just as earlier taxpayers paid for children to be immured in institutions – taxpayers today are paying for someone to give a listening ear to those same children, now grown. Out of sight, out of mind. It may be a legitimate, even a positive expenditure of money, since talking about their trauma is a visceral need of survivors. It does, nonetheless, raise a discomfiting question about current society, suggesting that paying attention, long-term, to survivors is a function the nation is prepared to unquestioningly outsource, just as it un-questioningly outsourced the care of children half a century ago.

Media has been more than willing to provide that ear in re-cent times. But the fact is that, for decades, when a few survivors of abuse were introduced to reporters and researchers, initial in-terest in their stories waned as fears of libel action grew, together with doubts about the emotional stability of the witnesses. Stories died on the vine and the silence continued.

Then came the conflagration, and now, only emotional infla-tion and even worse stories will do. Because that's how we in media operate. Once we've seen the tears and given space to the victims, we move on, looking for the next worst story. Because that's the way we are.

Over time, therefore, the media chariot will leave the child abuse story behind. Media people who have covered the story in recent months are likely to be contacted, more than once, by the survivors with whom they have dealt. They will listen intently to the first few calls. After a while, they will continue to take the calls but multi-task at the same time, checking their emails as they listen. Then they will arrange, in the event of a phone call, to be interrupted by a colleague after a decent period of time lis-tening. Then they will begin not to take the calls. The law of di-minishing returns applies very brutally to victimhood, and eventually, in another sad irony, some of the survivors will go back to the congregations, because the congregations will con-tinue to listen.

While listening is a fundamental part of good communic-ation, it is not the totality of it. Speaking and being a real pres-ence, informing public thought, is another aspect of it, and this is where the failure of the Catholic Church, in the latter half of the twentieth century, to fulfil the imperative of communicating the Christian message through the media best situated to reach the masses left a vacuum carrying catastrophic consequences, not just for the church, but for the wider public.

Because the thinkers in the church had run away from the challenging possibilities of electronic media, nobody was available to it, throughout the perfect storm of the child abuse story, to analyse the economic circumstances which caused an influx of grievously unfit people into ministry, to delineate the power relationships regnant within big church institutions which drew sexual abusers to them or to discuss the group dynamics which turn good intentions into bricks on the road to hell.

Because, within some of the female congregations, the infra-structure created in previous centuries, whether in healthcare or education, had become inextricably enmeshed with the state and state funding, they lost the credibility to talk of a mission to the poor. That was greatly complicated by three other factors. One was the ageing and shrinking of the membership. One was the morphing of the notion of humility into a sense that letting people know what you were doing was in some way blowing your own trumpet. The third was the growth of an internal lang-uage wherein the most frequently used terms – such, for exam-ple, as 'charism' – meant nothing at all to outsiders, or – in the case of words like 'discern' – had a quite different meaning to non-religious.

The bottom line is that the church finds itself a despised stranger in its own land, its massive contributions devalued, its voice largely missing, not just on the child abuse issue, but on any of the significant issues of our time. That tragedy is arguably better understood, at this point, by the congregations than by the hierarchy. The hierarchy operates within the comfort of an infinite continuum. In sharp contrast, the majority of the congreg-ations operate within the certainty of proximate extinction.

They face a brutal choice, at this point.

They can go into that dark night silenced and stereotyped, silently bearing the blame for their predecessors, acquiescing in the destruction of the reputations of thousands of present and past colleagues. Or, even at this late stage, they can learn to tell their wider story and have the courage to seek opportunities to do it. As Tzvetan Todorov, in his exploration of moral life in the Nazi concentration camps put it, 'This is the paradox: stories of evil can create good.'

The processions and the programmes on radio and television and the speeches in Leinster House were the outward and visible sign of a nation offering long-overdue vindication to thousands of abuse survivors. It would be a compounding of that tragedy to allow the understanding of abuse to be boiled into a vengeful soup that would prevent Ireland from learning the broader lessons necessary for us to become the egalitarian caring society we believe ourselves to be.

Handing over money is one part of the future for the church. Communicating with humility and courage about what has been learned is just as important.

CHAPTER SIX

Responding to Institutional Abuse: The Law and its Limits

Tom O'Malley

One hallmark of the present age is a strong belief in our collective capacity to right past wrongs, particularly through the medium of law. We see this reflected in events as disparate as the civil litigation being undertaken in the United States to hold large corporations responsible for slavery in the pre-Civil War period, and the constitutional annulment of 20-year-old amnesty laws in Argentina. Closely connected with this trend is the phenomenon of the political apology as exemplified by the British Prime Minister's apology in 1997 for the Irish famine which occurred 150 years earlier.[1] Most of these events, apart from the political apology, share one characteristic: a strong faith in the law's capacity to provide effective redress for historic wrongs. Sometimes, of course, the law can provide a remedy that is reasonably commensurate with the wrong suffered although it can seldom, if ever, completely annul the wrong. Personal injuries law, for example, is designed to provide accident victims with a measure of compensation reflecting the injuries received and their likely impact on the victim's future life and wellbeing. But there are times when the wrong suffered is so deep and complex that no purely legal remedy will come close to providing adequate redress. In such cases, the law may be able to provide some form of help but it can seldom, if ever, deliver healing. Victims of violent or traumatic experiences typically look to the law for a variety of remedies such as compensation for themselves, punishment for the perpetrators and, increasingly, public investigation of the nature and causes of the harmful events in question. In Ireland, in recent times, adults who suffered severe physical and sexual abuse during childhood have quite legitimately sought all of those remedies and the state has, for the most part, responded positively.

These reflections are obviously prompted by the recent publication of the Report of the Commission to Inquire into Child Abuse, or the Ryan Report as it commonly known. Like many similar bodies established about the same time, such as the tribunals of inquiry into planning malpractice, payments to politicians and so forth, it had a limited purpose which was to investigate, to find facts in an objective and dispassionate manner and to make appropriate recommendations. Even when headed by a serving or former judge, a tribunal or a commission is not a law court which means that it may never make a finding of criminal or civil liability. Its sole and essential purpose is to investigate. The Ryan Commission certainly investigated the matters within its remit, and it did so thoroughly. Although initially intended to last for two or three years and to cost a few million euro, it ended up lasting ten years and, by a recent estimate from the Auditor and Controller General, will cost a total of €165 million. The five-volume report runs to about 2,600 pages which in turn represents a cost of more than €48,000 a page. It may seem churlish to dwell on the financial cost of the report, given the heavy price paid over many decades by thousands of young victims who did nothing wrong, but who had the misfortunate to be born into poverty or to have been orphaned. My purpose in raising the matter is connected with a point to be developed later about our collective expectations from exercises of this nature and from other forms of redress.

In the fourth century BC, Aristotle wrote of Greek tragedy producing in its audience a sense of catharsis.[2] This has proved to be a troublesome concept but it is generally accepted to indicate the creation of a sense of pity and fear and other intense emotions which have the ultimate effect of purging, renewing or revitalising those subjected to them. It is not too far-fetched to apply a similar analysis to investigation exercises such as the Ryan Commission. For many victims of institutional child abuse, appearing before the Commission and recounting their childhood experiences was doubtless a very painful and traumatic experience. And a reason-

able expectation might have been that the experience would ultimately be psychologically beneficial. Reading the final report must
also have accentuated and reawakened similar feelings. Indeed, it
made very painful reading for the public in general. But did it produce the supposed benefits of catharsis? If I might be permitted a
brief autobiographical excursus at this point, I should explain why
I have a particular interest in this dimension of the Ryan Report.

In the mid-1990s as I was putting the finishing touches to a
book entitled *Sexual Offences: Law, Policy and Punishment*,[3] victims
of institutional abuse were beginning to make their voices heard
for the first time. When invited to contribute to this book, I revisited
what I had then written in the concluding pages of *Sexual Offences*
and this, in turn, reminded me of the rationale for the tentative rec-
ommendation made there. Former residents of Goldenbridge had
just been speaking of their experiences, though few members of
the general public could have imagined the scale and intensity of
the abuse that would come to light in the years ahead. It just so
happened that I had been reading one of Austin Clarke's autobiographical works, *A Penny in the Clouds*,[4] where at one point he describes a group of orphans being marched along a Dublin street
with jibes, taunts and insults being shouted at them by some members of the public. This naturally led to reflection on who was truly
to blame for the suffering of these children and thousands of others
like them. Certainly, those who assumed direct responsibility for
their care were primarily to blame, but there was a broader issue of
social responsibility at stake as well. Many of these children might
not have received the kind of nurturing or affection which they
needed within the institutions in which they were held but, by the
same token, there was even less concern about them within the
broader community where they were generally unwanted. By the
mid-1990s, and this remains true today, there was a significant
group of people, former residents of institutions, who clearly and
justifiably carried a great sense of hurt and anger at the manner in
which they had been treated during their childhood. We often
hear victims of intra-familial sexual abuse claiming that they were
robbed of their childhood. This was certainly true, but to an even

deeper extent, of those who spent their childhood in the unforgiving and often abusive environment of certain institutions. In any
event, at the very end of *Sexual Offences*, I suggested that something modelled on a truth commission, of the kind which had just
been established in South Africa, might be a more effective way of
providing a forum of expression, and possibly some redress, to
those who had suffered institutional abuse. What they needed,
first and foremost, was an opportunity to be heard, to tell their
story. The concluding sentence of the book reads: 'But in terms of
the venue for the telling of these stories, a reconciliation centre
would provide a far more constructive atmosphere than a court-
room.'[5] To the best of my knowledge, this was one of the earliest
recommendations made for something equivalent to a commission of inquiry.

In retrospect, it was probably naïve to suppose that something
akin to a truth commission or a reconciliation centre would be sufficient in itself to offer redress, psychological or otherwise, to the
majority of victims. It was only in the following decade that we became truly aware of the extent, the depth and the complexity of the
abusive experiences which had marked the childhood of so many
of our fellow citizens. Of course, it would be equally naïve to assume that such experiences were confined to institutions. Most of
the more horrific cases to come before the courts during the past
ten or fifteen years have involved serial child abuse within the
home, the school or the neighbourhood. The abuse in some of
these cases was so frequent, prolonged and intense that, by the
time the matter came before court, nobody involved, including the
victims, could recall how often exactly the abuse had occurred.
Yet, institutional abuse is different because it is characterised by
the absence of an escape route. Children held in industrial schools
and orphanages of various kinds were essentially prisoners. There
was seldom anybody to whom they could turn even for moment-
ary respite. This, indeed, was sometimes true of intra-familial
abuse as well, but the custodial dimension of the institutional experience made it all the more inhumane.

During the late 1990s and in the early years of this decade, the silence surrounding child abuse was well and truly shattered. In some respects, it is still too early to undertake an informed assessment or analysis of the way in which narratives of childhood abuse came to light and the manner in which the state responded to them. Future social historians will doubtless find this era one of great interest. If, perhaps, there is anything positive to be said of that era of disclosure it is that it happened to be one in which the country was experiencing unprecedented prosperity. The state was therefore in a position to respond in a manner which would not have been possible in earlier decades or, for that matter, today. How wisely and constructively the resources were deployed is again a matter which future historians will doubtless analyse, though even today some of us may have misgivings in that regard. One thing, however, must be admitted. Decades of silence were broken within the space of a few short years and the government had to react quickly. Two major initiatives were undertaken, the establishment of a statutory commission to inquire into institutional abuse and the establishment of a redress board. Before considering the work of these bodies, however, a further development must be noted and that occurred in the courts.

Criminal prosecutions

The under-reporting of sexual offences in general is a well-recognised and near-universal phenomenon. For a variety of reasons, many victims of rape and other sexual assaults never formally report the matter to the police or any other official agency. As might be expected, this is particularly true of child sexual abuse and, obviously, all the more so when the abuser is the very person from whom a child might otherwise naturally seek protection. A survey of official statistics in this country from the 1920s right down to the late 1980s would suggest a remarkably low incidence of child abuse. During the period 1971 to 1993, approximately 300 cases of unlawful sexual intercourse with females under the age of 15 years, and approximately 220 cases of unlawful sexual intercourse with females aged between 15 and 17 years became known to the Gardaí. The recorded conviction rate was approximately one-third in both categories. In earlier decades, the number of offences which might now be classified as involving child sexual abuse, although that expression was not used at the time, would have been even lower. It is sometimes alleged that there were few, if any, prosecutions for child sexual abuse during the first half century of the state's existence. This is not true, as official statistics and law reports reveal. However, what the law reports also reveal is that complaints were most commonly made and prosecutions most commonly initiated in response to what might be called 'stranger abuse'. Typically the victim would be a teenage girl who had become pregnant as a result of either a consensual relationship with an older male or an act of rape. While it now seems that there may have been some awareness of sexual abuse occurring within the home or within institutions, prosecutions for such offences were very rare to the point of being virtually unknown.

From the early 1990s onwards, the Gardaí began to receive complaints of childhood abuse committed many years, sometimes decades earlier. This created a serious dilemma for prosecution authorities and courts because to permit such cases to proceed appeared to violate the right to a speedy trial as it was then understood. Justice delayed is justice denied. Yet, child sexual abuse cases clearly called for special treatment. Delayed reporting was often due to the fact that the abuser was the very person, or one of the very few, to whom the child might otherwise have looked for protection while the abuse was taking place. Even after reaching adulthood or attaining some measure of independence, victims found themselves confronted with a culture of disbelief, and there was little enthusiasm for taking their complaints seriously. All of this changed radically in the mid-1990s when the Director of Public Prosecutions began to institute criminal proceedings against persons alleged to have sexually abused children in the past, sometimes indeed in the distant past. The accused persons routinely brought parallel legal proceedings to have their trials prohibited on the ground that, owing to the lapse of time, they could no longer receive a fair trial. The High Court and Supreme Court spend several years struggling with these cases, and attempting to reconcile the rights of accused persons to a fair trial with the rights of victims to some vindication in respect of the abuse which they had suffered. For several years, the resolution of these applications for restraint of trial involved a detailed and complex assessment of whether the complainant was justified in not reporting the alleged abuse earlier and whether that delay could properly be attributed to the impact of the alleged abuse itself. Eventually in a landmark decision in 2006, the Supreme Court decided that it no longer needed to examine the reasons for failure to report because experience over the past decade had shown that the effect of abuse could have a serious inhibiting effect.[6] From then on, the sole question has been whether the effect of the delay was such that the accused person ran a real and serious risk of an unfair trial.

Even before that Supreme Court decision, there were many convictions in so-called delayed child abuse cases. Many of those convicted and sentenced to imprisonment were quite elderly. Criminal courts were routinely faced with difficult legal and moral dilemmas over the extent to which age and infirmity should save an offender from the custodial punishment which they would otherwise deserve. For the most part, these factors, unless they were present to a very pronounced degree, did not save offenders from imprisonment though they often led to a reduction in otherwise deserved custodial terms. The experience for victims was often prolonged and traumatic. As a result of the judicial review proceedings commonly undertaken by accused persons seeking to restrain their trials, several years, sometimes five or six years, might elapse between the time of the initial complaint and the ultimate verdict or appeal decision. This has now improved considerably as a result of the Supreme Court's decision in 2006.

Criminal proceedings are, of course, entirely separate and independent of any general investigations such as that carried out by the Ryan Commission. Appearance before such a commission or tribunal does not in any way confer immunity from prosecution. Witnesses summoned to appear before a statutory investigating body, such as the Ryan Commission, must answer any questions put to them. They cannot invoke the right to silence; if they could, the investigatory process would be entirely frustrated. However, as a *quid pro quo* for that, any evidence which they give to a commission or tribunal cannot be used against them in subsequent criminal proceedings. However – and this is a point on which there is often some misunderstanding – there is nothing to prevent witnesses appearing before a statutory commission or tribunal being prosecuted provided there is evidence independent of that which they themselves have given to the commission.[7] The obvious source of such independent evidence is the complainant.

We have now reached a new stage in this general process and it is one which brings new challenges. Many of those who were convicted and imprisoned have served their sentences and have been released back into the community, though sometimes under supervision. Understandably, victims often experience renewed anxiety and distress once this happens, but no further formal punishment can be visited upon the offender. Those of us who have practised in this area of law will have witnessed some fairly consistent pattern of emotions and reactions on the part of victims. Between the making of the initial complaint and the ultimate court verdict, there is a sense of hope and expectation that justice will be done and that a guilty verdict will bring 'closure', to use a rather overworked word or, at least, some element of vindication. Needless to say, when prosecutions are dropped or result in an acquittal, victims can experience a great deal of distress and disappointment. For many, the conviction of the abuser following trial can be a source of some comfort, at least to the extent that it represents a clear official declaration that it was the offender, and not the victim, who did wrong. That alone can sometimes have a therapeutic and beneficial effect. For others, the conviction and sentencing of the offender leads to a feeling of 'what next?' Unfortunately, there is usually nothing next, because the process has now been completed and, unless the conviction is quashed on appeal and a retrial ordered (something which brings its own share of trauma), the matter cannot be re-opened.

There is admittedly an element of speculation in what has just been said though it is grounded on some practical experience of dealing with victims and offenders. The essence of a crime is that it represents a wrong against the community as well as (in the case of a sexual offence) a wrong against one or more individuals. It is the state, through its police, prosecution and judicial agencies, which assumes responsibility for the prosecution and trial of defendants and the punishment of those found guilty. Under our constitutional scheme, every sentence imposed on a convicted offender must be proportionate, not only to the gravity of the offence, but also to the personal circumstances of the offender. Granted, the sentencing judge must take account of victim impact but all other relevant considerations must also be given due weight. The ultimate sentence will sometimes therefore appear lighter than the particular victims might have deemed appropriate. This connects with the central message of this paper which is to suggest that we have so far paid insufficient attention to the long-term needs of victims. The mistake, I suggest, has been to cultivate the assumption that the initiation and conclusion of legal proceedings, whether civil or criminal, can provide a complete resolution to the many varieties of injury, hurt, loss, grievance and harm which have resulted from past abuse. This is not to imply that such proceedings are pointless. On the contrary, they can serve a number of useful purposes. From a deontological or just deserts perspective, conviction following trial may result in the infliction of deserved punishment on the offender. From a more utilitarian perspective, it may serve to deter future offending, whether on the part of the particular offender or others. It may also result in the incapacitation of persons who pose a serious threat to others within the community. And, as already mentioned, it may provide some degree of solace or satisfaction to victims.

The problem, I suggest, is that we have singularly failed to follow through in terms of measuring the medium- and long-term response of victims to the various legal mechanism put in place to address their grievances. We tend to assume that, once the offender is convicted and sentenced (and especially when he is imprisoned), the victim is subjectively satisfied and has been objectively afforded sufficient redress. This is a matter about which we know very little for want of adequate research. A great deal of effort and advocacy has been devoted to the encouragement of crime reporting, and with good reason. However, it is now time to revisit many of the victims whose cases have long since been completed in the courts or before the Redress Board in order to assess where they stand today. What do they feel they have gained from the process? Did it meet with their expectations? Would they go through the experience all over again? Is there is a better way? In a major study conducted in Oxford in the early 1980s, Shapland and Duff followed a large sample of victims of a variety of offences through the criminal process, and at each point interviewed them about their responses to the various decisions taken (e.g. in relation to prosecution, bail, mode of trial, verdict and so forth).[8] What emerged most strikingly from this study was that punishment and retribution did not rank highly on victims' order of priorities. Information and, to a lesser extent, compensation were far more important to them. A similar study could usefully be undertaken in Ireland at this point covering those victims of child sexual abuse who have been through one or more of the formal systems which, for this purpose, include criminal proceedings, the Redress Board and the Ryan Commission. The purpose of such a study would be to identify the views and responses of victims in light of their experience of interacting with those systems. How beneficial has the experience been? Is there a better way?

The Commission to Inquire into Child Abuse

At the core of the Commission's report is a series of detailed chapters on each of the institutions which were subject to investigation. Included also are some background reports on the creation and operation of the residential child care system, though some of these reports are rather uneven in quality. Overall, the Report aims to be balanced, in terms of setting out the conditions in which the various institutions operated and in recounting positive as well as negative experiences. If it has a weakness, it is the failure to stand back and survey its overall findings in a more analytical and contextual fashion. In fact, the five volumes of the report as published might have been more appropriate as an appendix to a principal report containing a thorough and reflective analysis of the matters which the Commission was appointed to investigate. That would have called for a particular set of skills and expertise which the Commission probably did not have at its disposal. Had the report this additional dimension, anchoring its findings more securely within their appropriate legal, historic, economic and social contexts, it would have been a more enduring and valuable piece of work. However, the report actually produced by the Commission remains of considerable value. It recounts, often in a vivid way, the experiences of children within the institutions covered. One rather shocking revelation is how recent some of these experiences are; once thinks in particular of Cappoquin where abusive practices appear to have prevailed right into the early 1990s. But the Report overall serves its formal purpose well by having investigated and recorded for posterity the intense suffering that many of our fellow citizens endured and the intense suffering that others of our fellow citizens showed themselves capable of inflicting, and all well within living memory.

Incidentally, it would be a mistake to assume that there was a complete lack of public or political awareness of the difficulties and possible abuses connected with the industrial and reformatory school systems while they were at the height of their powers. It is particularly instructive to read the Dáil and Seanad debates on the Children Bill 1940, at a time when the quality of parliamentary debate was generally higher than it is now. Consider, in particular, the following contribution from Deputy Allen during the Second Stage of that debate:

> That is a tendency which I have seen very much in operation. When the mother of a family dies, and the children are left on the hands of the father, the father is approached by some interested person and is encouraged to have his children committed to an industrial school. I have known very many cases where that has happened, and I think it is all wrong that the father should be encouraged to send those children to an industrial

school for three, five or seven years. It would be much better if that man were given some other means of maintaining his children. If he were given an allowance by the local authority or otherwise to maintain those children, and have them nursed in their own homes or boarded-out in the rural community, it would be far better. I believe the system is wrong in that respect. I have no views on the matter of children who may have committed an offence, or in regard to whom, for certain other reasons, it is believed important that they should be detained in such places as industrial schools, but I believe the Minister will find, if he investigates the matter, that two-thirds of the children at present in industrial schools have committed no offence whatever. That is my own belief; I do not know how correct it may be.[9]

This must surely reflect one of the great scandals of the era: the cynical manipulation of bereavement and family tragedy to prop up the finances of institutions controlled by religious orders. The practice reflected in this allegation becomes all the more egregious now that we know what children would have endured had they been committed to an institution. John Philpot Curran famously said that eternal vigilance is the price of liberty. What the Ryan Report teaches is that eternal vigilance is also the price of personal safety. If we must permit the committal of children or adults to institutions (and that is sometimes necessary for good reasons), we must remain collectively vigilant to ensure that they are free from maltreatment, abuse or neglect. For that lesson alone, the exercise, however expensive, was worthwhile.

State-funded redress scheme

For the sake of completeness, brief mention may be made of the Residential Institutions Redress Board which was established in December 2002 under the provisions of the Residential Institutions Redress Act 2002. A detailed account of the background to the Act is provided in the Report of the Compensation Advisory Committee which was submitted in 2002.[10] As it happens that Committee was also chaired by Mr Sean Ryan SC (now Mr Justice

Ryan). This Redress Board was given two essential functions. The first was to make every effort to ensure that former residents of institutions were made aware of the Board's existence so that they could consider making an application for redress. The second was to consider any such applications received and to determine the amount of any appropriate reward. This system has obvious advantages. It saves former residents from having to undertake the cumbersome and stressful process of initiating civil proceedings in the courts and, in some cases, having to surmount the obstacles posed by statutory limitation periods. While legal representation seems to be the norm, former residents can still have their applications dealt within in a relatively expeditious and informal manner, at least when compared with court proceedings. The closing date for receipt of applications was 15 December 2005 although some late applications were accepted. According to the Board's Annual Report for 2007, the most recent to hand at the time of writing, it received a total of 14,549 applications. Some of the awards made were as high as €300,000 but the average is in the region of €63,000. The Board also makes a reasonable amount available for applicants' legal costs. Legal costs to date are running at close to €100 million. To date, the Board has completed 13,000 cases and has made awards totalling €787 million.[11]

Assessing the official responses

Thus far, the state's response to complaints of institutional abuse has been three-dimensional, involving prosecution, investigation and compensation. Prosecutions are obviously undertaken strictly on a case-by-case basis, and are only viable where the evidence available to the Director of Public Prosecutions reveals a realistic prospect of conviction. Needless to say, there can be no question of a prosecution where either the accused or the complainant has died in the meantime. Investigation and fact-finding were assigned to the Ryan Commission, and compensation to the Redress Board. The level of financial resources committed by the state to these various responses is obviously very significant indeed, but then so is the underlying human problem. Despite all of this, the response of victims and of the general public to the Ryan Report demonstrated anything but a sense of general satisfaction with the treatment of victims by church and state. My concern here is solely with the state response.

A leading American constitutional lawyer once drew an un-likely, but rather compelling, parallel between certain decisions of the United States Supreme Court and New Testament parables.[12] His point was some of those parables appear unsatisfactory as nar-ratives because they end just as they should be getting interesting. The parable of the prodigal son, for example, ends with the return of the prodigal and with his much more dutiful brother eventually being persuaded to come in and join the festivities. Likewise, bod-ies such as the United States Supreme Court, which is a uniquely powerful institution, sometimes make highly consequential and sometimes unduly broad decisions which later prove very divisive. But the court, once it has made them, need not worry about them any further. In a similar way, it might be argued that in this coun-try, once we adopted certain strategies for responding to child abuse, institutional or otherwise, we failed to examine their impact in any detailed manner. No doubt, many victims have benefited materially from the compensation offered by the Redress Board. Yet, there is some anecdotal evidence to suggest that some applic-ants felt that the experience re-opened wounds which they felt were beginning to heal. Care must obviously be taken not to over-generalise on these matters, but it would be surprising if some who appeared before the Child Abuse Commission did not have rather similar experiences. Clearly, we are faced with a serious dilemma here. A failure to create these institutions would have resulted in many instances of serious and prolonged abuse being ignored and that would probably be a greater evil. But we are now presented with an opportunity to embark upon a valuable learning experience, an experience that involves no more than questioning and listening.

It is only during the past quarter of a century or so that victims have become recognised as important stakeholders in the criminal process. A great deal of law reform has been introduced and implemented during that period in Ireland and elsewhere in the name of the victim, and much of it was long overdue. To take but one example, the Criminal Justice Act 1993 introduced victim impact statements at sentencing, prosecution appeals against unduly lenient sentences and court-order compensation from offenders to victims, though the last-mentioned innovation has not been very successful. Looking back on the various developments mentioned earlier in this paper, such as the Commission on Child Abuse, the Institutional Redress Board and the prosecution of so-called historic cases of child abuse, all of these were inspired by a well-justified concern for victims. Moreover, they were at times enthusiastically advocated by victim support groups and by some individual victims.

When reports and allegations of child sexual abuse in institutions and elsewhere began to surface in large numbers a decade or so ago, state agencies had to think fast. The natural reaction was to establish procedures and structures to investigate the extent of the abuse, to offer some compensation to those who had suffered and to punish those responsible. The underlying assumption, held in good faith, was that these measures would assist victims, to some degree at least. The challenge now facing us is to undertake an honest assessment as to whether they did or not. Perhaps they have been effective in affording to victims some sense that justice has been done, and also in terms of providing some form of material assistance. But there is also evidence that many victims have been left with an enduring sense of dissatisfaction at the outcomes of the various strategies put in place for their benefit. For some, the dissatisfaction may be a question of degree in the sense that they have received insufficient compensation, or they feel that offenders received less punishment than they deserve. That, at least, would mean that the structures and institutions were themselves sufficient and appropriate but that particular decisions reached were a source of dissatisfaction. But one cannot help suspecting that there is a deeper problem involved, and that the strategies themselves may have created expectations which they could not realistically meet. This makes it all the more imperative that we open and maintain an ongoing dialogue with victims in order to learn from their experiences and to gain better insights into the drawbacks as well as the merits of the ways in which we have so far responded to their needs.

Notes:
1. Likewise, on 11 May 1999, the Taoiseach formally apologised to those who had suffered abuse while in residential institutions under state supervision.
2. Aristotle, *Poetics,* trs Malcolm Heath (Penguin Classics, London, 2003).
3. Round Hall/Sweet and Maxwell, Dublin, 1996.
4. Moytura Press, Dublin, 1990.
5. *Sexual Offences: Law, Policy and Punishment,* p 449.
6. H v DPP [2006] 3 I.R. 575.
7. This is illustrated by the prosecutions of George Redmond and Frank Dunlop both of whom appeared as witnesses before the Planning Tribunal.
8. Shapland and Duff, *Victims in the Criminal Justice System* (Gower, Aldershot, 1985).
9. Dáil Debates, Vol 81, col 1127 (11 December 1940).
10. *Towards Redress and Recovery, Report to the Minister for Education and Science by The Compensation Advisory Board* (Dublin, 2002).
11. Information about the Board's work including its annual reports can be found on its website: www.rirb.ie
12. Burt, 'Constitutional Law and the Teaching of Parables' (1984) 93 *Yale Law Journal* 455.

Who was Responsible?

Donal Dorr

Who was responsible for the church scandal that has been laid bare by the Ryan Report? Let me begin by saying that *I* was responsible in some degree. I and many others like me were priests and theologians during some of the time that the abuses were going on. Ever since the great renewal of Catholic theology that came out of Vatican II in the 1960s, I knew that the Catholic teaching on sexuality had been seriously warped. I had come to realise also that a distorted notion of God as primarily a harsh judge was fairly widespread in the Catholic community – even in some priests and members of religious congregations. I now believe that these two aspects of seriously inadequate theology must have contributed to some extent to the harsh atmosphere in which cruelties of all kinds took place. Furthermore, I was increasingly aware of how seriously flawed our understanding of religious authority had been in the past. And it is quite obvious that this played a large role in the mishandling of complaints and the lamentable failures to deal with abuses and abusers.

Over the forty-eight years of my priesthood I tried, through teaching, workshops and in my writings, to communicate what I saw as a more genuinely Christian understanding of religious authority, of sexuality, and of God. In doing so, I focused on the future, believing that it would be counter-productive to harp unduly on the faulty theology and spirituality of the past. But I see now that as a priest and theologian I should have taken more seriously the fact that the defective, inadequate or distorted spirituality of the past contributed to causing a serious lack of compassion and even to gross injustices – and that these failures were particularly scandalous when they affected the treatment of children for whom Christ had a particular concern.

As I reflect now on that failure it pains me to acknowledge that I never thought very much about the situation of those who had been sent into institutions. So I only had a vague memory of the sense we had as children that 'the iron bars school' (which is what we called Letterfrack) was a place of harsh punishment. It did not occur to me that such institutions were still operative during the early years of my priesthood. And it was only quite recently that I became aware that sexual abuse had been prevalent in many of the institutions. Even when these issues began to come into the public arena I too readily assumed that they were being dealt with – I did not think that I personally had any particular responsibility to do or say anything about them. Of course, even if I had adverted to the legacy of the past, it is doubtful whether I could have done anything effective to change the situation. But that is not the point. I feel that my failure was not so much in regard to what action, if any, I could have taken, but rather in not letting the issue trouble my conscience. I want now to say that I take responsibility for this failure and to say how deeply sorry I am.

Shared Responsibility

Having acknowledged my own partial responsibility, I want now to look closely at the responsibility of others. In particular I shall try to name the different kinds and levels of responsibility of different agencies. My main purpose in doing so is to challenge the kind of scapegoating which has taken place, where the blame for the radical failures in the system has been loaded unfairly on just one segment of those who were responsible.

I begin by making a clear distinction between, on the one hand, the role of the eighteen religious congregations and other agencies which owned, staffed and ran the institutions, and, on the other hand, the role of the Irish government which, having inherited the system of 'reformatories' and 'industrial schools' from the British administration, kept the system in place for decades after it had been replaced by a more humane system in other countries.

Responsibility for the Continued Existence of the System

A whole variety of agencies were involved in maintaining the system of reformatories and industrial schools. The National Society for the Prevention of Cruelty to Children (as it was then called) played a major role in the rounding up of children to be sent to institutions. Many of the Gardaí were also involved in this process – and so too were members of the diocesan clergy. The children were committed to the institutions through the courts, so many members of the judiciary played a key role in the process. But, above all, it was successive governments which failed to change the system, long after this had been done in other countries. All of these different agencies should take responsibility for their part in continuing the system of the *committal* of thousands of children into the institutions – and this is a different issue from how the children were treated once they found themselves *in* the institutions.

The ISPCC has apologised for its part in the process. It would seem appropriate that official spokespersons for each of the other groups should also acknowledge the part that was played in the past by their members and should apologise specifically for what was done by their members. In view of the repeated and apparently wilful failure of successive governments to change the system to a more humane one, as other countries had done, it must be said that successive governments bear primary responsibility for the continued existence of this cruel and unjust system as a whole. Consequently it is only right to demand that the present government acknowledge the failures of past administrations and offer a major apology not only to those who suffered obvious abuses, but to *all* of the children who went through the system over the past seventy years.

It may be said that the former Taoiseach, Bertie Ahern, has already issued an apology. But, as I understand it, that was for the various abuses which took place once the children were already *within* the institutions, rather than for the continued existence of the whole system. We are entitled to ask for an apology from the government for the repeated failures of past administrations to reform the system.

It appears to be the case that very many of the children (such as orphans or children of needy or dysfunctional families) who were sent forcibly to 'industrial schools' (as distinct from the two 'reformatories') were in fact treated as, or named as, 'delinquents' and many of them had this on their records for years afterwards. This was a serious injustice – one for which the state owes these children a further apology.

Even in the case of those who were being committed to 'reformatories' and could therefore legitimately be called 'delinquents' (in the language of the time), it seems to be true that the courts in which they were sentenced did not give them the basic protections which would have been given to adults at that time. Indeed it seems that very few, if any, of the children who were sent into either 'reformatories' or 'industrial schools' were offered any adequate representation in the courts which 'sentenced' them. This was grossly unjust. There is even a case for saying that it constituted criminal negligence (or worse) on the part of the state, even by the standards of the time. If that is the case, then the state has an obligation not only to apologise for this injustice but also to offer some form of recompense or compensation to all of those who were subjected to this unjust treatment. (It might take the form of some monetary compensation, or an offer of some advanced educational or training course, or of counselling.)

Furthermore, many of the children were sentenced to excessively long periods of detention (effectively for all of their childhood) for relatively minor offences or misdeeds (e.g. failing to attend school regularly). It has even been alleged that judges frequently sentenced children to periods of detention much longer ·than was allowed by the law of the land – though it is not easy to know whether this was the case. It is very regrettable that the terms of reference of the Ryan Commission did not require that they investigate the extent to which these very serious allegations are justified by the facts. It is not too late to have them investigated even now – and it could be done quite quickly and at minimal cost.

Responsibilty for the Running of the System

I come now to the second aspect of the question: the responsibility of those who owned and were running the institutions where cruelty was common and abuses were prevalent. Here, it may be helpful to begin by making a clear distinction between, on the one hand, legal guilt and a rather more general moral obligation.

It needs to be said that where there is evidence that particular members of religious congregations were guilty of sexual abuse of the children in their care, or of gross and illegal physical abuse, they should be prosecuted. In these cases it seems right and appropriate that the statute of limitations should not be used to enable the offenders to avoid prosecution and, if found guilty, to be sentenced in accordance with the law of the land.

Next we come to the issue of the kind of physical and psychological punishments which were common in schools and even in many families in the Ireland of the time. Very many of the children in institutions were subjected to these kinds of punishment. It seems likely that quite frequently some of these children were subjected to punishment of this kind to a greater extent than was allowed by the law of the time. However, I know from my own experience that this also happened in the regular National School system. And it is obvious that the law was not strictly enforced at the time either in the institutions or in the regular schools. So it would seem unfair to target just the staff of the institutions in regard to the physical and psychological punishments which were so common even outside the institutions that they would have been seen as 'normal' – even though these punishments would have had a far more damaging effect on the children in institutions because they did not have families to return to for support, comfort, and redress.

It can be argued, then, that it would be unfair to make a legal demand that compensation be paid by the current leadership of the congregations, for these fairly common kinds of punishment. On the other hand, it would seem to be appropriate for each of the religious congregations to offer some compensation to those who were punished in this way and who also suffered from being unduly regimented and being treated coldly by religious staff. This compensation would come not so much as a legal obligation but as a recognition by the congregations of their failure, and of the failure of many of their members in the past, to live up to their very high Christian ideals. It would be an acknowledgment of the shame and painful regret felt by present-day members of the religious congregations, and their leadership. They would be showing corporate repentance for the fact that their congregations, and their members – whose fundamental purpose was to be witnesses to the love of God – had agreed to own and staff institutions which were inherently inhumane, and where so many children were subjected to cruel and sometimes criminal treatment; and, especially, that they had continued to operate the system long after it had become clear that far better alternatives should have been put in place by the governments of the time.

It seems clear that at least some of the members of religious congregations who were running the institutions put pressure on government and government agents to ensure that there was a regular flow of new entrants into the institutions. They felt that the numbers had to be kept up because the government funding was based on the number of children in the institutions. Undoubtedly, this was wrong. But it must be said that the primary responsibility for this wrong rests with the governments of the time, for continuing to hold on to a system where the viability of the institutions depended on having all the available places filled.

Because the religious congregations are registered as legal bodies, it seems there is no doubt that the present-day leadership of the eighteen religious congregations can be held responsible, in a strictly legal sense, for the criminal offences of some of their members in the past. However, that is very different from their being morally responsible for those past offences. There seems to have been a widespread failure, in the media and elsewhere, to make this distinction. What the present leadership should be held morally responsible for is not the past offences but how well, or how badly, they are handling the issue at the present time.

Responsibility for Supervising and Reforming the Institutions
It needs to be clearly acknowledged that it is successive Irish governments which must be held responsible for consistent failure to adequately inspect and supervise the various institutions where children were held. Furthermore, the state must be held responsible for the failure by past governments to act on the various reports which called for major changes in the system – reports going back to the 1930s and 1940s as well as more recent ones.

The state must also be held responsible for the repeated failure of the Departments of Education and of Justice to take sufficiently seriously the various complaints of abuse that were made by the children themselves or by others on their behalf.

The Ryan Report points out that, on various occasions, complaints of serious abuses were made to the religious authorities (provincial or local superiors) of the congregations whose members staffed the institutions; these complaints were made by the children themselves or by others on their behalf. It appears that it frequently happened that these complaints were not taken sufficiently seriously or were not adequately investigated or appropriate action was not taken. Where this occurred, the relevant superiors must be held responsible.

The staff of the institutions, and the religious authorities of the congregations whose members staffed the institutions, must be held criminally responsible for not reporting to the Gardaí the criminal actions of known abusers and for allowing or even facilitating the abusers in finding employment in other similar institutions. It should be recognised, however, that such failures were by no means confined to these particular institutions. Similar criminal failures were very widespread in a whole variety of spheres of life in Ireland at the time.

Who should Pay Compensation?

There is a prima facie case for saying that the primary legal responsibility for compensation to the children who went through these institutions rests with the state. This is because it was successive Irish governments which continued to maintain the system long after it should have been replaced by a more humane system. I note an important point here, namely, that the compensation in question here is one that ought to be made to all of the children who went through these institutions, and not just to those subjected to criminal abuse by staff of the institutions.

It seems to be generally accepted that the religious congregations who were the owners of the institutions now bear legal responsibility for crimes committed in the past by staff of these institutions. However, this strictly legal obligation applies only in cases where the abuse has been proved, and in cases where the offence has been formally admitted, even if not legally proved. In many cases it would be difficult if not impossible to prove legally that particular crimes of sexual abuse or serious criminal physical abuse took place. Furthermore, the attempt to do so would add further to the distress of those making the claim. For these reasons it seemed appropriate to attempt to resolve cases in a less confrontational manner through a redress board. It was hoped that this approach would obviate – or at least lessen – the need to have teams of legal experts on either side. This hope was not realised. Lawyers and barristers got involved both on the side of those making claims and on the side of the religious congregations.

In my opinion, the original offer of €128,000,000 made by the religious congregations was not an unreasonable one, since they might well have had to pay less if they had insisted on going down the legal route. The state has to take primary responsibility for the decision not to have each claim judged on strictly legal criteria. Consequently, it is not at all clear to me that there is any solid case for the state, or the media, to demand that the religious congregations should repay the government half of the €1,400,000,000 which has been paid out in compensation and legal fees.

However, it seems right that the religious congregations should make a further very generous contribution to a Support Fund. There are three reasons for this. Firstly, it would show that the present leadership and membership of the congregations acknowledge some sense of corporate moral responsibility for the criminal activities and moral failures of some of their members in the past; and it would be a practical gesture to show their sorrow for these past failures. Secondly, it would be a mark of their concern for the present welfare of those who went through the system. Thirdly, it would be a way of showing that the present-day mentality and spirituality of the membership of the congregations is more enlightened and Christian than that which prevailed in the past.

The Irish church failed to offer a truly Christian witness and challenge to the government and to the general Irish society on this issue of how marginalised children should be treated and treasured. In fact the church as a whole, with some exceptions, passively acquiesced in – and sometimes actively colluded in – a system which treated children very cruelly and unjustly. In acknowledgement of this, it would be appropriate for the Irish church, through its leadership, its ministers, and its regular members, to acknowledge this failure publicly and to contribute generously to the Support Fund for all of those who went through these institutions. This would not be a legal obligation but a recognition of having some level of corporate moral responsibility for its failure. It would be a practical way of showing its sorrow and regret. Furthermore, it would seem appropriate that the present-day leadership and members of the ISPCC, the judiciary, and the Gardaí should contribute to the Support Fund as a way of showing their regret for the role which these agencies played in the unjust and cruel system to which so many children were subjected. All of these contributions should, however, be seen not as a matter of strictly legal obligation but as based on a sense of moral responsibility, since these agencies were all to some degree morally responsible.

This would be an appropriate time for the leaders of the Irish

Catholic Church, while acknowledging their own past failures, to join with the leaders of other churches and religions, and the leadership of other prominent institutions in Irish society in asking – even demanding – that the present Irish government issue a strong and clear statement of apology. The statement would be an apology for repeated failures by successive Irish governments: firstly, the failure to reform the system for decades after other countries had moved to a more humane system; secondly, the wilful failure to implement the recommendations of reports which called for radical reform; thirdly, the failure of successive governments to monitor the system effectively; and fourthly, the ignoring or downplaying or mishandling of the many credible complaints about abuses in the institutions.

An apology of this kind by the government would balance the apologies which have already been made by the religious congregations. It would go a long way towards ensuring a more equitable recognition of shared responsibility for the scandalous abuses which were inflicted on many of the more vulnerable children of Irish society.

CHAPTER EIGHT

Putting Children First

John Littleton

A flawed understanding

The well known saying 'Children should be seen and not heard' was used in the past to indicate what was expected – and some-times demanded – of children by their parents and other desig-nated adults (including relatives, guardians, teachers, clergy and healthcare professionals) who were responsible for the vari-ous aspects of their wellbeing. Unfortunately, the interpretation of the adage was frequently misguided because, although well intentioned, it suggested that children had no right to express their opinions and concerns. Good children generally adhered to the maxim, whereas those who were boisterous and trouble-some were chastised and often disciplined.

Thus children were effectively silenced and they quickly learnt to know their place in society. They were to be seen and not heard. The majority of adults did not think of putting child-ren and their safety first. In hindsight, this was a flawed under-standing of the dignity and rights of children.

Nowadays, however, much is changing. Particularly during the past two decades, people in Irish society have been under-standably horrified by the almost non-stop revelations about child sexual abuse in domestic settings and the institutional abuse of children and vulnerable adults. Many children paid a heavy price for society's refusal to listen to their repeated cries for help in circumstances where they were exploited and abused.

The revelations have focused especially, but not exclusively, on the Catholic Church. The hypocrisy, criminal behaviour and gravely sinful actions of individual priests and members (both men and women – although, it has to be admitted, mostly men) of religious congregations have rightly been publicised. But even more scandalously, the incompetence, denial, lack of trans-parency, conspiracies of silence and shameful efforts of the institutional church at self-preservation (especially by moving known abusers from one community to another) have shattered the faith of many Catholics.[1]

Likewise, people who do not espouse Catholicism have been dismayed by the appalling disclosures, while the credibility and moral authority of the institutional church have been so badly damaged that they may never be completely regained. Nevertheless, the practice of putting children first has not been satisfactorily implemented and a cultural shift is urgently required not only in the church but throughout all strata of society.

Children in the greater schema

A few days after the publication of the *Commission to Inquire into Child Abuse Report* (widely referred to as the Ryan Report), I received an unsolicited e-mail inviting me to join a campaign to save elephants from circus abuse. I presume that many other people also received the same communication. The message was somewhat unsettling, obviously written to shock recipients into giving it favourable consideration and responding appropriately. Part of it read:

> Baby elephants are ripped away from their mothers and forced into a circus life of abuse and humiliation that is reinforced with bull hooks, whips and electric prods. Don't allow animal abuse to continue at the circus.
> Join people from around the world who are speaking out against animal abuse. Abusing circus animals for our entertainment is unnecessary and wrong. Thank you for showing that you do not support this inhumane practice.

On an initial reading, I immediately imagined that, if the words 'children' and 'institution' were substituted for 'elephant' and 'circus' respectively, the e-mail would be similar in content and tone to the Ryan Report. For example, the e-mail's phrases 'ripped away from their mothers', 'forced into a life of abuse and humiliation' and 'lengthy history of abuse' could refer to many children placed in the care of institutions operated by religious congregations and others just as easily as they refer to animals in captivity.

Therefore, the modified e-mail could be an extract from the Ryan Report, except that the phrases in the report, referring to children (human beings), are even more distressing: 'hit and beaten', 'flogged, kicked and otherwise physically assaulted', 'scalded, burned and held under water', 'broken bones, lacerations and bruising', 'inadequate heating, food, clothing and personal care', 'lack of attachment and affection', 'loss of identity', 'deprivation of family contact' and 'humiliation, constant criticism, personal denigration'.[2]

Most people are familiar with numerous campaigns to support animal welfare, especially regarding the use of animals in research by the pharmaceutical and cosmetic industries, and with campaigns to protect wildlife (for example, the Save the Dolphins movement) and the environment. Advocating animal rights and defending the human and civil rights of diverse groups (especially minority groups) in society is common. But explicitly promoting the rights of children is not as much to the forefront of most lobby groups, although there are such agencies and charities as Barnardos, the Irish Society for the Prevention of Cruelty to Children (ISPCC) and Childline (part of the ISPCC). Regrettably, public awareness has not always acknowledged the obligation to be concerned about the welfare of children. If it did, the Commission of Inquiry into Child Abuse that produced the Ryan Report would not have been necessary.

The legitimate but often inordinate attention devoted to guarding animal rights raises an important question: Do I have to think about how I would treat an animal before I can know how to treat a child? Surely the answer must be an emphatic 'No'. Ironically, the only similarities between animals and children are their trust and vulnerability, which are easily exploited.

Right-minded people could never freely engage in tormenting and torturing animals. They cringe when they hear about brutal acts being inflicted on innocent birds and animals. Yet the Ryan Report confirms beyond all doubt that ostensibly good and right-minded people knew about and, in some cases, colluded with the physical, psychological, sexual and spiritual abuse of countless innocent and defenceless children who, through no fault of their own, were effectively imprisoned in various institutions around the country where the abuse was chronic. Ironically, in many instances where children were sent to these institutions, the initiative was taken by the ISPCC, an agency specifically dedicated to eradicating cruelty from children's lives. However, that agency is severely criticised in the Ryan Report.

How could this happen in Catholic Ireland?
Because of the complex nature of such abuse, it defies a simplistic analysis. It is almost beyond human comprehension. This is not to suggest that we should not seek to understand it; we most definitely should. However, all explanations are invariably partial and inadequate.

Perhaps the best that can be said is that the institutional abuse was, in the words of the poet Robert Burns, a tragic example of 'man's inhumanity to man' (allowing for the sexist language). Or, in the famous words of Edmund Burke, it was an instance of 'all that is necessary for evil to thrive is for good people to do nothing'. These quotations are more descriptive than explanatory. They provide little consolation because they convey facts rather than causes, summarising succinctly the terrible reality in which so many children found themselves. But it would be unfair to demonise all those who worked in institutions because there were also decent and kind-hearted staff members – and this cannot be forgotten. Also, it is important to acknowledge the potential for evil that is within each one of us.

Nonetheless, we can state unequivocally that the evil perpetrated on children in institutional care was totally inexcusable. No situation could ever justify such maltreatment of human beings. Yet that is precisely what happened. Innocent children became victims of this *mysterium iniquitatis* (mystery of iniquity), a phrase used by Pope John Paul II to describe the sexual abuse of children by priests. How was it, then, that some religious brothers, sisters and priests, assigned to their congregations' institutions, were transformed from being ordinary men and women into people who engaged in depraved behaviour that traumatised so many children?

In general, people did not become priests or religious brothers and sisters to gain easy access to children so that they could abuse them. Most men and women who joined seminaries and religious congregations did not leave home to escape from neglect, torture or other types of abuse. Undoubtedly, in the late nineteenth and early-to-mid twentieth centuries, the relatively poor Irish economy had an undue influence on people's vocational choice. This combined with the difficulty of leaving after perpetual commitment – which was mirrored in marriage. Furthermore, parents frequently encouraged their children to consider the priesthood and religious life as career options (although they might not have been perceived as careers in the same way as other professions) for reasons of piety and status. Consequently, many young men and women, who were not entirely convinced of their vocation, entered seminaries and joined religious life.

But candidates were predominantly from safe, religious homes. In other words, they were mostly normal, healthy, integrated human beings. The evidence for that is obvious from meeting them and talking to them, although it is seldom newsworthy today. Infrequent visits home usually guaranteed them great deference and spoiling because their families and neighbours considered them to be holy and special.[3] So how could some of them lose their sense of compassion towards the children to whom they ministered and who were less privileged than themselves? Why did some priests and religious become serial abusers?

The strategy of abusers and the silent collusion

From talking to survivors of sexual abuse, I have learned that paedophiles are complex people who know what they are doing, whatever they might pretend. They keep their activities secret while inflicting pain and shame on innocent, vulnerable victims. They project the blame for their habits onto victims through clever manipulation and control. Initially, they carefully groom their victims by focusing on their vulnerability to discover what they need and fear most. Then they move in, having persuaded victims that there is nowhere to escape and that they will not be rescued or believed. Victims then helplessly became part of the vicious cycle, convincing themselves that the abuse will not kill them and that they can cope with it. In this way, the abuse and its devastating effects continue relentlessly.

Some fellow-religious and other staff members genuinely did not know about the abusive situations and the reasons for this must be investigated. Perhaps it was due to overwork and exhaustion. Obviously, it was at least partly due to clever manipulation by the abusers.[4] However, what about those who knew but, through their silence and inactivity, colluded with the abuse (whether sexual or physical) in religious-owned institutions? By ignoring what they saw and heard, by refusing to believe and act adequately, they conspired with the abusers. Naturally, they would refute the charge that they also abused the children through their indifference and their sins of omission.[5]

By doing nothing, colluders did something seriously damaging: they gave evil the permission to reign with fear and terror. Accordingly, the whole lives of abuse victims have been affected by the way they were treated in the institutions (for example, the ripple effect of low self-esteem, self-harming, alcoholism, broken marriages and dysfunctional family lives). So why did nobody shout 'Stop!'? Where were the whistle-blowers? Those who colluded claimed that they did not know about the abuse, that they did not recognise the signs. The reality, however, is that they ignored the signs. Their sin of omission could be depicted as the sin of 'not knowing' – for which they are personally culpable. The sin of not knowing was an instance of structural sin insidiously infiltrating the institution's levels of organisation.

Abolishing institutions

In responding to the Ryan Report, several commentators have suggested that all religious institutions should be shut down and that priests and religious should be removed completely from every school and hospital where they minister.[6] Others have advised people to abandon Catholicism. But, quite apart from being inequitable towards institutions that operate to the best of their ability, that decision would not solve the scandal of child abuse (particularly sexual abuse) because, as statistical research indicates, it occurs mostly in the family context and is most often perpetrated by family members or their close acquaintances. Nonetheless, people are entitled to expect very high standards of behaviour from priests and those in religious life.

The concept of 'institution' is a sociological phenomenon. An institution is basically a movement, an organisation of people who work together for a common goal. The institution assists and benefits human society at a communal level because its purpose is to perform tasks that transcend the competence of any one person. The main risk associated with an institution is that, unless it has a definite mission, proper structures and appropriate monitoring, it may simply perpetuate itself, working for bad instead of good. Institutionalism then takes precedence while the institution becomes an end in itself rather than a means to an end. Tragically, this is what had happened in those institutions that became the subject matter of the Commission to Inquire into Child Abuse. Institutionalism (and clericalism, which is another form of institutionalism) can never be justifiably tolerated by the church.

The facts are that the vast majority of Irish clergy and religious have tirelessly dedicated their lives to helping needy and vulnerable people. Through their varied ministries, they have preached the Christian message of forgiveness and hope. Sometimes they have been supported by specially established institutions so that their work is more effective. This is particularly true of Irish missionaries working abroad who have established in South American countries, for example, hospitals, orphanages and care homes that respond to the needs of those local people living in dire poverty. Those people have often been abandoned by their families and are alone. The institutions provide them with a refuge and give them a sense of belonging. Therefore, shutting down all religious institutions is certainly not the solution to the difficulties discussed in the Ryan Report. Instead, appropriate opportunities for healing are required.

Towards healing[7]
The first stage in being healed from the effects of institutional abuse is disclosure of the truth. The basic truth about institutional abuse is: many residents in institutions administered by church and state suffered unspeakable cruelty and violence. This truth must be recounted and put into the public domain so that victims and survivors know that they are finally being listened to and believed. The truth demands to be told so that the perpetrators are confronted by their criminal and sinful behaviour, and by the devastation they have caused in their victims' lives. Revealing the truth ensures that abusers will never again be able to deny – with any authenticity – what they have done and, hopefully, they will begin to accept responsibility for their actions. Finally, the truth must be told so that the wider society will learn from the frightful happenings in the past and resolve never to let such incidents occur again.

Significantly, the Ryan Report, along with the earlier Ferns Report[8] and other reports that will follow,[9] is a major contribution to the first stage of healing because it compels all of us to acknowledge the truth of what happened. At this disconcerting time, we need to be encouraged by the words of Jesus: 'The truth will set you free' (John 8:32). Everyone, not least the victims and survivors, needs to be liberated from the scourge of every sort of abuse, and the first step is disclosure of the truth.

The second stage of healing is justice being done and being seen to be done. This means that abusers must be made accountable for their actions. Criminal and civil proceedings must be pursued against them, where possible, in the courts. In addition, victims and survivors are entitled to compensation for being abused while in the care of church and state institutions. The relevant church authorities and government departments need to accept responsibility for their negligence.[10] They must be prepared to deal honestly and respectfully with the consequences of that negligence. There can be no more obfuscation.

Monetary compensation is crucial because it demonstrates sorrow on the part of the perpetrators and the offending institutions. Simultaneously, it helps the victims to avail of facilities that will alleviate the effects of their abuse, thereby enabling them to evolve from being victims to being survivors. That is why merely saying 'Sorry' is never sufficient. It would be too easy, perhaps even meaningless. In addition, other compensations are necessary. These include the provision of adequate counselling and psychotherapy services, and the offering of opportunities for further education and professional development. Otherwise, we cannot claim that we live in a just society.

The third and most difficult stage in the healing process is forgiveness, which is one of the most demanding challenges for Christians. Forgiveness does not necessarily entail forgetting, as many people mistakenly assume. Actually, it is sometimes very important not to forget harmful episodes in life so that they can be avoided in the future. Forgiveness, then, is essentially about letting go – letting go of the hurt caused by the abuser so that he or she can no longer harm the survivor. Forgiveness is made easier for human beings when expressions of sorrow are accompanied by gestures of atonement. Actions demonstrate genuine sorrow and remorse which may eventually lead to reconciliation. This makes the risk involved in forgiveness worthwhile for the victim.

Finally, it is worth noting that the need for healing is not confined to the victims and survivors of institutional abuse. Healing is desperately needed in the lives of most priests and religious who, themselves, have been betrayed and scandalised by the abusive behaviour of some of their colleagues that is detailed in the Ryan Report, and who yet again have nearly abandoned their hope for transparent and honourable church leadership in these troubled times. Also, while there is little or no sympathy for the perpetrators of institutional abuse – and that is understandable – they too need to experience healing and forgiveness, but only within the wider context of disclosing the truth, and justice being seen to be done.

*Another part of the story*There is another part of the story about institutions, the part that focuses on goodness rather than evil, which is not treated extensively in the Ryan Report, and that part of the story must also be told more fully.[11] But now is not the time because many people are unable or unwilling to listen to it. They are outraged by the predominantly sordid details contained in the Ryan Report, so it may take a while before they will be ready to accept additional information that will complement what has already been revealed. Those other facts must also be put in the public domain so that the entire story becomes known and so that it will be possible to make an overall assessment that will be reasonable and fair to all members of staff. While it is deeply regrettable that children were abused, it is sad that the reputations of many good men and women who worked in the institutions were tarnished by the crimes and sins of some of their colleagues.

I believe that most priests and religious are fundamentally good people. My experiences of those whom I have encountered over nearly half a century have generally been pleasant and wholesome. During my childhood and teenage years (I received my early schooling from the Mercy Sisters and I was an altar server in my local parish church) and my priestly ministry (I have been a priest for 23 years, with varied ministries in several countries), I have met and worked with some wonderful priests and religious. They were 'the salt of the earth': decent, normal human beings whose lives radiated the joy and kindness of the gospel.

Not surprisingly, I have dealt with some priests and religious who were impatient, grumpy, lazy and cynical – just like the rest of humanity. However, aside from occasional rudeness and sarcasm, I have never experienced physical, psychological, spiritual or sexual abuse from any priest or religious. Neither have any of my closest priest friends. We all know priests and religious against whom allegations of abuse have been made and some of whom have been prosecuted and convicted in court, but none of us have personally been abused by a priest or religious.

Let me go further. I know a few priests and religious who have saved children from being abused by adults because, on discovering the abusive situations, they did exactly what every law-abiding citizen would do: they reported the abuse to the proper authorities and offered appropriate pastoral care to the victim. This typifies the untold part of the story.

Putting children first
There are several important lessons to be learned from the Ryan Report. Undoubtedly, the one that requires urgent implement- ation is that children must be put first by giving them a voice in society. Thus, for example, the proverb 'Children should be seen and not heard', quoted in the opening paragraph of this essay, needs to be modified to read 'Children should be seen and heard'. This means that acknowledging children's status must now become a priority. We all need to learn to put children first.

If children had been put first during the decades of institut- ional abuse, the abusers would have been detected quickly and brought to justice. Their depraved behaviour would have been stopped and they would have been removed from ministry, thereby posing no further threat to the safety of vulnerable children, many of whom would not have had to endure tortured and troubled lives. Hence the practice of putting children first must become enshrined in the culture of Irish society and in the ethos of the church.

The Ryan Report will have a considerable impact on church and state. Its lessons will reinforce the contemporary under- standing that childhood is an integral part of human life and not just a preparation for adulthood. Children are no longer per- ceived to be underdeveloped adults. Child protection must be a priority and nothing must ever be allowed to happen again that could jeopardise the integrity of childhood.

In the context of putting children first, the reflection, Children learn what they live, by Dorothy Law Nolte merits se- rious and humble meditation:

If children live with criticism, they learn to condemn.
If children live with hostility, they learn to fight.
If children live with fear, they learn to be apprehensive.

If children live with pity, they learn to feel sorry for themselves.
If children live with ridicule, they learn to feel shy.
If children live with jealousy, they learn to feel envy.
If children live with shame, they learn to feel guilty.
If children live with encouragement, they learn confidence.
If children live with tolerance, they learn patience.
If children live with praise, they learn appreciation.
If children live with acceptance, they learn to love.
If children live with approval, they learn to like themselves.
If children live with recognition, they learn it is good to have a goal.
If children live with sharing, they learn generosity.
If children live with honesty, they learn truthfulness.
If children live with fairness, they learn justice.
If children live with kindness and consideration, they learn respect.
If children live with security, they learn to have faith
    in themselves and in those about them.
If children live with friendliness, they learn
    the world is a nice place in which to live.

Notes:

1. The classic New Testament example of an attempt at institutional self-preservation is found in John 11:50 when Caiphas, the high priest, said to the other religious leaders: 'You don't seem to have grasped the situation at all; you fail to see that it is better for one man [Jesus] to die for the people, than for the whole nation to be destroyed.'

2. See Ryan Report, Executive Summary, p 13. These phrases could equally be used to describe the documented abuses of adult prisoners that have occurred in Abu Ghraib Prison (Iraq) and Guantánamo Bay Detention Camp (Cuba) during the past few years.

3. For example, Christian Brothers were allowed five days at home every five years (the quinquennial visit). This was an austere concession by today's standards.

4. There is, for example, the recent case of the Austrian woman, Rosemarie Fritzl, who claims that she was unaware that her husband, Josef, had kidnapped their daughter and imprisoned her in a cellar for 24 years during which he behaved violently and incestuously towards her.

5. Sins of omission are committed when people do not do what, morally, they are obliged to do.

6. It must be remembered that the events and happenings discussed in the Ryan Report are historical, not contemporaneous. Thus automatically removing priests and religious who are currently working in such institutions could not be justified.

7. In 2005, the Irish Catholic Bishops' Conference published a Lenten reflection, entitled *Towards healing*, which dealt with child protection.

8. The Ferns Inquiry, which identified more than 100 allegations of child sexual abuse made between 1962 and 2002 against priests in the Diocese of Ferns, presented its report to the Minister for Health and Children in October 2005.

9. For example, the report into the handling of clerical sex abuse in the Archdiocese of Dublin, due to be published in autumn 2009. There may be others in the future.

10. Victim support groups have expressed serious misgivings about the confidentiality requirement in the legislation establishing the Residential Institutions Redress Scheme. This requirement has undermined people's confidence in the Scheme.

11. See Ryan Report, vol III, chapter 10 and sections of chapters 13-18 which deal with positive experiences and happy memories reported by residents.

Reflections of a Layman on the Ryan Report

Eamon Maher

It was a pleasant surprise to be asked by the editor to contribute a chapter to this book on the Ryan Report. To me it was a sign of how far Ireland has travelled in recent years that a layman be approached by a priest to share his views about a report that is damning of the treatment meted out to children in religious-run institutions to which they were committed, often for the simple reason that they were from poor families or born out of wedlock. My opinions will be as measured as possible, in spite of my belief that it is not wise to deal in too dispassionate a manner with the physical violence and sexual and psychological trauma that were visited on vulnerable children a few mere decades ago in these establishments.

Writing in *The Irish Times* on the 23 May 2009, Fintan O'Toole drew an analogy between how people reacted to the incarceration of 170,000 children in our 50 or so industrial schools to Hubert Butler's account of Drancy, the camp in Paris where, during World War II, children were held before being transported to Auschwitz. Butler wrote: 'Had four or five children only been killed or burned ... we would have responded emotionally and their fate would have been carved on a marble tablet.' Relating this to the Irish experience, O'Toole observed: 'Had seven or 17 or even 70 children been enslaved by church and state, we could weep for their fate. But 170,000 is too many and the things inflicted on them too vile.'[1] I had not actually realised that so many had passed through these institutions: it is indeed a lot of human suffering to come to terms with.

It is important to recall in the survivors' own words exactly what did happen to them. Here is a selection of comments taken from the *Report of the Commission to Inquire into Child Abuse* and quoted in Irish newspapers on May 21, 2009:

The worst thing was seeing a young boy die. He was 12 years old … he was beaten by brothers on the landing and he fell over a banister.

I was beaten and hospitalised by the head brother and not allowed to go to my father's funeral in case my bruises were seen.

I was beaten until knocked out and my head split. My finger was placed in boiling water until all feeling was lost.

I was stripped naked by a nun and beaten with a stick and given no supper and humiliated.

I never gave my daughters or my sons a hug. I associate touch with sex, I could not put my arms a round them. I am always wary if I bump into someone. I am always saying 'sorry, sorry, sorry' … I feel so dirty, afraid …

At six I was raped by a nun and at 10 I was hit with a poker on the head by a nun.

I was tied to a cross and raped whilst others masturbated at the side.

I wouldn't stop crying. I was down in the ground. The first thing he could lay his hand on was a hammer and he hit me and damaged me.

One brother kept watch while the other abused me [sexually] … then they changed over. Every time it ended with a severe beating. When I told the priest about it in Confession, he called me a liar. I never spoke about it again.

I was beaten stark naked for wetting the bed, two or three different people would beat me. They liked beating kids naked.

The horrors that took place behind the walls of these hellish in-stitutions were kept silent for far too long and often for reasons similar to those that prompted clerical authorities to keep hidden the clerical abuse scandals: the pathological fear of compensation claims pouring in. Attempts have been made by certain commentators, many of them sympathetic to the religious orders, to explain away the abuse within the industrial schools and reformatories by saying that these things occurred in a very different Ireland to the one that exists today, at a time when the attitude to corporal punishment was ambivalent, especially when it came to those who were viewed as being low-lifes, the spawn of criminals and whores. Also, the argument that the majority of sexual abuse occurs in the home is a sinister way of detracting from the degree to which men and women of the cloth, who were revered in Ireland as the upholders of the gospel message of love, indulged in horrible practices with minors. That they should be guilty of heinous crimes against innocent and defenceless children goes completely against what their vocation was supposed to consist of, and hence the level of opprobrium the revelations inspired in people towards the perpetrators.

There is a feeling of guilt also. Essentially, we in Ireland allowed prison camps to be created for children, places where male and female religious acted outside of the rule of law. In fact, they were allowed establish and enact the laws according to which these corrective schools were run, with little or no interference from the state. In addition, there was undoubtedly collusion on the part of the agencies of the state, most notably the Judiciary, the social services and the Department of Education. Very few dared to speak out against how the schools were run. The Catholic Church in Ireland at the time enjoyed too much power and prestige to be challenged in any meaningful way. Those who tried to break the silence, like the Artane chaplain, Fr Henry Moore, were either not taken seriously or else were excoriated. Thus the violence continued unchecked, the isolation and suffering of the inmates exacerbated by the knowledge that their cries for help would not be heard. It was a question of 'offering it up', surviving as best one could in the midst of systemic abuse and violence. At this juncture, I cannot help thinking of the former Director of One in Four, Colm O'Gorman, and his experiences at the hands of Fr Sean Fortune. In his compelling memoir, *Beyond Belief*, he wrote:

> In order to escape I would have to name the abuse and that couldn't happen because to do so would destroy the very fabric of the society I lived in. It's no exaggeration to say that it would mean the end of the world ... or at least the end of the world as the Ireland of the early 1980s knew it.[2]

O'Gorman discovered at an early stage that to 'name' the abuse he was suffering at the hands of a sinister and manipulative priest would bring shame and disgrace on his family and himself. The fact that from the age of 14 a Catholic priest was using his body for sexual gratification, that he was being raped, forced to perform oral sex, degraded in the worst possible ways, all this had to be hidden from public view because no one would believe him, because society was complicit in keeping the lid on such sordidness. As was so often the case of the victims in the Industrial Schools, the victim was treated as if he/she was responsible for what had happened: 'This sex is worse than bad, it is evil. But he is a priest and cannot be evil, so I must be evil.'[3] Then there was the difficulty in finding the words to describe what had happened:

> Words like abuse are easy to use. Words can't show how it was. Words can't describe the smell, the sounds, the taste of it all. Words can't tell how it felt.
>
> It was sordid and degrading and hateful. Hateful is an important word here ... it was full of hate. Full of hatred of himself and of what I was to him. I believe he hated the boy, the boy he had been and the boy I was before him now. He destroyed that boy. He seduced and sickened him. He defiled and destroyed him until he was no more.[4]

Many of the testimonies in the Ryan Report record similar hate on the part of the male and female religious. On several occasions, the sexual abuse was followed by a savage beating, with the children being told they had the devil in them, that they were the source of temptation and evil. Unlike so many victims, Colm O'Gorman grew to appreciate that he was not to blame for what had happened to him and, more importantly, he had the intelligence and the facility with words to communicate his message in a forceful and unambiguous manner. The inmates of Letterfrack, Goldenbridge and Artane, to name three of the more notorious institutions, did not in general possess these skills. Their spirit was broken along with their bodies. They felt worthless, a shameful blot on society.

Much of the awfulness that is chronicled in the Ryan Report had its origin in an ambivalent and unhealthy attitude towards sex. Tom Inglis points out how it was almost impossible to mention sex in the Ireland of three or four decades ago. Sex was associated with sin, impurity, lack of control. As such, it was viewed as being dangerous. Sadism and sexual perversion, as they became manifest in the reformatories and industrial schools, were the result of a repressed sexuality among a large number of the male and female religious who were in charge of these places. They were the pawns of a power structure that brokered no challenge to its authority. Inglis writes:

> They were caught in a regime of Catholic thought and practice from which, effectively, there was little escape. There was no mechanism by which they could talk about themselves, their desires and frustrations. They took their anger out on the children. The children became their scapegoats.[5]

Patsy McGarry develops this point further by showing how the clergy preached the virtues of the celibate life, which was viewed as superior to the married state. He continues: '[…] sexual activity outside marriage was evil, and even within where the intention was not procreation. Sexual pleasure was taboo, powerful evidence of an inferior animal nature that constantly threatened what was divine in the human.'[6] The sermons given in most Irish churches concentrated on issues associated with sex, rather than on the readings from scripture, and in a way that always promulgated an unhealthy distrust of the flesh. Sex thus assumed the characteristics of a national obsession. Tony Flannery is very forthright on this issue: 'The Catholic attitudes to sex that my generation grew up with were oppressive and guilt-ridden. The ridiculous idea of associating all sexual thoughts and desires with mortal sin was seriously damaging to the person.' Indeed it was! But, even more damagingly: 'It led to a great deal of sexual repression, and when sexual attitudes and desires are repressed at an early age, they tend to emerge in gravely unhealthy and perverted ways.'[7] Those working in the industrial schools and reformatories were the products of this skewed view of sexuality. In many cases, the religious cloth served as a convenient means of having untrammeled access to vulnerable children. Absolute authority, allied to a problematic sexuality and complete control over those in their care, formed a toxic cocktail, the results of which have emerged in recent weeks and months. This type of attitude needs to be placed in a broader context, which is what I hope to do now in an effort to explain how the male and female religious working in these institutions carried with them certain values and traits that proved so dangerous to children.

A good place to start might be the work of one of Ireland's most loved and respected writers, the late John McGahern. McGahern was acutely aware that the Irish approach to sexuality was inherently unhealthy. He wrote in *Memoir*:

> Authority's writ ran from God the Father down and could not be questioned. Violence reigned as often as not in the homes as well. One of the compounds at its base was sexual sickness and frustration, as sex was seen, officially, as unclean and sinful, allowable only when it too was licensed. Doctrine separated body and soul.[8]

With the artist's sensitivity, McGahern was able to link the violence to sexual frustration. A classic example of this can be seen in the opening lines of his second novel, *The Dark*, which was banned on its publication in 1965 and caused the writer to lose his job as a primary school teacher in Clontarf. The young protagonist, Mahoney, is heard to utter a curse under his breath and is forced to strip and bend over a chair while his father brings the leather down on the chair in a simulated beating that causes the son to urinate on the floor in terror. The older man is sexually aroused by this feeling of power: 'He didn't lift a hand, as if the stripping compelled by his will alone gave him pleasure'.[9] The abuse of power is one of the main causes for the events that are related in the Ryan Report. Elaine Byrne, in an article on this topic, quoted a passage from the Book of Proverbs that reads: 'When the righteous are in authority, the people rejoice: but when the wicked beareth rule, the people mourn.' According to Byrne, the Catholic Church in Ireland felt it 'was above reproach, without question and beyond criticism'. She quoted a Sr Carmella, a Mercy nun who was principal at St Joseph's Industrial School in Cliften who followed the instructions of the Reverend Mother because 'she was that kind of person that her word was law, she was an authority and that was it'.[10] Many of the religious working in the institutions came from relatively humble backgrounds and the power they assumed in the schools was a heady drug which a good number found impossible to resist. In McGahern's fiction, the father exerts power only in the home and the victims are as often as not the children. The beatings are not as traumatic as the sexual abuse:

> The worst was to have to sleep with him the nights he wanted love, strain of waiting for him to come to bed, no hope of sleep in the waiting – counting and losing the count of the thirty-two boards across the ceiling, trying to pick out the darker circles of the knots beneath the varnish.[11]

A lighted match that is pushed at the child's eyelids, the prelude to a conversation that will end up with the massaging of the thighs and later the groin, leads to what Mahoney refers to as 'the dirty rags of intimacy'. The father says: 'You like that – it's good for you – it relaxes you – it lets you sleep. Would you like me to rub you here? It'll ease wind. You like that? It'll let you sleep.'[12] Approaching such a taboo subject in 1960s Ireland was very daring and McGahern paid a heavy price when he lost his job as a result of the banning. I sometimes wonder how he could have expected any other outcome given that the church at the time was completely in control of the Catholic schools in the country. The then Archbishop of Dublin, John Charles McQuaid, campaigned strenuously for McGahern to be removed from his teaching position after the banning. Whatever about alluding to child abuse in the home, dealing with the prospect of clerical child abuse, as McGahern did in *The Dark*, was totally unacceptable. Mahoney made a promise to his mother, now deceased, that he would become a priest and one day say Mass for her. He travels to see his cousin, Fr Gerald, with a view to discussing his vocation. At the start of the stay, the pair pay a visit to the Ryans' house where his sister Joan has found a position helping in the shop that is owned by this family. Mahoney is disturbed when told by Joan that 'It's worse than home' and he later discovers that Mr Ryan has been making lewd observations to her as well as putting his hand up her dress. Her brother resolves to take her home with him in a moment of rare decisiveness.

Fr Gerald has a boy of around Mahoney's age keeping house for him, something that seems unusual, even untoward. Why would a boy be employed to do this type of work? Mahoney is then perplexed when his cousin joins him in his room late at night and proceeds to question him in an intrusive manner about his sexual fantasies and problems with masturbation. Mahoney feels he is not worthy of the priesthood because of his impurity and the presence of the semi-naked priest in the bed alongside him strikes him as being uncomfortably similar to the abuse he endures at his father's hands. After admitting his weakness to Fr Gerald, he asks the priest if he ever had to fight that particular sin himself when he was younger. The question is met with a silence that the adolescent finds shameful: he has revealed all and gets nothing in return. At a certain point, the shame turns to anger:

> What right had he (Fr Gerald) to come and lie with you in bed, his body hot against yours, his arm around your shoul-

ders. Almost as the cursed nights when you father used stroke your thighs.[13]

While nothing happens on this occasion, the boy spots enough resemblances between the behaviour of his father and the priest to be aware of the potential for a repeat of the abuse. He abandons all thoughts of the priesthood at this point and leaves the priest's house sooner than expected, accompanied by his sister whom he saves from the lascivious Mr Ryan, a pillar of the local church. What is most striking about McGahern's novel is his courageous decision to tackle a subject like abuse at this time and in this manner. From *Memoir* we know that the writer's father also interfered with him. Note how similar the description is to what occurred in the Mahoney household:

> He never interfered with me in an obviously sexual way, but he frequently massaged my belly and thighs. As in all other things connected with the family, he asserted that he was doing this for my own good: it relaxed taut muscles, eased wind and helped bring on sleep … Looking back, and remembering his tone of voice and the rhythmic movement of his hand, I suspect he was masturbating. During the beatings, there was sometimes the same sexual undertow, but louder, coarser.[14]

You may feel as though we have drifted a long way from the Ryan Report, but it is my contention that McGahern did much to alert the public about certain dark aspects of Irish society as early as the 1960s, when such topics were never openly discussed. A puritanical church inspired an irrational hatred of the body in Irish people at the time. This resulted in the crimes of their parents being visited on the children. Hence illegitimacy was dealt with in a forceful manner, with the children usually being taken from their mothers shortly after birth. Poverty was another 'sin' in the eyes of Irish society, possibly as a result of the economic problems that followed our newly-won independence from Britain and the long shadow cast by the Famine. For whatever reason, the poor did not enjoy anything like equal rights to the professional classes and those with money. When they arrived in the corrective institutions, they were viewed as subhuman, lesser beings, an outlook that made it possible to treat them like animals. Writing shortly after the three-part documentary entitled *States of Fear* (1999) exposed the horrors of what went on in these institutions, the journalist Mary Kenny wrote:

> The scale of the cruelty seemed so systematic that it was as though it was inherent in our history: not only were the religious who ran these institutions accused before the bar of history, so was the Irish state, which utterly failed to take responsibility for those in its care. So, indeed, were the complacent middle classes, who used these reformatories as a source for servants, and so too was the media, which remained indifferent to the punitive regimes around them.[15]

The fault certainly did not lie entirely with the religious orders, which may be what prompted the then Taoiseach, Bertie Ahern, to issue a formal government apology on behalf of the government and its citizens to the victims of this system in May 1999. The reaction of the religious orders to the revelations mirrors closely the approach of the bishops when it came to clerical child abuse: they circled the wagons, proclaimed ignorance of what was going on, denied that things were as bad as the media were making them out to be. (There was collective amnesia also about the decision to take out insurance against potential compensation claims some time before the full extent of the abuse was revealed). Mary Raftery sums it up well when she writes:

> When protecting their own (usually financial) interests, the religious orders displayed a zeal and even ferocity notably absent in their attempts down the years to control the criminal battery, assault and rape perpetrated by their member brothers, priests and nuns against small children.[16]

Similarly, the Irish bishops, shocked by the extent of the claims that poured in during the clerical abuse scandals, tried to protect their own interests by forcing victims to bring their cases to court or feigning disbelief that there could be any substance to allegations against priests who were known to have a track record of paedophilia. With the publication of *The Ferns Report* in 2005, there could be no more denying that certain bishops sent priests who were known abusers from parish to parish, where they repeatedly inflicted pain on innocent and powerless victims. As their power began to slip, the desire remained to hold on to its vestiges by whatever means possible. When the public reacted angrily to the improper and reprehensible acts that had been perpetrated by some priests, the hierarchy behaved like rabbits caught in the car headlights. They attempted to minimise at all costs the potential damage to the institution to which they had pledged their lives. Tom Inglis wrote on the publication of *The Ferns Report*:

> There was a time when people trusted the church. It supposedly told us the truth about life and death. While other organisatons had material interests, the church was only interested in proclaiming the truth. Now we see that it has an almost pathological inability to tell the truth about itself.[17]

Fair analyst that he is, however, Inglis also stipulated that the Catholic Church in Ireland merely showed itself to possess the same weaknesses as those displayed by any group that enjoys a monopoly of power. Recently, politicians, the Garda Síochána, lawyers, bankers, journalists, teachers, developers were also seen to have corrupt and evil members in their ranks. That said, the trust placed in priests has a special significance, as they are supposed to act in a Christ-like manner. What was particularly annoying to Irish people was the way in which the hierarchy attempted to avoid facing up to their inept mismanagement of the crisis. After *The Ferns Report*, certain measures were put in place by the church to ensure that children's safety would be paramount in the future. However, in recent times, the Bishop of Cloyne, John Magee, was found by the National Board for Safeguarding Children to have mishandled cases of alleged sexual abuse by priests in his diocese. It was another clear case of a bishop acting as sole arbiter in allegations of abuse being brought against priests. Cardinal Seán Brady's initial reaction seemed to indicate dissatisfaction when he stated that the first concern in these matters must be the protection of innocent children. But as the weeks went by and Bishop Magee refused to resign, the mood changed perceptibly. On the 13 January 2009 Cardinal Brady rejected calls for Magee's resignation, declaring that he had known this man for over 50 years and found him to be a 'reliable and dependable person'. (In his handling the allegations of abuse, he had shown himself to be anything other than 'reliable' and 'dependable'.)

On 6 March 2009, John Magee finally agreed to step aside to make room for the Archbishop of Cashel and Emly, Dermot Clifford's appointment as apostolic administrator of the Cloyne diocese. The gesture was far too little, far too late. The Cloyne debacle was just one more in a long line of self-inflicted disasters by the Irish hierarchy and once more it came in the highly emotive area of child protection. The Ryan Report has again exposed the Catholic Church to the glare of public scrutiny, a scrutiny that is not at all welcomed by the religious orders that are implicated. It has strong links to the clerical abuse scandals and really cannot be dissociated from them. Archbishop Diarmuid Martin seems to be the one member of the hierarchy with his finger on the pulse of public opinion. He has stated on numerous occasions that the first thing the church has to do in cases like these is to acknowledge its responsibilities and accept the liabilities that come with them. An article he published in *The Irish Times* will not have endeared him to many of his clerical colleagues. Here is a sample of what he had to say:

> The first thing the church has to do is to move out of any mode of denial. This was the position for far too long and it is still there. Yes, there was abuse in other quarters. Yes, childcare policy in Ireland at the time (when Industrial Schools and other institutions were operational) was totally inadequate. But the church presented itself as different to others and as better than others and as more moral than others.[18]

Martin echoes in these lines the sentiments of Tom Inglis already quoted. Pointing out inadequacies in other areas does not free the church from supplying moral leadership and providing a more Christian approach than secular bodies to areas like child protection. It is supposed to promote virtues such as love of others, generosity, Christian sacrifice, humility. At times it appears very far removed from such ideals. However The Ryan Report is another stage in the dismantling of what was an all-powerful Irish institution, the Catholic Church. Rather than seeing this necessarily as a bad thing, there is a sense in which this fall from grace could be the beginning of a purification and the emergence of a leaner, humbler, listening church that would be closer to the model favoured by its founder. The French priest-writer Jean Sulivan (1913-1980), wrote in his spiritual journal, *Morning Light*: 'Like the storm clouds of the exodus, the church's face is more luminous today than when it seemed to rule. It has found glory in its humiliation.'[19]

This is exactly what the Irish Church is going to have to do; find 'glory in its humiliation', admit its past failings and set about rebuilding trust and confidence and renewing its commitment to the example of Jesus Christ. Perhaps when it does this, the victims whose horrors are chronicled in the Ryan Report will find some solace. One of these victims, Christine Buckley, stated: 'To promote healing, it is important to learn why abuses occurred and who was responsible.' It is also necessary that there be no repeat of the culture of denial and desire for self-protection that have been the hallmark of the representatives of the Catholic Church when confronted with the sins of their past. Only time will tell whether or not it is up to this particular task.

Notes:
1. Fintan O'Toole, 'Law of anarchy, cruelty of care', in *The Irish Times*, 23 May 2009, Weekend Review, p 1.
2. Colm O'Gorman, *Beyond Belief* (London: Hodder and Stoughton, 2009), p 61.
3. *Beyond Belief*, p 50.
4. *Beyond Belief*, pp 48-9.

5. Tom Inglis, 'How we became an international disgrace', in *The Irish Times*, 30 May 2009.

6. Patsy McGarry, 'Roots of a warped view of sexuality', in *The Irish Times*, 20 June 2009.

7. Tony Flannery, 'Attitudes to sexuality and power made for disastrous cocktail', in *The Irish Times*, (Rite and Reason), 26 May 2009.

8. John McGahern, *Memoir* (London: Faber&Faber, 2005), p 18.

9. John McGahern, *The Dark* (Loondon: Faber&Faber, 1965), p 8.

10. Elaine Byrne, 'Irish society shot through with debased authority', in *The Irish Times*, 26 May 2009.

11. *The Dark*, p 17.

12. *The Dark*, p 20.

13. *The Dark*, p 74.

14. *Memoir*, p 188.

15. Mary Kenny, *Goodbye to Catholic Ireland* (Dublin: New Island Books, revised and updated edition, 2000), p 309.

16. Mary Raftery, 'Taxpayers pick up the bill while abusers get secrecy and protection', in *The Irish Times*, 22 May 2009.

17. Tom Inglis, 'Something rotten in the barrel itself', in *The Irish Times*, 3 November 2005.

18. Diarmuid Martin, 'Tarnished Orders have a last chance of redemption', in *The Irish Times*, 25 May 2009.

19. Jean Sulivan, *Morning Light: The Spiritual Journal of Jean Sulivan*, trs Joseph Cunneen and Patrick Gormally (New York: Paulist Press, 1988), p 149.

PART THREE

WHERE DO WE GO FROM HERE?

'A Lingering Shame'[1]

Fainche Ryan

The Ryan Report has been published, and as I write (July 2009) the Dublin Report is still to come. People are shocked, the Pope has been informed, and the normal quiet discomfiture between diocesan priests and religious congregations has been made public through comments made to the media by a prominent church leader following the report. Children in Ireland have been systematically abused in living memory. The most vulnerable of Ireland's children have been abused by those given the responsibility of care, people who took on this responsibility in the name of God. This is indeed a scandal. Moreover, it seems that 'even the dogs on the street' were aware that all was not well, and yet few responded actively, and perhaps this is the real shame. 'We' knew, and we did little. Perhaps this is an underlying cause of our outrage, and indeed of our 'scapegoating'.

While this chapter does not attempt a comprehensive analysis of the issue of abuse, or of Irish society past or present, it will seek to explore some of the questions raised above, the scandal of physical and sexual abuse of children and the shame of no response, by asking 'why?' Why did this happen? Why and how could this happen in an Ireland which saw itself as Christian, an Ireland which was just learning to come to terms with the management of a newly independent state? More controversially, and uncomfortably, I will seek to address the question of 'Why are we so surprised?' Why are Irish people so shocked that children were abused and neglected in the past when they continue to be abused and neglected today?[2] The daily papers regularly report instances of parents, or sports coaches, or neighbours, abusing children but we somehow let this pass without too much comment. Why did we do little or nothing in the past, why do we continue to fail to act? It is said that we failed to act because the church in much of 20th century Ireland was a formidable and powerful institution, virtually unchallengeable. There is undoubtedly truth in this, however it does not adequately explain why we continue to refuse to act today, nor does it address what is perhaps a much more troubling question: 'Why is there so much abuse in our homes and family networks in the 21st century?'

These are hard and difficult words, for the topic we are dealing with is a hard and difficult one. Words are insufficient, perhaps the most insufficient word of all is 'sorry' and yet it is the word that needs to be said again and again, until we tire of hearing it. Hopefully there will be a time when it no longer needs to be said, when child abuse is a thing of the past. History indicates otherwise, but Christian history should help us to hope against hope for this time, and in the meantime to do our best to safeguard the vulnerable in Irish society, and indeed throughout the world.

In an attempt to seek to understand, but by no means to justify, what happened, it is helpful to look at who these people were who committed these serious crimes, these very grave sins. Like the majority of Irish people of the time they were born into situations of poverty, in a poor country full of large families and small farms. Poverty, like affluence, has its levels, and while those who entered religious life were in general not as destitute as the children who were destined to live some of their lives in Reformatories and Industrial Schools, the majority of Irish people were poor by international standards. We know that in this era, before the advent of free secondary education, most pupils finished their education with the completion of primary school. In 1957 records tell us that only 10,000 completed the Leaving Certificate.[3] To some an opportunity came to get second level education and at the same time unburden their families of some of the expense of bringing them up by entering a junior seminary, a novitiate, or a school designed to foster vocations. The

Christian Brothers, the Ryan Report tells us, actively recruited boys 'for their novitiates across the country and sent them to their boarding schools ... where they studied for their Leaving Certificate' (Vol 1, 6.08). Other male congregations had a similar practice. Many left after receiving their education, but many more stayed, some with great idealism, some to escape poverty or emigration, some because they lacked the courage to leave. With young girls I am sure there is a somewhat similar story. I remember a very fine Mercy Sister who taught us describing early religious sisters as amongst the first feminists, and indeed they were. To join a religious community meant one could escape the alternative path of marriage, children and farm work. Even if a person did manage, without joining a religious congregation, to become a teacher, or join the Civil Service and enjoy the 'high living' of Dublin for a while, she had to retire when she got married. I find it difficult to relate the words of Diarmuid Martin, Archbishop of Dublin, with this understanding of life in Ireland in the 30s, 40s, 50s and indeed right into the 60s. He suggests that the question the Ryan Report puts to these congregations is 'What happened that you drifted so far away from your own charism?' (*Irish Times*, 25 May 2009). Charism is by and large a post-Vatican II word when used of religious life. The question seems inappropriate, anachronistic ... most religious who worked in the industrial schools and orphanages knew little of charism, or founders, or theology. Their understanding of God, and of vocation, would by and large have been far removed from that which is promulgated today.

As the nation wonders, in common with the archbishop, how the Christian message of love could become so distorted amongst those who had vowed themselves to follow God's teaching in a particular way, I would like to explore a little what Irish religious of the period in question (largely prior to the 1970s) might have known of God. To use modern parlance, what was their image of God? As the Sisters of Mercy and the Christian Brothers were revealed as the two greatest offenders by the report, they will remain the focus. The Brothers we read, 'received instruction in theology and philosophy' (Vol 1 6.17), but this would have been the scholastic mode of doing theology which presented God as the detached unmoved mover. They would not have had the opportunity to engage in years of study, as was (and is) canonically required of those preparing for ordination. Speaking to one brother I learnt that much of their theology was based on the *Exercises of St Ignatius of Loyola*, and that the God they came to know, although not particularly frightening, was a God who valued fidelity and discipline. Indeed discipline and rule keeping could be said to be characteristic of most religious orders in the 19th and 20th centuries. Discipline and rule keeping were the foundation stones on which the various institutions were run, a level of discipline beyond the capacities of most, if not all, children.

Few of the Sisters would have received any worthwhile theological formation. Who was God to them? Who, or more correctly speaking, what was God to Irish people in 20th century Ireland? God was undisputedly male, and by and large this male God was a powerful one, a judge, a jealous God who was seen by some as vindictive and punitive. He was an old man with a beard sitting up in heaven noting bad behaviour in his notebook, and punishing it in this world or the next. Some of us are lucky never to have known him, but even still many are crippled with this vision of God. As a teacher of theology it is a regular shock to discover, as I begin to work with a new group, that this image of God is still alive in people's thoughts and prayers. This God is waiting to pronounce judgement on our death, to decide our punishment for our sins, and so naturally he is to be feared while we live. This monarchical model of God where God is sovereign King and Lord of the Universe, omnipotent, and all seeing is a God much removed from the God of Pope Benedict's first encyclical, *Deus Caritas Est*, God is love. If this was the God of many of the general mass of the faithful, it was also, and at times even more so, the God of many religious. The religious, Sisters and Brothers, were of the people, and from the people. Why fearing God might lead one to neglect and abuse children remains unclear to me; however it does reinforce the fact that fear is not a proper foundation for good behaviour.

What is remarkable, and what is lost amongst the stories of great evil we hear, is that abuse and neglect were not universal. Some knew a God who loved and invited one to a life of celibacy, a Jesus who could be a companion and who understood the difficulties of human living. Even amongst the many for whom God was a male, all-powerful judge, giving stability and order to the world, great good was done. This is recognised in the report in a chapter entitled 'Positive memories and experiences'. The issue of abuse is a complex one; the Christian God is not at fault. Responsibility does indeed lie with the church, a man-made institution both human and divine, and with a society which seems to have chosen to remain silent. The God that was professed and preached, and the world that was Ireland, was rather insensitive, somewhat ruthless and, as we know from the many stories passed down, this God was not too fond of sex. Those who entered religious orders were, as is always the case, a mixture. Many were young, too young we would say today for the type of decision they were asked to make. Some were idealistic, full of good desires, and at the same time hoping to gain an education, and a level of security difficult to gain elsewhere in the Ireland of the time. Few, one would suspect, wished to end up working in large institutions or reformatories, where to use modern parlance, the student-teacher ratio was far from ideal.

Fr Vincent Twomey in conversation with *The Irish Catholic* (28/5/2009) wondered 'How is it that the conscience of these religious was never touched by their daily religious rituals? How is it that they never engaged in self-criticism?' Probably precisely because they were simply following rituals, doing what everyone else did, doing what they were told. Keep the rule and the rule will keep you, or so the popular saying went. The notion of fostering a relationship with a loving and living God was not really part of the formation of the time; the idea of questioning a superior's decision was outside the understanding of most. The daily regime followed by the Sisters and Brothers was tough, harsh and demanding. Everything was regulated. The Sisters were to obey the directions of the Mother Superior as her authority comes from God, and they were to 'obey the call of the bell as the voice of God' (Vol 2, 6.48; citing from the 1926 edition of the *Rule and Constitutions*). Although commanded to love and respect her, it is hard to see how they might do this. Just as society in Ireland was hierarchically governed, so too was the church. The convent became a microcosm of the hierarchical church. The Mother Superior and those in management were the elite, and at the lowest rung of the hierarchy were the lay sisters (the Mercy Sisters had both Choir and Lay sisters, the latter were to spend their life largely in manual labour). The Brothers too would have had a similarly harsh regime, and a strictly hierarchical leadership system. A notable difference, however, is that while the Brothers, as a Papal Institute, were relatively autonomous when it came to governance, the Sisters, prior to 1983, were subject to the authority and jurisdiction of the local bishop. Obedience rather than conscience or virtue was the norm of life. And yet why did people abuse so violently? Many others lived the same strict life, prayed to a paternalistic, all powerful God and yet were capable of kindness, of goodness, of love, of giving a child a precious sweet every week.

To try to understand what might have led someone to abuse, and to repeatedly abuse, it may be of help to look again at their life. We have noted it was harsh and demanding, for religious as well as the children. The religious, it has been suggested, entered for a variety of reasons – to escape poverty, marriage, to get an education, to do good, to serve God. The Brothers and Choir Sisters received an education, and many were trained to be teachers, some of whom ended up in Industrial Schools and Reformatories. It is not fair or just, *pace* Vincent Twomey (*The Irish Catholic*, 28/5/2009), to describe them as the 'dregs of traditional Irish Catholicism'. They too were human beings created after the image and likeness of God, born into a harsh and cruel Ireland, and placed by those in authority over them in situations of high stress, and little rest. The Ryan report speaks of 4 or 5 adults being responsible for 100-150 children, of a Sister sleeping surrounded by 6 little cots of babies needing feeding during the night (Vol II, 6.25) … is it any wonder that some broke under the stress and strain, that children suffered? We read of children being punished for bed wetting … imagine having 6, or 10, beds to change every morning, with no end in sight for there would always be young children coming fresh into care. Perhaps given such a context even the best amongst us might lose patience, might punish, might think the children were wetting the bed vindictively, or out of laziness? This is not in any way to take from the suffering of the children, but to ask of us today to seek to understand also the vulnerability of those placed in difficult situations, with little or no training.

For indeed at this time there was a lack of formal training in childcare. Care is needed in making judgement here as the science of 'childcare' is a relatively new one, and as one Sister commented it was regarded more as 'common sense'. It is however of interest to read Sr Bianca's (a pseudonym for the Resident Manager of Goldenbridge) lecture on childcare given in 1953, where enlightened and progressive views are to be found, and to compare them with the stories of abuse which we hear today. Similarly we read of the Christian Brothers' awareness of the danger of excessive or abusive physical punishment. A letter of the Superior General, Br Moylan, in 1900 shows us this (Vol I, 6.208ff). A few years later in 1906, a letter written by his successor, Br Whitty, indicates that excessive punishment was being used, and that it 'could not have the blessing of God' (6.210). He once more advocated great restrictions on the use of corporal punishment. All this shows that knowledge and guidelines are clearly not enough. This is a salutary lesson for society today as we seek to implement laws and guidelines, to educate people so that these horrendous forms of abuse may never again occur. Just as in the past the discipline of the rule was insufficient, so too today knowledge and guidelines are not enough. If we put people in highly stressful situations, and do not support them, and if they too are vulnerable, anything may happen and someone, or many, will be hurt. Laws and rights are necessary but not sufficient to keep the vulnerable safe. Something more is needed, and this is where the church might respond, a point we shall return to. For now I would just like to say that we speak so much of the past, of neglect and physical abuse in the past, of dreadfully abusive paedophilia, and we seem blind to the fact that this is happening today, as I write, in families throughout our country. The papers report some of it, the law seeks to prevent it, but it is happening.

Four types of abuse are identified in the report – physical, sexual, neglect, emotional. People today continue to be abused physically, sexually, emotionally, and many in Ireland in 2009 suffer from neglect, and not all of them are children. It is all too easy to condemn and judge the past. To scapegoat, or blame, comes easily to many of us. The religious are easy scapegoats. In Ireland by and large they are elderly, and somewhat lost. They rattle around in big houses, and many today probably wonder in the light of all the reports if they have done anything worth-while with their lives. Religious Sisters and Brothers do not have a sacramental function in the church, and much of the work they used to do is now being done by the state. One can only hope the state is doing a better job, although when Peter McVerry speaks of young men being locked up for long hours in overcrowded prison cells and when one sees young children wandering our streets, homeless, one wonders. We still have a scandalous level of child poverty. The Celtic Tiger seemed to help mainly the powerful and rich. Future generations may judge us very harshly. Perhaps this is why we seek to focus on the ills of the past, on the crimes and sins of a clearly identifiable group of people, public members of a church which was powerful and abusive to many. Many prominent church members speak eloquently and author-itatively about the arrogant, superior, proud, and abusive church of the past, and so it was in too many cases, but they seem to fail to see, and respond to the abuses of today. Blindness, spiritual blindness is difficult to heal. The Sisters in Africa who are abused by priests come to mind,[4] the official response to the AIDS pandemic, the abusive nature of the bond between a woman and a priest who are in a clandestine relationship in a church which continues to mandate celibacy despite so much evidence to the contrary, the enforced hunger for the Eucharist in a world in need of spiritual food by an institutional church unwilling, perhaps even unable, to change its vision of who might or might not be ordained. Abuse is not a thing of the past; the abuse of the present should concern us as much, if not more. Only here can we really begin to make a difference.

Perhaps it is precisely our awareness that abuse is not only of the past that leads us to so vehemently accuse and judge the past. The reason, the 'why' we judge the past with such severity, righteousness and, yes, real pain, is because we are afraid to look at the present. In our newspapers we read of sexual abuse within families, of the neglect of children, of children as young as eight being used by criminal gangs. We have homeless children, both Irish and non-national, in a relatively prosperous country. The neglect of children and their abuse is not a thing of the past. Yet, we remain silent. In my silence I am as culpable as the priest, bishop, religious superior, doctor, lawyer, judge who knew, or suspected that all was not well in our industrial schools or orphanages. I am as guilty as the parents who rejected their daughter when she became pregnant outside of marriage, as guilty as the man who impregnated her and walked away, as guilty as the society who spurned the unmarried mother, and her child. The statistics showed us that a significant number of those in care were born out of wedlock, or were the children of a widowed parent. We were too 'religious', too law abiding, to countenance any degree of deviance, even when it happened to be our own children who were deviant.

Today, in the 21st century, many Irish people speak a different language. For some the language of 'rights' has replaced that of religion, and the rest of us are bilingual, using 'rights' or 'religious' language depending on our context. Yet little seems to have changed. We scapegoat the past, and use blinkered vision in the present. We rightly seek to find the truth from the past, to try to rectify some of the wrong that was done, in so far as that can happen, but care needs to be taken that all our energy is not expended in the past, nor simply in bringing those whom we label 'religious' to account. Might not, indeed *did* not, abuse take place in our own families, especially amongst those living six or more people in one-room accommodation (in 1926 we had 6,000 such households, 1946 3,000; by 1961 this had reduced to 321, still too many)? As late as 1950 'there were 6,300 tenements housing 112,000 people, or nearly one-third of Dublin Corporation population' (Vol IV, 3.08). It is likely, possible, and indeed probable, that physical, sexual and emotional abuse happened in these households, as indeed it happened in families across all class levels. It happens today, surely it also happened then.

Some of our abhorrence at the wrong done by religious can be explained by our understanding of religious, and priests. We have seen them as holier than us, and perhaps their biggest fault is that they have allowed us to do this. What is even more disturbing is that some of us, perhaps those most vehemently critical of the church, continue to live out of a vision which purports that those who profess religious vows, or opt for ordination, are holier and better than the run of the mill Christian. We continue to pray for 'young' people to courageously decide to dedicate their whole life to following Christ by joining a congregation, or for those 'bravely' choosing to be ordained. This church year has been dedicated as a year for priests, who are evidently holier than other baptised Christians, since if their behaviour is not up to the mark, at least sexually, they may be laicised or, as used to be said, '*reduced* to the lay state'. Celibacy continues to be seen as a higher calling. This week we have celebrated the feast of St Maria Goretti, a young woman, a girl, whose holiness is officially recognised by the church because she choose to defend her chastity rather than give way to a 'man attempting to violate her' (*The Divine Office*, Vol 3, p 103*). She was stabbed to death.

To try to explain from a theological perspective the fact of abuse, and the judgemental response of the Irish people, one must return to the notion of 'original' sin. The apostrophe on the term 'original' is important. With a renewed understanding of what it means to be human, of Christian anthropology, and a recovery of some of the theological insights prior to the Reformation, Catholics are invited to remember that each one of us is created after the image and likeness of God, a God who is good, true and beautiful in ways beyond our ability to understand. Jesus the Christ, one of the Trinity, was goodness incarnate, living truth, the beautiful one ... and we crucified him. This is the greatest sin of all time, the crucifixion of goodness and truth, while most followers of Jesus walked away. Perhaps this may be seen in some ways as the 'original' sin, occurring in the middle of time but with implications throughout all created time, just as the gift of eternal life, of redemption, happened once only for all peoples whenever they live. This is the world in which we are invited to truly grow into the image of God, a world created and judged 'very good' (Genesis 1:31), a world gifted with the very freedom that can choose to reject goodness. We are not born with the stain of Adam on our souls, but we are born vulnerable, fragile, weak, with great potential for growth in goodness, a potential which can also manifest itself in great badness, often termed evil. Some of us seem more fragile than others. To return to our focus, many of those who worked in the industrial schools survived great stress and strain, and a harsh daily regime, without doing any great harm to anyone. Some broke, and did great damage. Psychologically damaged, they hurt others, vulnerable children, in a way we cannot understand. Some of these people did what may be termed great evil, but we must be slow to label them evil people for they too are created after God's image although the image has been greatly tarnished. And some, we must not forget, managed to do good, to be gentle and kind on occasion, amidst a harsh regime in a poor and judgemental country.

Sin did not die with the closure of the last industrial school or reformatory; it is as alive today as ever, although not so often spoken about. Recent financial scandals in Ireland show that we remain vulnerable, in a world and lifestyle which cannot be

deemed as harsh or tough, physically at any rate. Keeping the
focus on the Ryan Report, sin is clearly manifest in the blindness
of congregations to believe that some of their members had done
great wrong, some continually over an extended period. This
blindness has almost lifted entirely now, and the time for restit-
ution has come. Today we can sin in our judging, our scapegoating, our claiming the high moral ground. In the past we, many of
us, chose to remain silent, non-judgemental although we knew
things were not right. Today we judge, we condemn, and we
choose to remain blind to a larger story. The abuse and neglect of
young people in our society and in our families needs addressing
now lest our children and grandchildren judge us as harshly as
we today judge the preceding generations. The past has been
judged and found wanting, let us now act in the present.

The institutional church could do a lot here, if it should
choose to do so. Firstly it could offer to educate its members in
their faith, in their images of God, and remind each baptised
person of their priestly, prophetic and kingly role. We could
begin to recognise all ways of life as valuable ways of following
Christ, and cease to posit some callings as higher than others.
Different yes, but higher or better, no! The church could try to
see women and children as equal in dignity to men, and make
this explicit in its action. Nice words and platitudes are insufficient – the abuses of the past have shown us how easily words
can be ignored. We could cease to see the celibate state as higher
than the sexually active one, and perhaps the Irish church could
be proactive in proposing the removal of the requirement of
celibacy for the ordained priesthood. We could refuse to be
silenced here, but we need the support of our bishops. We could
cease to abuse those who work in and for the church by paying
them a just wage, just work conditions, and we could begin to
preach more honestly from our pulpits, addressing the real issues of the day. We could condemn paedophilia in the family
while continuing to visit the condemned person in prison. We
could teach women that they should not suffer physical or sexual
abuse from their partner, and neither should their children.

Likewise for men, we should alert them to the fact that it is not a *sine qua non* that a mother loves and treats her children well – women too can damage horrendously. Let us be alert, aware and active. The list is endless. As Christians, more specifically as Catholics of the Latin Rite, let us be alert and active today. Let us not dissipate our energy in judging the past, or bury our heads, and refuse to see what is happening and what needs to be done and said today. Perhaps the invitation to each one of us, whatever our status in the church, is to 'listen to the signs of the times', to read the words Jesus wrote in the ground in the story of the woman caught in adultery (Jn 8:1-11), and to make real those words in our lives and in the lives of those who share our world. Each one of us has to find our own way to respond to these words which are

> Impossible words,
> wondrous necessary words,
> words longing to be more than words,
> longing to be more like silence
> or like action.
> Words in the face of unspeakable beauty,
> of unspeakable anguish,
> words of shame and of hope
> blushing at themselves.[5]

Notes:
1. Title taken from an article by Ethna Regan CHF, '"But now You Speak at last." The Rights of the Child after the Shadows of Hiberno-Christendom' in *Doctrine and Life*, July/August 2009, p 19.
2. 6,500 children at risk do not have an assigned social worker, and neglect continues to be the primary reason (approx 60%) of why children are taken into care. There is still no comprehensive nationwide out of hours social work service. See 'Voice of Children must never be silenced again.' Barnardos responds to Report of the Commission to Inquire into Child Abuse Dublin, 20 May 2009. "http://www.barnardos.ie/media_centre/our-latest-news/voice-of-children-must-never-be-silenced-again.html" http://www.barnardos.ie/media_centre/our-latest-news/voice-of-children-must-never-be-silenced-again.html
3.http://www.muckross-house.ie/library_files/ireland_in_the_30s.-htm Accessed 8/7/09.

4. In 1994 a report by Dr Maura O'Donohue FMM gave this form of abuse official recognition, that it was followed by a second report by Sr Marie McDonald MMM in 1998, entitled 'The Problem of the Sexual Abuse of African Religious in Africa and Rome', indicates that the response to the report has been lacking.

5. The words of Paul Murray OP, poet and friend, shared during a conversation on abuse and the Irish Church. *Words of the Poet* is published in *Religious Life Review* Vol 48 no 258, Sept-Oct 2009.

Some Ideas on
a New Approach to Catholic Sexual Teaching

Tony Flannery

In trying to analyse the reasons why so many people, dedicated to following Christ in priesthood or religious life, were involved in the sexual abuse of children, many of us are provoked into questioning even more seriously than we may have done in the past the traditional church teaching on sexuality. Seán Fagan, in his chapter in this volume, outlines some of the history of this teaching, and the various influences that were at work in its development. Many of these influences, unfortunately, were far removed from the teaching of Jesus, and led the church in ways that can now be seen to have been harmful. Donal Dorr uses the phrase 'seriously warped' to describe his understanding of trad- itional Catholic sexual teaching. Marie Keenan's study of sexually abusing clergy also raises questions about the theology of sexu- ality they received in the seminary. My hope is that all the revel- ations of recent years about clergy and religious involved in various forms of abuse might provoke the church into looking again at its teaching on sexuality, and maybe beginning to re- shape it more in accordance with the mind of Jesus, and more in tune with the daily struggles of his followers in the twenty-first century.

I am aware that a great deal of work has been done in this area since the Vatican Council, and that a lot of new thinking has emerged, softening the harsh, judgemental attitudes and teach- ings of the past. But this work has been patchy and difficult. The famous encyclical of Pope Paul VI on contraception, *Humanae Vitae*, which was published in 1968, put a big spanner in the works, and largely took the momentum out of the movement for change. Indeed, in hindsight, I am inclined to see that event as probably the biggest catastrophe for the Catholic Church in the last century. And what makes it really sad is that, while it was presented as a carefully considered and conscientious decision, many people would now accept that it was more the result of a power struggle between those who wished to move on with the reforms of the Council, and those who were trying to hold on to the old ways. Since then I think it is fair to say that there has been a constant battle (or maybe more a type of sniper fire) between what are usually referred to as the liberal moral theologians and the church authorities, both at national and Vatican level. In the process some of the more daring and imaginative voices have either been silenced or pushed to the fringes. I think of people like Charles Curran, or indeed even the great Bernard Haring in his later years. The result is that, while there have been changes in Catholic sexual teaching and some of them very significant, because of the ambivalence of the authorities they haven't been communicated effectively to the ordinary believers. As a result no real dialogue has taken place between the purveyors of theology and the lived experience of the people. This has been crucial.

For Christian teaching in any area of life to be really effective it seems to me that it needs two essential qualities. It needs to be as close as it possibly can be to the spirit and the teaching of Jesus, in so far as that can be interpreted from the New Testament. Here we must be careful to avoid any form of literal interpretation, because that would immediately exclude the second essential element. It also needs to be in constant interaction with the experience of the followers who are trying to live it out in their daily lives. If it does not have the first it suffers from the sort of problems that Seán Fagan has outlined. If it does not have the second it is dead, useless knowledge, lying in a bookshelf and gathering dust. Historically this has been the weak aspect of Catholic theology. It had a tendency towards dogmatism, handing the teaching down for a docile faithful to accept. I know that there are people, and some theologians, who believe that there is a corpus of teaching on this and other subjects dating back to the Bible, and that it is fixed and unchangeable for all time. I do not see it this way. I think that Jesus gave us basic principles on which to work, and that each generation, both the leadership and the faithful, have to interact with the culture and circumstances of the age, and try to work out how exactly these might apply in the particular time and place. To some this might sound like relativism, the type of thinking that Pope Benedict is so opposed to, that it could lead to 'a la carte' morality, with people picking and choosing what they want to believe, and leaving us without any objective principles. We do of course have a very fundamental principle on which all our actions must be based, that all the follower of Jesus must constantly try to love one another.

I would like to make an attempt at outlining here some of the characteristics on which a new theology of sexuality might be based.

A basic fault of traditional Catholic sexual teaching was its perceived negativity. We were always more sure of what it was against than what it favoured. And the general perception was that it was against sexual activity of all types, only tolerating the very essentials for the preservation of the species. We were made to feel that our sexual nature was part of our fallen selves, and prone to sin of such gravity that it would lead us to eternal damnation. Maybe this was not the intention of many of the teachers down through the ages, but it was undoubtedly the reality of most people's experience. Setting up the celibate life as superior to that of marriage was also reinforcing the same message, a point made strongly by Fainche Ryan in this book. Celibate clergy were the only people allowed to preach and we now know that these very same people were struggling (sometimes successfully, sometimes not so successfully) with their own sexual desires; and when we are struggling we often overstress the point of the argument where we see ourselves failing. For this reason, the supposedly celibate preachers sometimes gave an excessively harsh presentation of church teaching on sexuality. So the first basis of a new theology of sexuality would be a positive acceptance of the beauty and goodness not just of our sexual nature, but of sexual activity in relationships. The notion of sex as being inherently sinful would have to be eradicated from our psyches. This would be a major task. It would take the church a long time to come around to really believing that sex is good and beautiful, part of the wonder of God's creation. There would be a lot of the baggage Seán Fagan has outlined that would have to be eradicated from our thinking and teaching. But this, it seems to me, is an absolutely fundamental starting point, even if it takes a century or two to really achieve it. Our sexual nature is good and sexual activity is good, not bad and sinful. Everything else should flow from this.

The second basic change would be to break the inherent connection, long part of traditional Catholic teaching, between sexual activity and marriage. To continue to hold that sex out-side marriage is always sinful is in my view a mistake. Marriage is ultimately a social rather than a religious institution. Historically it has been promoted as part of the good ordering of society, and as a way of ensuring that children are brought into a safe and secure environment. The church, surprisingly more in tune with the needs of society then than now, tried to reinforce this social ordering by declaring sex outside of marriage to be seriously sinful. In the era during which this teaching developed people got married much younger. Often they were betrothed to each other as young as twelve years of age, and came together after puberty. They had many more children than today, be-cause infant mortality was high, and in order to ensure that three or four offspring would survive and grow to adulthood they needed to give birth to about ten. Life expectancy was short, and people died young, most often in their late thirties or forties. For women in particular the bulk of life was absorbed by the bearing and rearing of children. In that context the teaching that sexual activity was for procreation purposes within mar-riage made somewhat more sense. Now things are radically dif-ferent. People mostly don't marry until their late twenties, have fewer pregnancies because infant mortality is rare, and will expect to live for many years after they have reared their children. It makes no sense to expect that a teaching, which was framed when life was so much shorter, and when bearing children was the main purpose of marriage, would be still meaningful when circumstances have so dramatically changed. Making a life-long commitment today, when a person can reasonably expect to live for fifty years or more in the marriage, and for maybe twenty or thirty after the children are reared, is a much different thing to making it when the realistic life-span of the couple in marriage was about twenty years, which would be spent in giving birth and rearing children. The great English theologian, Jack Dominion, suggested some years ago that it might be more realistic to ask people to make a commitment to each other for a specific period of time, for instance until the children are reared, and then to see if they wished to renew it for the next stage of their lives. I am not saying that there should be no moral principles applied to marriage. Of course there should. Commitment, dedication, fidelity – these are essential qualities of a relationship, and they are as important today as they ever were. But we change so much in the course of a lifetime that it is unrealistic to expect that every couple will continue to love and cherish each other until death. As long as we hold to this rigid notion of life-long fidelity as the essential norm we will inevitably be excluding many people from full participation in the church, and branding them as failures. Undoubtedly keep it as the ideal, which of course it is, but do not make it a condition for full membership of the church

If we can accept that relationships of love can happen also outside of marriage, and can be appropriately expressed in a sexual way, then we will be in a position to influence the debate and have a voice in shaping the accepted moral ethics of society. We will be freer to delve into what exactly is the nature of the sexual act, what does it express and where will it find its full meaning. Then we can begin to talk about the true nature of a relationship, the degree of commitment a couple have to each other, the real unselfish love that they are trying to grow into, and their understanding of the difference between enduring love and romantic feelings or unadulterated sexual desire masquerading as love. I would wish to see the Catholic Church once again having something important to say on this subject, except that this time it would be a positive, life-enhancing message that we would be presenting to the people of today. We would certainly find a hearing, because there is a stark dearth of moral guidance in this area, and many lives are being damaged or destroyed. Selfishness is part and parcel of human nature. Sex, because it is so intensely pleasurable, is possibly more prone to selfishness than most human activity. To the extent that it is selfish it is divorced from love, and becomes destructive of people. When it is in a context of real love it is a great promoter of human growth and development. Catholic sexual teaching, if it is to have any relevance, must help people to grow through their sexual relationship, and not to cause hurt or destruction to themselves or others.

Breaking away from the rigid connection between sexual activity and marriage would also give us a way out of the bind we find ourselves in with couples who are involved in second relationships. The failure of the church to respond to the many people who are getting married for the second time is scandalous. More often than not they are good, sincere people, and all we can offer them is a blank refusal of any religious ceremony, even a blessing, coupled with a mostly unstated, but implied belief that they are living in sin and no longer pleasing to God. I am advocating that the church's attitude to people in second relationships must change. Such persons deserve to have their union sacramentalised in the church, if they so wish, and must never be excluded from the Eucharist.

The third basic change that I would look for is in our attitude to artificial contraception. With the advent of various ways of preventing conception, sex is no longer necessarily connected with pregnancy. For the past half century or more, the church has lamented this, and fought against the use of any form of artificial conception with all its might. It is, in my view, tilting at windmills. Freely available contraception is part of the new reality within which our church teaching has got to make some sense. I have met very many people who are fully committed to the Catholic Church, who attend Mass regularly, who believe that the church still has the ability to transmit the message of Christ, who want their children to be fully practising members of this same church but who use artificial contraception and see no problem with it. Sometimes I even wonder if these people are aware that, according to our present church teaching, they are sinning by doing so. It is ludicrous to uphold a teaching that brands such people as sinners and, precisely because it is ludicrous, the church has lost its credibility when it comes to discussing anything to do with sex. Church teaching has officially conceded now that sex has a purpose other than procreation, namely to nourish and develop a relationship of love between two people. In a previous book, *Keeping the Faith*, I have outlined the principal that for church teaching to be fully valid, it must be not only preached by the church authorities but generally accepted by the bulk of the faithful. If we apply this to artificial contraception, it is obvious that its use cannot be considered sinful. If the church could accept this, it might begin to actively encourage its use in the most responsible way possible. This would be done in the interest of ensuring that couples would only bring a child into the world when they are ready for the responsibility, and willing to make the commitment to bringing it up. Children deserve no less.

Some form of sexual guidance is very important for the adolescents. This is a time when they discover their sexual nature, and are experimenting with it. It is a time that can be very frightening for their parents and many of them feel at a loss as to how to provide guidance and moral direction to their teenagers. We know that if sexual development goes awry at this time of young people's lives serious damage can be done, and we equally know that promiscuity in the lives of young people can have detrimental effects. So our children must be protected. But that is ultimately the responsibility of parents, and nobody, either church or state, should try to take it away from them.

This brings me to the last point where I would like to see a basic change of attitude from the church. We should trust the believing community much more than we have done. We should trust their good nature, their desire to live by right principles, and their good intelligence and common sense. So the church's role in this whole area should be one of guidance and assistance rather than that of law maker, judge and punisher with eternal flames. In this way the Catholic community, large and diverse as it is, working together would come up with good principles and attitudes which perhaps would be a lot healthier and better for the promotion of human living than we have managed in the past. This same believing community would want to hear what the church has to say about sexuality and responsible sexual activity and may be much more receptive to its message. However, this will not happen unless we change our present teaching on sex.

In summary, then, I am looking for four basic changes in church teaching on sexuality:

Firstly, that we begin from a positive rather than a negative position.
Secondly, we break the rigid connection between sexual activity and marriage, allowing for appropriate sexual relationships between people who are not married, when the quality of the relationship merits it.
Thirdly, we no longer teach that the use of artificial contraception in a loving relationship is sinful.
Fourthly, church leadership learns to trust the believing community, and develops its teaching in partnership with them, rather than handing it down in an authoritarian manner.

I know that all of this amounts to radical change. People will say that the church does not change. Historically this is not true. It has changed, and in ways even more radical than I am suggesting. It eventually withdrew its support for slavery; it ceased to tolerate the awful excesses of the Inquisition; after some hundreds of years it accepted that it had treated Galileo badly.

In our church nothing happens quickly. And yet in the course of my lifetime I have seen enormous changes of attitude, which have gradually led to real change in teaching. Life has taught me the power of ideas, and how something that seems to be outrageous can gradually become part of people's thinking. The revelations of sexual abuse by clergy and religious, and the efforts by the authorities to cover it up have in a real sense changed the whole landscape. Out of evil good can come. There is a possibility now that the ancient structures and thought-processes of the church might be shaken up, and that new thought, energy and life might be breathed into them.

A Young Person Reflects on the Ryan Report

Joe O'Riordan

Detachment. Such a cold clinical word. In this context almost a dirty word. It is not an emotion, if indeed detachment can be called an emotion, which readily springs to mind when you think of the Ryan Report. You will find no newspaper headlines, no emotive speeches that will speak of detachment from the Report. But it is what I feel.

Please do not misinterpret me. I am not cold-hearted or unfeeling. I agree that what happened in these institutions was a terrible crime that should never be allowed to occur again. The detachment I feel comes not from lack of empathy but from distance. The world that the Ryan Report describes is beyond the limits of my experience. A chasm exists between me and the sufferings and horrors of these regimes. The pain felt by those abused is something I can only imagine. I was twenty seven years old when the report was published. Corporal punishment was never a feature of my education. I attended a Christian Brothers' secondary school where no Christian Brother was teaching. These institutions were either no longer in existence or were being wound up when I was born. I suspect that I am not the only one, that in fact a lot of my generation feel like this.

For two weeks after the Ryan Report was published every form of national media was saturated with responses. After so many years of not being believed, this recognition must have been an enormous release for those who were abused. But only two weeks! That's all the attention we had to give. Yes, the ramifications of the findings will still be reported but the news cycle and the public interest have moved on. Two weeks, and even within that time we did not give our full attention. In my experience the Report was given only cursory discussion before the conversation moved on to topics closer to people's hearts, such as the economy. The world moved on secure in the knowledge that a report had been written and all, therefore, was taken care of. On any given day, make your way through the radio stations and hear how few of them still mention the Ryan report. Why? Because they realise their average listener is more interested in current topics. The majority paid attention for a while and then washed their hands.

I am disconcerted not so much by the Report but by our reaction to it; by the fact that we could move on so quickly. It frightens me that such an attitude could allow abuse to occur again.

The Ryan Report revealed deep flaws within the systems and procedures of church run institutions but it also raises deeper questions as to whether such flaws exist in other areas of our social fabric. Let us get one thing clear from the start: this report is not just about the church. Society cannot stand aside and condemn. None of these abuses took place in a vacuum. They occurred in a world similar to today's, where it was easier to look away than take a stand against a large organisation, especially one where issues pertaining to sexuality and sexual abuse were not dealt with in an open and understanding way. We need to look at the underlying ideological causes which contributed to creating such abuses. We need to examine the individual's relation to authority and how we deal with issues of sexuality. These issues must be addressed unless we are to find ourselves in this situation again.

All that is necessary for evil to triumph is that the good do nothing. People knew and did nothing. I cannot understand that. Why was no one screaming from the rooftops? Where were the good men and women of the clergy and religious? Where were the investigating reporters? Where was the state? Where were we?

Let us look at the church bodies that ran these institutions first.

In Vol II Chap. 6.48, where the Report quotes the 1926 version of the *Rules and Constitution of the Mercy Order* it is stated that the

Sisters 'have forever renounced their own will, and resigned it to the direction of their superiors'. I consider this directive detrimental in that it removes personal responsibility and individual autonomy. Questioning anything becomes a sign not only of weakness but of disobedience (See 6:50). By removing the channels for the free exchange of ideas, an institution developed which was entirely closed to new ideas, whose purpose was to preserve itself in an unchanged form. Without freedom of expression the value of what it was preserving was never open for debate. This is why the Report refers to abuse being systematic rather than caused by individual breaches of conduct. Once you remove personal autonomy and responsibility you create a group mentality which is more concerned with uniformity than values or people.

Where loyalty is the ultimate value in an institution you will always have abuse. In the church this abuse took the form of physical and sexual maltreatment, but we mustn't forget that all organisations based on a group mindset are equally open to unethical behaviour. We can see illustrations of this in the banking scandals or the various scandals that have emerged in our health system. There were people in these organisations who knew improper behaviour was taking place, but loyalty to the system came first, and they remained silent. This attitude is apparent in Vol 4 chap 6.23 of the Report where it states that no attempts were made to address the underlying systematic nature of abuse; or again in 6.20 where cases of abuse were handled in such a way that would minimise 'the risk of public disclosure and consequent damage to the institution and the Congregation'. The attitude of an organisation that wishes to keep its wrongdoings out of the public eye, for fear that the group's reputation would be damaged, is a common failing.

Failure to report the wrong-doings of a colleague is not the sole preserve of religious organisations. Even in discussions on the need to protect those who come forward with information on the misdeeds of their co-workers the phrase used to describe such people is 'whistle blowers' – language which conjures up images of the playground tell-tale rather than a courageous individual bucking the trend of conformity. We have created a culture where the parcel of responsibility is passed around until the music stops.

How do we create a society in which people are more willing to take personal responsibility and adopt a critical attitude? I am a teacher and it bothers me when people place responsibility for curing all society's ills at the door of schools. But in relation to the two issues we are discussing here, education *can* play a vital role. In our system a good student is still one who listens to the teacher and accepts the facts given. A good member of society is one who accepts whatever authority offers. This must change. Children must be encouraged to adopt a critical attitude to the information they receive and must be given the freedom to question authority. A child is not an empty vessel to be filled with prescribed information. By taking away their initiative and responsibility children are domesticated to accept the world as it is, and so a culture of silence is developed. We should cease the practice of depositing pre-packaged units of knowledge in our student's heads, and should instead focus on problem-posing in the context of the person's lived experience of, and relation to, the world. This problem-posing should not be the kind one finds at the end of a chapter of a maths book, but rather should be a reflection on the world in order to discover solutions to the real problems of our existence. Through dialogue between students and educators students become critical learners instead of passive receptors. To become 'agents of change' students should be encouraged to play an active role in the governance and operation of their own education programmes. Children need to be encouraged to express their opinions even though they may run counter to the teacher's views. This vocal awakening against authority does not mean we will create a society of rampant individualism. Conflict will lead to mutually agreed positions which are open to revision. In promoting the vocal awakening of our children we can hope, in the future, to defeat the culture of silence that allowed abuses like the ones in church institutions to occur.

For the younger generation to which I belong, the church is in danger of becoming irrelevant. It no longer has the status it had in my parent's time. It is seen as out of touch and out dated. To rectify this it needs to follow the same principles outlined above. The relationship between the church and its followers needs to become a dialogue of equals. The church can become more relevant by increasing parental and community involvement in the structuring and running of the local church community. This dialogue cannot be dictated by the church, rather it needs to be a relationship that transforms both parties. The voice of the church is not being listened to because it says too much and does too little. A gap exists between pronouncements from the altar and practice on the ground. This is most evident regarding the topic of sexuality. We try to change events in order to avoid changing ourselves.

Sex, sexual expression and the body have long been issues on which the church has taken strong and unchanging views. In its conclusion the Report maintains that attitudes towards sexuality made it difficult for members of church organisations to deal candidly with abuse (Vol 4, 6:28). What is needed is not so much a change in systems but a change in attitudes and actions. Church teachings on sexuality are held in low regard by the majority of my peers. These teachings speak to a world that is, for better or worse, long since gone. There is also a large element of hypocrisy when an organisation which has been found responsible for incidents of child abuse, and which practises sexual inequality within its own structure, presents itself as the moral guardian of sexuality. The church has to stop believing it has all the answers. It is in a sense the proverbial 'hurler on the ditch' removed from the flow of life but still regarding itself as all knowing. It needs to cross its own Rubicon and change not only its mindset but also its actions. Simply put, I believe clergy should, if they so wish, be allowed to marry. Such a move would help them to be more in touch with reality and with their emotions. It is a move which the majority of people would support. A married priest, or indeed nun, would still be able to dedicate their lives to God. If presidents and prime ministers of large nations are able to fulfil their tasks while married, I see no reason why a parish priest can not. I am no theologian, but I do not see how celibacy brings someone closer to God. The best way to be close to God is to love others and to let them know that they are loved, and sexual expression is an integral part of this. Allowing clergy to have intimate relationships could represent an example of a Christian union. Giving advice, for example, on the ideal of marriage is not the same as showing how that ideal can be put into practice.

Society also has a role to play in developing appropriate sexual attitudes. Sex is in and of itself entirely non-moral, it is the context and our attitude towards it which determines its moral value. It must be taken seriously, but currently we are treating it with the wrong kind of seriousness. Instead of dealing with it openly we have mystified and placed it on a false throne. Sex is treated as if it is an entity in itself because we have given it so much respect and invested it with so much power. It is becoming a controlling force rather than something we control. There is a tendency sometimes, when discussions of sex arise, to equate the idea of openness towards sexuality with promiscuity and moral looseness. The sexual drive is like any other human desire – it must be kept in balance. The fact that so many adults still have a problem in saying the word *penis* in adult conversation indicates that society still does not have an open, mature attitude towards sex. None of us are the result of celibacy or an immaculate conception, yet some still get squeamish at the thoughts of their parents having sex.

To develop an appropriate attitude towards sexuality we must look again at education.

Currently in Britain the government is being criticised for a policy which would make sex education mandatory. As a primary school teacher, I believe such a policy should be introduced here. The current Relationships and Sexuality programme in Irish primary schools is quite good, but unfortunately in most schools it is not being fully implemented. The programme recommends that sex education begin in the infant class and continue right throughout the primary school years. What happens in most cases is that the whole course is covered in fifth or sixth class in an intense lesson or two. Beginning sex education in infants would not, as some fear, sexualise our young children. Rather it is an opportunity to create an open and informed attitude to sexuality. Early sexualisation arises due to lack of information rather than excess. It is a bravado picked up from the manner in which sex is portrayed in the media and the fact that it is still a mysterious subject rarely discussed openly. Children, as they grow older, are encouraged to stop using 'baby talk' and to use correct terminology. Unfortunately this attitude does not extend to the naming of the sex organs. We are all sexual creatures who have sexual organs but we act as we if didn't. The RSE programme recommends that in infants the children are encouraged to call sexual organs by their correct names. The level of information increases year on year until in sixth class puberty and sexual intercourse are discussed. Children have no problem in learning this information, it is natural to them. By starting at a young age these issues can be dealt with without the baggage of previous generations. By removing false information, children can grow up to see sex as it truly is and to treat it with the correct kind of seriousness, seriousness which can discuss it openly and realise fully its implications and effects.

One final point: The Ryan Report revealed terrible child abuse and we all hope such incidents are never repeated. The protection of children from abuse is extremely important but such protection cannot be at the expense of positive adult-child interaction. A crying child who has hurt a knee does not want or need a sterile and detached response from the carer. However, in our present social milieu, fear of how action might be misinterpreted is preventing a true caring relationship between many adults and the children in their care. I do not know how we can strike the balance between normal protection and giving an opportunity for abusive behaviour. Perhaps in time and through a process of trial and error an appropriate middle ground can be reached.

It is easier to blame others. It is easier to say that it is someone else's responsibility. It is easier to talk of changing events than changing people. However, the easier path is seldom the right one. The Ryan Report is just that – a report. Words never changed anything unless they stirred individuals to action. We cannot allow ourselves the comfort of passing the responsibility to yet another commission and another report. We must 'be the change we want to see in the world'. What has happened is beyond our control; what is to come is our responsibility.

PART FOUR

UNDERSTANDING CHILD SEXUAL ABUSE

'Them and Us':
The Clergy Child Sexual Offender as 'Other'

Marie Keenan

Since the late 1980s there has been heightened public awareness of child sexual abuse in Ireland, which in no small way has shaped child welfare and legislative provision for the last twenty years. In that time, child sexual abuse has become a significant issue on the Irish social and political agenda, which may have come about in part due to the interest of the media in this issue and the publicity given to 'high profile' cases. Childhood experiences of sexual abuse recounted in the press and in the course of television documentaries have caught public and political attention in a way not experienced in Ireland before. Stories of child sexual abuse by family members, members of the clergy and by other individuals in positions of trust have sent shock waves through Irish society (McGuiness, 1993). In particular, child sexual abuse by Catholic clergy has received significant public attention, leading to the collapse of a government, the resignation of one bishop,[1] the stepping aside of another,[2] two state inquiries into the handling of abuse complaints by members of the Roman Catholic hierarchy[3] and one commission of inquiry into abuse of children in residential facilities run by the Religious Orders on behalf of the state.[4] It has also changed the lives of many clerical and religious men and women and men in positions of leadership in the Catholic Church.

Although disclosures of sexual abuse by Catholic clergy have been reported in many countries throughout the world,[5] and the Catholic hierarchy in the United States has experienced severe public criticism for its handling of abuse complaints, the relationship between church and state in Ireland has made the Irish experience fairly unique. Inglis (1998, 2005) argues that the Irish take on sexuality, and the historical position of the Catholic Church in Ireland, has contributed to this situation. My view is that the changing understanding of childhood, and the form that professional discourses have taken in relation to abuse perpetrators in the United States and Ireland, also created a background for the manner in which child sexual abuse by Catholic clergy is currently narrated. On this issue, Irish professionals are inclined to follow closely what happens in the United States – a situation that I regret. There is much to be learned from the Scandinavian countries on how to handle crime in general, and I think we could do well to look to Berlin rather than Boston if we need guidance on sexual abuse in general. We must also situate and understand our own problems within our uniquely Irish context.

This article investigates child sexual abuse by Catholic clergy in two jurisdictions, Ireland and the United States. These jurisdictions are selected because most of the research on this topic emanates from the United States and my own research with Catholic clergy is situated in Ireland. The article begins by taking a critical look at the dominant discourses[6] of child sexual abuse, as these discourses form part of the context in which sexual abuse by Catholic clergy is currently understood in Ireland. Drawing on sociological and psychological perspectives as well as my own research and clinical experience,[7] the article then examines what is reliably known about Catholic clergy who have sexually abused minors and about the role or otherwise of the institution of the Catholic Church in relation to these abuses. Whilst much of the literature from the United States provides the quantitative data on the nature and scope of the problem, my research provides the qualitative picture of the lived experiences of Catholic clergy who have sexually abused minors. The article concludes by arguing that if we truly want to help children and create a safer society for all men, women and children in Ireland, then we need to get beyond a blaming stance and towards more preventative and rehabilitative/restorative perspectives.

The Power of Language

Many scholars argue that language and its usage are central to the emergence of social problems (Hacking, 1999: 27; Jenkins, 1998: 7; Best, 1995: 2; Berger & Luckmann, 1991: 39; Kincaid, 1998: 5). How a problem is 'languaged' will influence whether or not it will be privileged over other issues and what 'core features' will become 'taken-for-granted' as central to the problem's depiction. Jenkins (1998: 9) argues that none of the words or concepts that are often used in relation to child sexual abuse represents universally accepted or 'objective' realities. Rather, many of the words used in relation to this problem's definition, such as *sexual abuse, victim, survivor, paedophile, molester, pervert, sexual deviant,* are rooted in the attitudes of a particular time and each carries its ideological baggage. Jenkins (1998) warns that it seems impossible to write on the topic of child sexual abuse without using language that appears to accept the ideological interpretations of a particular school of thought. In so doing, it forecloses the exploration of other avenues of interpretation.

Interpretation is hugely important when it comes to sexual abuse by Catholic clergy, especially when it comes to assessing the motivation of individuals who acted or failed to act in relation to children in times gone by. Whilst it is objectively correct that many children are and have been exploited sexually and that many suffer as a result, many other 'taken-for-granted' assumptions in relation to the issue certainly require further debate and analysis. Different eras have produced different perspectives on child sexual abuse and in each era the prevailing opinion is supported by professional discourses that present what is described as convincing 'objective' 'empirical' research that is said to represent more advanced thinking than what went before (Jenkins, 1998). What appears to be the case is that one 'reality' prevails until another replaces it, and each formulation is presented as progressive, claiming that the contemporary beliefs are 'true' whereas the previous ones were not (Jenkins, 1998). To say that political and ideological agendas are not influencing how the problem of child sexual abuse is construed would be to neglect that which is most obvious.

Several scholars (Jenkins, 1998: 2; Hacking, 1999: 127; Johnson, 1995: 22) observe a tension in the professional and social field in relation to current discourses of child sexual abuse in which the holders of the 'truth' of the situation, those who are seen to have the 'correct' interpretation of events, are juxtaposed against those who are said to be 'in denial', or whose interpretations are seen as suspect. Protagonists for one side argue that recent realisations of the size and nature of child sexual abuse are made possible by the growing accumulation of 'objective' knowledge and the lifting of taboos that limited research in the past. Those who disagree are seen as 'in denial'. This attempt to silence opponents who do not agree with one's particular version of events is a central feature of the public discourse of child sexual abuse in Ireland and in the United States. Such positioning gives rise to a singular highly policed discourse (Kincaid, 1998: 8) in which many voices and perspectives are marginalised and silenced. Kincaid (1998: 8) argues that in writing on the subject of child sexual abuse every author feels compelled to state '[p]lease don't misunderstand me; I know millions of children are sexually molested'. He argues that the very feeling of being compelled to ward off such misunderstandings suggests a very narrow range to the current discourse, one that is 'conscientiously policed' (p 8). Only minor variations on a single story can be told.

Kincaid (1998: 13) argues that Western culture has 'enthusiastically sexualised the child while denying just as enthusiastically that it was doing any such thing', such as during child pageants in the United States and in certain spheres of the pop music industry. According to Kincaid (p 20), a society that regards children as erotic, but also regards an erotic response to children as criminally unimaginable, has a problem on its hands. In his opinion, the true nature of the abuse of children is still denied, largely because the complexities involved in the interplay of childhood, sexuality and adulthood[8] are also denied, whilst attention is focused on the 'monster' who is seen as 'other' (Kincaid, 1998: 20). Kincaid argues that if a society wants to protect children from sexual abuse and understand how the problem is constituted, then the discourse must change to one in which the problem of child sexual abuse is located within the general adult population and not with a few individuals who are identified as 'monsters'. Ultimately, a better understanding of the complexities of adult and child sexuality will lead to greater protection for children (Kincaid, 1998: 22) and less marginalising of men. In Kincaid's (1998: 6) view, many children suffer in the current situation: those children who are sexually abused and those who are denied a nurturing relationship with adult men. Perpetrators of abuse suffer too when they are sentenced to live their lives as 'evil monsters' by an unforgiving adult public.

Changing Understanding of Childhood

Since the mid 1970s changes have occurred in how childhood is understood, which may have a bearing on current day perceptions of abuse victims and indeed on abuse perpetrators. In most Western societies, childhood is seen as an age-related phenomenon which prescribes legal rights and responsibilities that take effect at different ages (Corby, 2000: 10). Despite these age related demarcations, children grow at different rates both physically and psychologically and there is not uniformity in how the child is seen throughout the world.

The most influential work on childhood in the twentieth century has been that of Philippe Ariès (1962) a French social historian. In *Centuries of Childhood* (1962: 125) Ariès argued that in medieval society the idea of childhood did not exist, but this was not detrimental to the child. Rather he thought the opposite was true. In the Middle Ages children mingled with adults as soon as that was physically possible and spent much of their time together in work and play (p 125). It was from the seventeenth century onwards, with the advent of a form of education dominated by religion-based morality, that children became separated from adults in the way known today. Ariès (1962: 126) saw this as a backward step and he argues that the concept of childhood is a limiting force for children, placing more restrictions on them in their formative years and placing them more at the mercy of adults than had previously been the case.

Other scholars (De Mause, 1976: 1; Pollack, 1983: 7; Wilson, 1984: 183) criticise the work of Ariès (1962) and argue that he does not have the evidence to back up his wide-ranging claims. They also argue that his view of family life in the Middle Ages is suspect. Some scholars (De Mause, 1976: 1; Stone, 1977: 70) see the development of the concept of childhood as highly progressive. They argue that developments in the concept of childhood heralded a time when children were now recognised as a distinct group from adults, with their own particular developmental needs and vulnerabilities that made them deserving of special rights. These scholars argue that developments in the concept of childhood did much to improve the lot of children. De Mause (1976: 1) argues that 'the further back in history one goes the lower the level of childcare, and the more likely children are to be killed, abandoned, beaten, terrorised and sexually abused'.

It is highly likely that there is no universal experience of childhood, nor has there been in the past, and it is highly possible that children of different classes, genders and races have had and continue to have widely differing experiences of childhood (Corby, 2000:15). As Corby points out, during the period of industrialisation in Britain in the nineteenth century, there was the development of greater sensitivity towards the children of the middle classes whilst, at the same time, appalling working conditions for children of the labouring classes were tolerated in the mills, factories and on the street. Scholars of childhood believe that as societies develop economically there is a tendency for childhood to be extended and to gain more attention as a separate category from adulthood (Corby, 2000: 12). In the Irish situation, Buckley *et al* (1996: 12) observed, if the period up to the 1970s was to be characterised by the era of the 'depraved child' (when child care interventions were viewed as a means of social control and of 'disciplining' the children of the poor) and the 1980s were characterised by the era of the 'deprived' child (when the influences of developmental psychology were being felt, emphasising emotional and psychological dimensions to the welfare of children), the 1990s and 2000s must certainly be considered the era of the 'abused child' and the 'sexually abused child' – and this era shows no signs of abating. However, it is also worth noting that as an Irish public gets rightly upset and angry about the childhood experiences of the children of the Irish industrial and reformatory schools of the 1950s, 1960s and 1970s, countless children live in poverty in Ireland in the year 2009, and services for children with disabilities and those in the care of the state due to family breakdown are grossly neglected and underfunded (O'Brien, 2009a; 2009b; 2009c; 2009d; 2009e).

The twentieth century has seen the concept of childhood become almost the exclusive preserve of psychology, with childhood experiences seen as a crucial determinative of the human character (Dunne & Kelly, 2002: 4). This has also led to the development of child welfare and child protection policies and to a range of child care legislation aimed at protecting children from adults. The changing concepts of childhood have had a significant influence on social change in Ireland since the 1970s.

Changing Concepts of Child Sexual Abuse
Jenkins (1998: xi) traced the history of adult/child sexual relations (today known as child sexual abuse) and argues fairly convincingly that although the term *child sexual abuse* has a long history it was not until the mid 1970s that it acquired its present cultural and ideological significance, 'with all its connotations of betrayal of trust, hidden trauma and denial'. In Jenkins's opinion (1998: 234) modern concepts of child sexual abuse are linked to what he sees as irreversible social, political and ideological trends (the vulnerability of children and their need for protection, political and social equality for women, and the power of medico-legal discourses of sexuality)[9] which make it likely that contemporary formulations of the child abuse problem will not diminish in the near future. This is a concept that has changed over time, and child-adult sex has not always had the same meaning and implications for the child or adult as we have come to accept as taken-for-granted truth today.[10]

Whilst Freud wrote of 'damage' to children who had experienced abuse, it is only since the 1970s that this idea has re-emerged as worthy of professional and public interest (Jenkins, 1998: 18). For some earlier periods of the twentieth century it was not uncommon for some of the clinical literature to suggest that that in many cases of adult-child sex the child was the active seducer rather than the one who was innocently seduced and the idea prevailed that children produced such offences for their own psychological reasons (Jenkins, 1998:2). Such thinking certainly influenced aspects of professional practice in the 1970s. Child sexual abuse was seen as an infrequent occurrence unlikely to cause significant harm to the vast majority of subjects. Today children who have been experienced sexual abuse are sometimes regarded as 'damaged for life' (Jenkins, 1998: 2) – a label I also find myself equally rejecting on their behalf. Just as children are not the active seducers neither are they 'damaged' for life – traumatised, hurt, angry, upset, maybe, but damaged I completely reject. For those people who are labelled as 'damaged', often by a well intentioned professional or public discourse, an additional burden to that already endured can be an unintended consequence. My professional involvement with individuals who have experienced all kinds of trauma and abuse has taught me that it is always possible for human beings to turn their tragedy into something that makes even greater human beings in the world, especially when the trauma and the wrongs inflicted are truly acknowledged and lamented. The potential for the human spirit to rise above adversity never ceases to amaze me.

Images of child sexual offenders have also changed dramatically over time. Once seen as benign molesters, 'a species of defective' individuals, known to all and not doing much harm, child sexual offenders are now seen as evil sex 'fiends' who possess the most dangerous and sophisticated criminal intellects. Child sexual offenders are also thought to have access to the latest form of technology and communication (Jenkins, 1998: 18) and to operate in 'rings'. The perpetrator of child sexual abuse, who was once seen as a 'harmlessly inadequate', is now referred to as a 'dangerous predator' (Jenkins, 1998:2; Hudson, 2005; Greer, 2003). In much public discourse, child sexual offenders are now seen as posing danger to every child in all situations and their behaviour and personhood is often little removed from the worst multiple killers and torturers (Jenkins, 1998: 2; Hudson, 2005: 26; Breen, 2004b: 9). The resultant public discourse is one of retribution, in which risk management and public notification of the dangers posed by certain individuals are preferred to the more rehabilitative or restorative ideals. Risk management rather than reparation and social inclusion become the focus of social policy and political action.

In the Irish situation, some men who have abused children and who have served prison sentences for these offences and benefited from treatment for their problems are often run out of their homes and sometimes out of their country. Men who are known to have perpetrated sexual abuse against minors find it difficult to secure employment, and if successful, employment can be terminated on the whim of a public campaign, such as the name and shame campaign orchestrated by the *News of the World* in 2002, which is available in Ireland. These men are often subject of attacks on their homes and their personhood, and their families can suffer for being seen to support a 'pervert'. I have met all of these situations in my professional life. Paradoxically, he who is seen as most threatening lives in a highly threatening and uncertain world. In Ireland and the United States, child sexual abuse has acquired a new moral weight and sexual offending has become the worst of all possible vices (Hacking, 1999: 125; Kincaid, 1998: 5). The child abuse victim is portrayed as damaged for life and the child sexual offender is viewed as the most evil of human beings.

The Creation of 'Types'
The primary focus of the psychological literature on the child sexual offender is an individual one, with a strong emphasis on understanding the causes of the crime and the vulnerability factors that might lead an individual down a sexually abusive path.

Generally the aim of a psychiatric perspective is to measure and classify, identifying the predictive personality variables that are seen to play a causative role in creating the phenomenon. The predominant focus of the psychiatric and psychological literature is one of individual limitation, resulting in a professional discourse based largely on ideas of deviance, deficit and individual pathology. Medical definitions have also influenced legal perspectives, leading to medico-legal dominance of the public discourse.

Within medico-legal discourses the child sexual offender is classified as a paedophile or conceptualised as suffering from 'cognitive distortions' or 'deviant sexual attraction'. At any rate he is conceptualised as different from 'normal' men, belonging to a different 'class' or 'type' – a member of a class apart. This construction of the sexual offender has been challenged by some scholars within the discipline of psychology (Marshall, 1996; Marshall *et al*, 2000; Freeman-Longo and Blanchard, 1998). However, despite this challenge, the power that professional disciplines exercise in the creation of knowledge appears to be rarely questioned, and with some notable exceptions it is rare that the social consequences of these particular 'findings' are addressed (Freeman-Longo and Blanchard, 1998; Marshall *et al*, 2000; Marshall, 1996).

Bell (2002: 83) offers some observations on the tensions between individualisation and 'types' and the techniques that are used in certain disciplines, such as psychology, medicine, social work and criminology, in order to produce information about individuals, which is then subsequently used to identify and govern others of the same 'type'. O'Malley (1998: 1) observes such a process in the Irish legal system, whereby as soon as a person is formally or informally judged to be a 'sex offender' or 'child abuser', he is socially classified under that heading only. O'Malley, (1998: 1) argues that the attachment of one of these labels has the effect of wiping out the offender's entire social and personal profile. As soon as a man becomes classified as a sex offender his earlier achievements and social contributions are deemed irrelevant. What matters is the very sexual nature of the offence and the classification that follows (O'Malley, 1998: 1; Hudson, 2005: 26; Bell, 2002: 83). Such classifications, which are often based on psychiatric categorisations, lead to marginalisation and demonising of individual men. The sexual offender's offending behaviour is disapproved of and also his very personhood is construed as evil (Hudson, 2005: 30). The man's identity becomes totalised as an abuser – an identity description from which there is no escape, no matter what else in life he does to make good, including never abusing again.

Bell (2002: 84) argues that the processes by which child abuse becomes known within the disciplines of medicine, psychology and social work and the techniques by which 'the population at risk' is constituted and governed, through law, social work or police practices, need to be analysed rather than taken-for-granted as 'objective' truth. The variety of figures that emerge from such professional discourses and labelling practices, such as 'child abuser', 'paedophile', 'child at risk', 'abuse victim', give rise for concern (Bell, 2002; Hacking, 1999; Mercer and Simmonds, 2001; Haug, 2001; Cowburn and Dominelli, 2001). Power is at play within such professional disciplines and in effect careers are built on developing new classification and categorisation systems for human beings. In the United States, psychiatric classifications underpin the whole counselling 'industry', and individuals cannot recoup the cost for counselling from their insurers unless they have been given a DSM diagnosis (a psychiatric classification) (Freeman-Longo and Blanchard, 1998). Classification systems serve interests beyond the people whose lives are subjected to such categorisations. Classification systems serve as instruments of objectification, measurement and economic gain. Classification systems certainly concern me, mainly because of their potential to contribute to further oppression, marginalisation and abuse, producing the very effects we are attempting to alleviate in the first instance. Such labels are also of little value when treating individuals who have experienced childhood abuse or individuals who have perpetrated sexual offences.

My argument is that attention must be paid to the practices and techniques that help construct child sexual abuse and the child sexual offender in particular ways, such as 'a danger to every child'; otherwise socially sanctioned practices of dehumanisation, oppression and marginalisation are endorsed in the absence of good data, but based on ideology and power. All of this takes place in the name of child protection. What is important here is that power relations and vested interests are concealed whilst the cast of villains are construed and elaborated.

In arguing for this I am arguing for a safer society for all and for a society in which all abuses of individuals can be abhorred and challenged, and not just the abuses that happen to catch public attention as worthy of intervention at a particular time. If traditional views of power are based on ideas of domination by individuals or groups, such as in feminist understanding of gender hegemony and patriarchal social structures (Herman, 1981: 177; Mercer and Simmonds, 2001: 171; Cowburn and Dominelli, 2001: 401; Kelly, 1997: 10), modern power is located in the strategies and techniques employed to bring forth consensus (Lukes, 2005). In producing 'apparent' consensus on a topic, by silencing certain voices and rendering invisible the power forces at play, a cultural narrative emerges that offers a very narrow range to the public discourse. Both traditional and modern practices of power must be kept to the fore in understanding how child sexual abuse comes to be and how it comes to be understood.

The Media and the Child Sexual Offender

Several scholars (Best, 1995a; Jenkins, 1996; Breen, 2004a, 2004b; Greer, 2003) have analysed the role of the print and electronic media in influencing public opinion on sexual offenders and in using shaming techniques and strategies to marginalise and punish. The mass media is said to play a significant role in setting public agendas on a wide variety of issues, and the media coverage of a story can also alter public perception of its central participants (Breen, 2004a: 3). The term *typification* is used to refer to the process by which 'claims-makers characterise a problem's nature', suggesting reasons for the problem, interpreting the motivations of its elements, and recommending solutions (Best, 1995a: 8). This is a process often evident in media representation of certain social problems. In most Western societies it has become common to use a medical model to typify social problems, implying sickness/disease, treatment and cure (Best, 1995: 14). Crime is often typified through the medium of a 'melodramatic' model, which sees 'victims' as exploited by 'villains' who must subsequently be rescued by 'heroes' (Nelson-Rowe, 1995: 84). In an extension of the melodramatic model, Johnson (1995: 19) argues that 'horror stories' serve a function in typifying the nature of child sexual abuse and many of its characters. Johnson suggests that the media's use of the 'horror' story is also a way of gaining privilege for child sexual abuse over other aspects of child maltreatment, child poverty and child neglect (p 20). The effect of typification of the problem's nature and of the motivation of its key elements and actors is that a single story gets told, usually presented in binary form (good/bad; innocent/guilty; protector/predator; victim/villain), and many alternative interpretations of the complexities of the issues involved are left unexplored.

In relation to the media coverage of child sexual abuse and its portrayal of the child sexual offender, the use of media templates is also most illuminating. According to Kitzinger (2000:62) media templates are routinely used to emphasise only one clear perspective, to serve as rhetorical shorthand/shortcut, and to help audiences and producers place stories in 'a particular' context. These templates have a threefold effect: (a) they shape narratives around specific issues, (b) they guide public opinion and discussion, and (c) they set the frame of reference for the future (Kitzinger, 1999, 2000). Even though the events once reported might have long since passed, they continue to carry powerful associations that have long outlived their potential immediate usefulness (Kitzinger, 1999, 2000). Examples of media templates are The Wall Street Crash of 1929, which serves as a media template for the reporting of financial issues and problems;

'Vietnam' for a failed or mired war; 'Watergate' for political scandals (Breen, 2004a: 5). This is such a strong template that the suffix 'gate' carries its own derived meaning (Breen, 2004a: 5). We once in Ireland had 'Bertigate' as a media template for discussing the financial affairs of former Taoiseach, Bertie Ahern, with the associated meaning that 'gate' implies.

The power of the media template lies in its associative force (Breen, 2004a: 5). Media templates are used to explain current events, but their main function is to highlight general patterns in particular social problems (Breen, 2004a: 5). The major consequence that follows from the use of the media template is that it too contributes to a strong single dominant discourse, representing what is portrayed as 'fact' and 'truth'. However, these 'facts' or 'truths' have been simplified or distorted and alternative readings of the 'facts' minimised (Kitzinger, 1999, 2000). Greer (2003: 4) argues that the image of the sexual offender portrayed in the press in Britain is that of an 'amoral, manipulative, predatory sociopath' who preys preferably on the most vulnerable. Such imagery succeeds in creating the picture of the sex offender as an inherently different person compared to other members of society. Even legislative and policy responses can be seen as stemming from such perceptions. Hudson (2005: 1) argues that the current trend in Britain of taking increasingly punitive measures against sex offenders, both in sentencing and in the community, derives from such created and constructed images. The same can be said of Ireland.

In Ireland, the coverage of sexual abuse by Catholic clergy led to the emergence of a new media template, 'Brendan Smyth'. Fr Brendan Smyth, a Norbertine priest, had been convicted in June 1994 on seventeen counts of sexual abuse of children stretching over thirty years. An investigative journalist, Chris Moore, reporting for Ulster Television showed that the clerical authorities had known for years of Smyth's crimes and had dealt with them simply by moving him on, with the suggestion that they covered up his abuses (Moore, 1995). A series of political events concerning the mishandling of the case in the Attorney

General's office led to political tensions which eventually brought down the government in the Republic in 1994 (Moore, 1995). While reporting this case, a new category of sexual offender, 'the paedophile priest', was invented by the media (Ferguson, 1995: 248; *Boston Globe*, 2002: 7). Furthermore, the media also relied heavily on powerful visual images. From the outset, the media had repeatedly used the same photograph of Brendan Smyth's bloated and angry face, staring straight into the camera, so that he became 'the living embodiment of the greatest demon in modern Ireland' (Ferguson, 1995: 249). Long after his death, this photograph often accompanied media reports of sexual abuse by other clergy. This is partly the context in which the child sexual abuse by Catholic clergy has gained public attention and in which the changing constructions of the abuse victim of Catholic clergy and the clergy perpetrators have taken hold. The media template has also led to a view of clerical men who have abused children as a homogenised group, whose offending histories are the same, and all of whom represent continuous danger to children in every situation. This view bears no relationship to the reality, but it is a view that carries much weight in influencing public opinion and in frightening church leaders to act as they do regarding the management of clerical men who have sexually abused minors.

Sexual Abuse by Catholic Clergy: The Extent and Form of the Problem
It is difficult to estimate the extent of sexual offending in the general population and it is equally difficult to estimate the extent of sexual offending by Roman Catholic clergy. Most estimates of sexual offenders are derived from forensic sources and some studies acknowledge that those arrested or convicted represent only a fraction of all sexual offenders (Abel 1987: 89; O'Mahony, 1996: 210). Sometimes the extent of sexual offending is gleaned from the extent of victimisation, but that too is difficult to estimate because of variations in the values, customs, definitions and methodologies that are used in international and comparative studies (Finkelhor, 1994: 409). Child sexual abuse is

also believed to be significantly underreported (McGee, 2002; O'Mahony, 1996; Russell, 1983). These factors make for difficulty in assessing both the extent of the problem of child sexual abuse and the actual number of sexual offenders in a given population. However a meta-analysis of a number of studies on victim prevalence in the United States is currently accepted as offering good baseline international data (Bolen and Scannapieco, 1999: 281). This study reported that the overall prevalence of male children who are sexually abused is 13% (one in six to eight boys) and the prevalence of female children who are sexually abused is 30-40% (one in three girls) (Bolen and Scannapieco, 1999: 281). In the Irish situation, McGee *et al* (2002: 67) reported prevalence rates of contact sexual abuse of male children as 24% (higher than in many countries), and rates of sexual abuse of female children as 30%. The number of perpetrators can only be surmised from these data, as some perpetrators have many victims and many perpetrators are never reported.

By far the most comprehensive study to date on the problem of child sexual abuse by Catholic clergy emanates from the United States (John Jay College, 2004, 2006) with longitudinal studies from a treatment centre in Canada (Camargo and Loftus, 1992; Loftus and Camargo, 1993; Camargo, 1997) also providing important data. In 2004, the John Jay College of Criminal Justice released the findings of the first-ever national prevalence study on child sexual abuse by Roman Catholic priests, in a study that was commissioned by the US Conference of Catholic Bishops (John Jay College, 2004). A supplementary study analysed some of the descriptive data (John Jay College, 2006). The study, based on survey responses from 97% of Catholic dioceses (amounting to 195 dioceses in total) and 64% of religious communities (representing 83% of religious priests across the country) produced a number of findings that give a sense of the pattern of sexual abuse by Catholic priests and deacons in the United States at least. Their relevance for Ireland or any other country would need to be empirically tested.

The total number of priests alleged to have abused in the

period 1950-2002 was 4,392, representing approximately 4% of the 109,694 priests in active ministry during that time. No significant differences were found between abuse rates in small, medium or large dioceses, with the average percentage of accused priests in a region ranging from 3% to 6% (Terry, 2008: 558). Approximately 4.3% of secular priests had allegations of sexual abuse made against them whilst allegations of sexual abuse were made against 2.7% of priests of religious orders. Other studies and reports have estimated that between 2.4% and 8.4% of Catholic priests and deacons in the United States and Canada were involved in sexual abuse of minors (Sipe, 1995; Greeley, 1993; Goodstein, 2003; Camargo and Loftus, 1992, Loftus and Camargo, 1993; Camargo, 1997). In the Irish situation, a very important study aimed at establishing the extent of sexual violence in Ireland, the SAVI study (McGee *et al*, 2002: 88) estimated that Roman Catholic clergy abused 3.9% of all adults who had been sexually abused as children in Ireland (5.8% of all male victims and 1.4% of all female victims). This study also included religious brothers. Data collated by an Irish journalist (Quinn, 2005: 26, 27) from a number of Catholic dioceses in Ireland, estimated that 4% of all priests in Ireland have been accused of abusing minors over a period of fifty years. The comparable figure of men in the general population who are said to sexually abuse children, although difficult to estimate, is put at 6% by one of the leading researchers in the world on this topic (Hanson, 2003).

The John Jay data suggest that the largest number of priests began abusing when they were between the ages of 30-39 years, on average after eleven years in ministry (John Jay College, 2006). (The men in my own study began abusing when they were somewhat younger, and usually within the first five years of ministry.) The majority of priests in the United States (55.7%) had one formal allegation of abuse; 26.4% had two or three allegations; 17.8% had four to nine allegations and 3.5% had ten or more allegations. Allegations in this instance refer to individual victims – there were in many cases several offences perpetrated against the same victim. Those men with one allegation made against them were more likely than those with further allegations to have a female victim and have a victim in the fifteen to seventeen year old age range (Terry, 2008: 560). The duration of abusive behaviour was calculated by using the date of the first incident of abuse and the date of the most recent reported incident and although these figures did not necessarily represent continuous abusive activity, the data calculated in this manner suggested that 31% of priests abused minors for less than one year. These data were reasonably stable during the period of 54 years (1950-2004) that the research team investigated (Terry, 2008: 562). Priests ordained in the early 1970s were more likely to have been accused of sexual abuse of a minor than priests ordained in any other period. Approximately 10% of priests ordained from 1970 to 1975 had allegations of abuse made against them, with a significant decline thereafter (p 565). Overall the John Jay data suggest that although the majority of incidents were not known until 2003, the data show a steady rise in the incidence of abuse between the 1950s and the 1980s in the United States and a sharp decline by 1990. Although abuse allegations were often reported many years after the event, the John Jay team controlled statistically for this occurrence in coming to the conclusion that they did.

Overall, 81% of the victims were male and 19% were female. Male victims tended to be older than females. Over 40% of all victims were males between the ages of eleven and fourteen. Approximately 78% of the victims (male and females combined) were between the ages of eleven and seventeen years; 16% were between the ages of eight and ten years, and 6% of the victims were younger than seven years old. Whilst some men abused both male and females, there were more male to female victims in all of the categories of offender (those with one, two to three, four to nine and over ten victims). In my own study, eight of the nine participants sexually abused post-pubertal males in the course of their priesthood or religious ministry, while one man sexually abused younger males between the ages of ten to fourteen years. However, there was one allegation of abuse by a post-pubertal female against one other man. Three of the men in my own research also sexually abused the post-pubertal male children of friends or family.

The John Jay team found significant delay in reporting of abuse cases by people who had experienced abuse to the church authorities (John Jay College, 2004; 2006). Prior to 1985, 810 cases had been reported to the dioceses and religious orders for the period 1950-1985, whereas the total now reported as having occurred during that period exceeds 9000 (Terry, 2008: 565; Smith et al, 2008: 575). Of the total number of cases known by 2003 (n=10,210), 33% (over 3000) had been reported in the single year of 2002, after an average delay of 30 years. Although many cases of sexual abuse were known by church authorities from the 1950s onwards, most of these events were unknown to civil authorities or church leaders before the year 2000 (Smith *et al*, 2008: 575). Because of the statute of limitations few cases went through the criminal justice system. Although information was not available on all cases, the available data suggested that 3% of all priests against whom allegations were made were convicted and 2% received prison sentences (Terry, 2008: 563). Nearly 40% of the accused priests participated in some form of psychological treatment.

The available data provide good support for the argument that the extent of the problem of sexual abuse of minors by Roman Catholic clergy is no greater than in the general population and one might reasonably argue that there is no case to be answered or understood in relation to sexual abuse by Catholic clergy. Whilst the population of priests are a highly selected, highly educated, highly formed group of men, there is in fact no evidence that child sexual abuse is less prevalent in the educated or highly educated male population. In fact, some might argue that the highly educated might be more able to hide their abuses and that it may be more prevalent in this group of men, although more hidden. However, I believe that sexual abuse by Catholic clergy is a subject that requires further research and understanding as Catholic clergy are distinguished from other men in a number of respects and the Catholic Church is one of the largest religious organisations in the world, representing an influential force in many societies and in the lives of its many members. For millions of people, Catholic clergy are, or have been, the spiritual, moral and ethical leaders.

Catholic clergy represent a group of men pledged to celibacy and the occurrence of sexual activity, especially of an abusive kind, contradicts everything that the institution publicly stands for. In addition, the strong emphasis on moral conscience and moral theology in religious and seminary formation, which takes place in an all-male celibate environment, makes the preparation for this professional and vocational life fairly unique. The accusation that church leaders responded in a similar manner to abuse complaints in Ireland and the United States, (as well as from what we know in Canada, Australia and England), a response that is now seen as having compounded the problem, raises questions about the systemic nature of the problem. Whilst the statistics suggest that 92%-96% of the Roman Catholic clergy did not abuse minors there is much to be analysed and understood about what distinguishes abusive from non abusive clerical men.

'Normal' Catholic Clergy

Since the 1970s a number of studies on 'normal' Catholic clergy have examined various aspects of clerical life, principally in the United States of America (Plante, Manuel and Tandez, 1996; Madden, 1990; Lane, 1997; Benyei 1998; Plante and Boccacccine, 1997; Keddy, Erdberg and Sammon, 1990; Loftus, 1999, 2004; Hoge, 2002; McGlone 2001). However, there remains a dearth of in-depth studies on both 'normal' clergy and seminarians and in particular on their sexual lives and experiences, although a small number of studies do exist (Nines, 2006; McGlone, 2001; Sipe, 1995; Kennedy, 1971, 2001). Loftus (1999: 16; 2004: 88) argues that without adequate data it is difficult to compare the lives of 'normal' and offending clergy accurately and in particular to compare their sexual lives. This is not to suggest that in all cases child sexual abuse is about sexuality – as power, anger and attempts at making contact are also said to play a role – however, every sexual offence has a sexual dimension, otherwise without consideration of sexual motivation it is difficult to explain why an offence is sexual in nature (Finkelhor, 1984: 34). My own research suggests that sexuality concerns are highly implicated in child sexual abuse by Catholic clergy, but it must be stressed that this is a problem that has no single cause. As most of the literature on 'normal' clergy emanates from the United States, the extent to which some of the themes apply to an Irish Catholic clergy population also requires further analysis. However, a number of themes emerge from the literature on 'normal' clergy, which may be relevant to our understanding of Catholic clergy who have sexually abused.[11]

The literature on 'normal' Catholic clergy describes as extremely stressful the conditions and expectations under which Roman Catholic clergy work, particularly as many clergymen discount their personal needs, do not ask for help and take responsibility for the well-being of others over whose lives they have little control (Lane, 1997; Brenneis, 2001; Cozzens, 2000). Brenneis (2001:23) found that when a priest takes a 'defensive' or 'repressive' stance towards his inner life, especially in relation to matters that pose an emotional threat, such as hostile, aggressive or sexual feelings, stress is significantly amplified. The problem is that clergy work within an emotionally demanding profession, in which the interpersonal boundaries are often not clear (Papesh, 2004) and if they adopt a perfectionist attitude towards the self, are defensive in relation to self-awareness, do not disclose personal distress, or are reluctant to identify vulnerability, significant problems may build up for these men. Brenneis (2001: 24) argues that if unresolved, these issues can bring a man into all kinds of acting out, including the sexual abuse of children.

The literature on normal clergy points to the fact that priests live in an environment that is beset with contradictions, such as a promise to celibacy, but inadequate preparation for living a healthy celibate life (Ranson, 2002a; 2002b); a need for intimacy, but inability to negotiate intimacy within the confines of a celibate commitment (Papesh, 2004); problems with sexuality and sexual orientation, but a need to conceal sexuality concerns (McGlone, 2001: 119). Considerable skill is required for living the life of the Catholic clergyman and one would imagine that the training for clergy would be hugely important in this regard. It is interesting, therefore, to note that the literature on 'normal' clergy shows consistently that clergy do not feel well prepared in the seminaries and houses of formation for their lives and ministries (Loftus, 2004:92; Sipe, 2003:277; Hoge, 2002: 98; Papesh, 2004: 70), nor do they feel adequately supported by church hierarchies in living that life (Lane, 1997: 62). This is a theme that also arises in the research on clergy men who have abused.

The literature on 'normal' clergy also suggests that the spaces for clergy in which to speak are few, leading some of them towards the protective environments of spiritual direction, personal psychotherapy and the confessional (McGlone, 2001: 119; Ranson, 2002b: 220). However, overall the picture is one of clergy keeping their personal, sexual and emotional lives private from other clergy. Cozzens (2004) argues that clerical culture supports such non-disclosure of emotion, including emotional distress. In my research the confessional emerges as the most important site for disclosure of personal distress, including sexual offending, and it emerges as the most important site from which the participants seek emotional support. Few of the men used spiritual direction.

A most striking feature arising from the examination of the literature on 'normal' clergy in the United States is the view that up to 50% of Roman Catholic clergy are sexually active at any one time, despite vows of chastity and a commitment to celibate living. Several studies (McGlone, 2001; Nines, 2006; Sipe, 2003) report this trend. This is an important finding because it indicates that sexual abuse of minors by clergy may be part of a bigger problem of celibate sexuality for the Roman Catholic Church. This is not to say that celibacy singularly 'causes' clergy to sexually abuse minors – but nonetheless celibacy may play some role in leading clerical men down this path. Clergy engaging in 'consensual' sexual relationships is merely a disciplinary matter for the Roman Catholic Church and of itself is not of civil or criminal concern. Neither can its effects be compared to the sexual abuse of children. However, the widespread lack of celibate practice in the Roman Catholic Church is relevant to the central issue of the sexual abuse of minors by Catholic clergy because an organisation that publicly proclaims the sexual abstinence of its members, whilst at the same time tolerating or denying their sexual activity, is itself already in trouble.

Celibacy – the state of non-marriage and the practice of perfect chastity – is a requirement for ordination to the Catholic priesthood in the Latin Rite (Canon Law Society, 1983, Canon 227). Celibacy is an on-going requirement for the active priesthood, an image that the church hierarchy, including bishops, religious superiors and the Vatican have diligently fostered. The fact that 'consensual' sexual activities take place by clergy in secret and within the institutional rhetoric of an all-male celibate clergy may suggest a systemic denial of the problems that celibacy poses, thus creating an unhealthy organisational culture (Cozzens, 2004; Ranson, 2002a, 2002b).

Clerical Men who have Sexually Offended against Minors
Sometimes the question is raised why individuals with a disposition to prey sexually upon minors gain admission to the priesthood and why they are not weaned out before they infiltrate the organisation. Examined closely this question suggests a number of assumptions: that priests and religious who come to be accused of the sexual abuse of children have a predisposition to do so, that such inclinations can be discerned at the point of entry to the seminary or while they are seminarians and that some men become priests and religious in order to gain access to children to abuse. By implication the assumption is that the sexual abuse of a child by Catholic clergy is the result of individual pathology or predisposition – a theory that is favoured by some men in

leadership in the Catholic Church. The response often suggests the need for better screening for clergy at the point of entry in order to pick up individuals with a disordered psychological state.

Whilst screening the clergy might be important for a lot of reasons, the assumption that it will pick up those men who might come to be accused of the sexual abuse of children is not borne out by available research and clinical experience. My research and that presented by other clinicians and researchers (Kafka, 2004; Marshall, 2004), including the John Jay team (Terry, 2008: 567; Smith *et al*, 2008: 580) lead to this conclusion. The John Jay College research team (John Jay, 2004, 2006) worked hard to be able to discern the evidence of pathology or predisposition to abuse children from the data that they studied of the clergy offenders in the US. They concluded that the data did not support the finding that most of these acts of child sexual abuse were predicated by pathology or paraphilic behaviour, such as paedophilia (Smith *et al*, 2008: 580; Tallon and Terry, 2008:625). Tallon and Terry (2008:625) argued that because clerical men wait several years before committing their first acts of abuse and because they do not target particular types of children (as the majority of clergy perpetrators in the John Jay Study abused victims with wider age discrepancies than 2 or more years and sometimes minors of both genders), whatever else is happening, it is not likely that most clerical abuse of children is driven by sexually arousing fantasies about prepubescent children or adolescents (which forms the basis of the definition of paedophilia). Tallon and Terry (2008: 625) found that very few priests who had sexually abused minors fit the typology of the 'paedophile priest' – a typology that is favoured by the media. Even those men who initiated sexual abuse soon after ordination and whose abusive pattern spanned a long duration did not meet what could be regarded as paedophilia, as they would not have waited so long to begin their abusive 'careers' if they were paedophiles. Many so called paraphilic interests, such as paedophilia, are said to begin in adolescence and if these men did have a diagnosable disorder on which they would act out, (even if one subscribed to such thinking in the first instance) it would be expected that they would have done so sooner (Tallon and Terry, 2008: 626). In my own study, in which eight of the nine men abused post-pubertal males (and one also abused a female), and one abused younger male children, I reached the same conclusion, based on an analysis of the men's narratives and of their case files. Tallon and Terry (2008: 625) also concluded that it is unlikely that clerical and religious men who have sexually abused minors have specifically chosen a profession in the Catholic Church so that they could have access to children to abuse. I have reached a similar conclusion (Keenan, 2006).

Several other studies have reviewed aspects of the psychological functioning of clerical men who have sexually abused minors, looking for clues to their abusive actions and decisions. Lack of intimacy and emotional loneliness is considered important by a number of clinicians and researchers (Loftus and Camargo, 1993: 292; Sipe, 1995; Loftus, 1999; Kennedy, 2001). Depression and difficulty expressing emotional concerns is seen as important by others (Plante, Manuel and Bryant, 1996: 135; Robinson, 1994: 365). Whilst McGlone (2001: 88) found that 59% of non-offending or 'normal' clergy identified themselves as having received some form of psychological treatment or counselling, mainly relating to depression, sexual orientation, sexual identity issues and alcoholism, Flakenhain *et al*, (1999: 330) indicated that only 1.8%-2.5% of sexually offending clergy ever sought psychological help prior to treatment for their sexual offending. Clergy who were identified as child sexual offenders simply did not seek help for their sexual and emotional problems. This is also something that emerges in my own research.

Anger and over-controlled hostility was also reported as part of the profile of clerical men who have sexually abused minors (Plante, Manuel and Bryant, 1996: 135). A style of relating that tended towards passivity and conformity and in some instances a tendency towards shyness is also reported in some of these studies (Rossetti, 1994:4; Loftus and Camargo 1993: 292). Anger was also implicated in the offending of the men who participated in my own research – anger that came from a lifetime of submission and attempts at living a life that was impossible to live. My research suggests that the practices of obedience and the absence of personal autonomy in clerical and religious life must be considered significant in the sexual offending of Roman Catholic clergy – especially if obedience becomes an instrument of oppression in the hands of church leaders who work in a spirit of power and control rather than a spirit of guiding leadership.

Some studies found that ignorance of sexual matters, lack of knowledge of the basic physiology of sexuality and of the emotional responses in sexually charged situations (Loftus and Camargo, 1993: 292, 300) and what is described as sexual and emotional underdevelopment (Flakenhain *et al*, 1999: 331) were all found in sexually offending Catholic clergy. However, Loftus and Camargo, (1993: 292) also found that all groups of clergy attending a treatment centre in Canada for a range of issues were ignorant of sexual matters and not just those who had abused minors.

Several studies have reported that clergy who have sexually abused minors have experienced sexual abuse themselves in childhood, sometimes by another priest or religious (Robinson, Montana and Thompson, 1993 (66%); Connors (1994) (30%-35%); Sipe (1995) (70%-80%); Valcour (1990: 49) (33%-50%)). This is also the case in my own research in which six of the nine participants reported a history of sexual abuse; five in childhood and one man was abused in the seminary. This is an important finding and although sexual abuse in childhood can never be accepted as an excuse for sexual offending in adulthood, and many people who experience childhood sexual abuse never abuse anyone, it is important that many clergy who had experienced sexual abuse in childhood had never discussed these experiences until they were in treatment for sexual offending. Perrillo *et al* (2008: 611), who analysed the John Jay data to try to understand repeat[12] offending by Catholic clergy, found that a history of childhood sexual victimisation was one of the strongest predictive variables for clerical men to become repeat offenders. This is an important observation as there is not over-all support for this finding in the general literature on other child sexual offenders (Hanson *et al*, 1993; Hanson and Morton-Bourgon, 2004, 2005). Priests and religious who have experienced childhood sexual abuse may be different in this regard. Priests who had experienced childhood sexual abuse were seen as particularly at risk for subsequent sexual offending against minors in the John Jay study and my own research has pointed to the role of childhood experiences of sexual abuse in the sexual offending histories of five of the men who took part in my research.

The implication of the fact that five of the men in my study had experienced sexual abuse in childhood is that they entered priesthood and religious life with feelings of shame and fear of speaking about their experiences. As in many situations involving child sexual abuse, the men in my study were drawn into secrets by their abusers, leading them to assume responsibility for the sexual 'relationship'. They believed themselves to be complicit in what was happening and therefore equally culpable. The main reason given by the men for the non-disclosure of their childhood sexual abuse was their conflicted understanding of what was happening to them. The men stated that they normalised the experience when they were children, especially if they knew the same thing was happening to other boys in school. They believed that the sexual abuse did not cause them harm, but that it reflected negatively on them and therefore it had to be kept as a 'shameful secret'. However, four of the five men who experienced sexual abuse in childhood subsequently abused boys using exactly the same techniques as those employed by their own abuser. The shame with which the men lived was likely to present problems for them in their priestly and religious lives, if not attended to, given that their priestly or religious ministries would give them access to the most intimate and vulnerable spheres of other people's lives. Two men, whose motivation for priesthood was in part an attempt to avoid sexuality altogether, following a history of childhood sexual abuse, also needed to explore these issues during the course of their formation, as their experience of life would show, avoiding sexuality altogether was an unrealistic aspiration. Unfortunately for the participants in my research their experiences of childhood sexual abuse were not discussed during their time in formation for priestly or religious life – neither they nor anybody else mentioned it.

Another issue that is often raised in relation to clerical men who have sexually abused minors relates to the question of homosexuality. Is the sexual abuse of minors by Catholic clergy the result of the ordination of men of a homosexual orientation? On closer examination this question assumes that homosexuality *per se* is responsible for the sexual abuse of minors by Roman Catholic clergy. However, this is not seen to be the case by much research on the subject. McGlone (2002) suggests that 46%-66% of Roman Catholic clergy who sexually abuse children and young people are of a homosexual or bisexual orientation. However, there is no evidence that sexual identity and sexually abusive behaviour have the same origins and whilst the majority of priests and religious have abused adolescent males, the picture does not represent a simple linear trajectory from child sexual abuse of males to homosexuality, or the other way round. In the general child sexual offender field, adult heterosexuality is still reported as the predominant sexual orientation of men who sexually abuse pre-pubertal children, both males and females, whilst adult males who abuse adolescent males are much more likely to be men of a homosexual orientation (Marshall, 1988: 383-391; Langevin, 2000: 537). However, it is not simply the case of heterosexual men abusing pre-pubertal girls and homosexual men abusing boys as heterosexual men also sexually abuse pre-pubertal boys and indeed these data may not be relevant anyway for clergy men who represent a distinct group (Marshall, 2004; Kafka, 2004; Terry, 2008).

Seven of the nine men who participated in my own research were men of a homosexual orientation. Their narratives suggest that for all of them their difficulties in coping with celibacy and sexuality were compounded by a denial and fear of their homosexuality. Without institutional support the project of construct- ing the 'clergy' man as a 'gay' man was a concealed affair and an individual and isolated journey. The religious and cultural mores of their day made acknowledging homosexuality some- thing the men could not contemplate. Whilst this situation created significant intra-personal conflicts for them, there is no sugges- tion by the men that their homosexuality caused them to sexually abuse minors, even in situations where they abused adolescent males. The analysis of their narratives suggests that aspects of their concealed sexuality and struggles with celibacy and emotional loneliness, and not sexual orientation *per se*, must be considered significant for their sexual offending. My research suggests that the challenges of celibacy were no greater or less for men of a homosexual orientation than they were for heterosexual men and concealment of sexual desire was evident for all men, re- gardless of sexual orientation. The fear of unmasking was, how- ever, a constant fear for men of a homosexual orientation, and their identity and self-confidence was severely constrained by such fear.

The existing literature on sexual abuse by Catholic clergy does not give enough prominence to the distinctly important issue of what might be referred to as homophobic tendencies within the Catholic Church and how this disables the develop- ment of human sexuality and the natural expression of sexual desire and relationship.[13] This is of particular relevance since what could be regarded as 'homophobia', certainly seeing homo- sexuality as dysfunction, is institutionalised by the Catholic Church and to some extent supported by social structures. Homophobia is a particular feature of male gender socialisation and sexual identity and is a central aspect of a complex range of internalised and externalised male behaviours. This is ever more so for a group of men who are socialised together into a life of celibate living in an all-male institutional environment.

The relevance of homophobia in the response of the Catholic

Church to clergy sexual abuse cannot be over-emphasised and in my forthcoming book on the subject (Keenan, (in press)) I give this issue due attention. In particular I am concerned about the hegemony of hetero-normative culture and the spiritual and emotional 'violence' experienced by clergy men in their development, largely perpetrated by a homophobic culture that is rigidly articulated – even today – through aspects of the Catholic Church hierarchy. The recent proclamations by the Catholic Church, which essentially links child sexual abuse by clergy to the issue of homosexuality, are fundamentally flawed and have no basis in empirical or respectable research, scientific knowledge, common social mores or a theology of justice. Indeed, this misinformation and the frequency of homophobic condemnation by church hierarchy contribute significantly to an obfuscation of the facts about child sexual abuse and human sexuality and *de facto to* opportunities for the recurrence of abusive behaviours.

Something that is not much reported in the literature on clerical men who have sexually abused minors, but that I found in my own research, relates to the role of fear. It is apparent from an analysis of the men's narratives that the participants in my study constructed their priestly or religious vocation on fear – fear of breaking their celibate commitment and fear of displeasing others (particularly those in authority). For these men the resultant way of 'doing' priesthood involved strategies such as adopting a submissive way of relating to others, avoiding relationships with women and avoiding particular friendships with men. In essence, these men avoided intimacy. Such strategies produced poor adult attachments, a fear of emotional and physical intimacy and prolonged emotional loneliness. Although three of the men in my study said that they learned their initial fear of displeasing others and of emotional disclosure in their families of origin and two of the men believe that they developed these patterns in response to childhood experiences of sexual abuse, all of the men believed that these problems were compounded by their experiences of seminary life and during their time in formation.

Based on an analysis of the literature on 'normal' and offending clergy and my own research on this subject, my conclusion is that individual pathology is insufficient to explain sexual offending by Roman Catholic clergy and alternative interpretations must be explored. When comparing clergy offenders with non-clergy offenders, a similar conclusion is reached. The broad consensus in the psychological literature is that Roman Catholic clergy sexual offenders represent an atypical group of child sexual offenders (Kafka, 2004: 49; Marshall, 2003) and that situational and contextual factors must be considered significant in their sexual offending (Marshall, 2003; Brenneis, 2001: 25; Tallon and Terry, 2008: 627). Following her exhaustive analysis of all of the available data in relation to sexual abuse of minors by Catholic clergy in the United States, Terry (2008: 567) concluded: 'There is little information that relates to identifiable pathologies of the offender (e.g. clear indications of paedophilia), and there is much information that indicates an opportunistic selection effect. Although the majority of victims were male, it is the group of children [and young people] to whom the priests had the most (and unrestricted) access.' As the kind of access that clergy are given is a product of their institutional identity, and the kind of safety that their roles suggest comes to them from the authority of the institution, it is important for the institution to examine itself to see what in its structure and history have contributed to this problem (Gordon, 2004: 110). At the same time, although access and opportunity are very important, my own research suggests that to see sexual abuse of minors as a problem of access and opportunity alone is to simplify what is a much more complex issue. Many clergy men who have unrestricted access to minors never sexually abuse anyone.

The Individual and the Institution

In order to understand clerical men who have sexually abused minors, one can come to no other conclusion but that their sexual offending must be understood within the unique context of their lives and ministries as Roman Catholic ministers within the

Roman Catholic Church. In the literature on this subject a number of institutional aspects of the Roman Catholic Church are seen as creating a climate in which child sexual abuse by Catholic clergy becomes possible, but an analysis of exactly how these factors contribute to the problem and in what way is beyond the scope of this article, but is fully articulated in Keenan (in press). The features of the institutional church that are said to contribute to a climate in which sexual abuse by Catholic clergy becomes possible includes the theology of sexuality, power and the ecclesiastical structure of power relations and hierarchical authority, clerical culture and seminary formation. These aspects of the institution are influenced in turn by its traditions and teachings, which are seen by some scholars to have rendered sexual abuse by clergy and the subsequent responses of the Catholic hierarchy almost inevitable (Frawley-O'Dea, 2004; Kung, 2003; Berry, 1992; Sipe, 1995; Cozzens, 2004; Papesh, 2004; Ranson, 2002a, 2002b; Dokecki, 2004; Oakley and Russett, 2004; Doyle, 2003, 2004; Gordon, 2004; Celenza, 2004). What is important here is the interrelationship between the forces of sexuality, power and power relations, governance structures and clerical culture and their enabling and constraining powers and potentialities on the lives of those men who became the clergy perpetrators, those men who became the church hierarchy and those men who are regarded as 'normal' clergy.[14] Whilst many within the leadership of the Catholic Church prefer to operate outside of conscious awareness of this fact and prefer to think in terms of individual pathology rather than systemic breakdown, the evidence seems to point otherwise (White and Terry, 2008; Keenan (in press)).

In addition, a church and social culture that prefers to focus blame on individuals – those men who have abused minors and those religious leaders who are seen to have failed in their duties in the handling abuse complaints - may do well to think again – and keep the institutional dimensions of the aetiology of the problem in focus, as well as the manner in which the problem is currently constructed in popular discourse. This is not to say that individuals are not responsible for their actions, but it is to point to the fact that in trying to understand the problem (and presumably seek solutions), an approach that merely focuses on the individuals who have been 'named and shamed' is to fail in a way that is regrettable. An approach to the problem that merely focuses on the named and the shamed will keep the institutional aspects of the problem in play, aspects that will contribute to additional human problems, if not to further abuse of minors. As the identity of the clerical male takes its shape from the institution of the Roman Catholic Church, breaching the boundaries of his identity (as in the case of the clergy perpetrators) or working for what he believed to be the best interest of the church (as in the case of church leaders who are said to have failed in the handling of abuse complaints) is, therefore, an institutional issue.

As the question of celibacy is often mentioned in relation to sexual abuse by Catholic clergy I will make reference to what the men in my research had to say in relation to celibacy and their subsequent sexual offending. All of the study participants believed they freely accepted their vow of celibacy, and they said had celibacy been a voluntary option at the time they might still have opted for a celibate commitment. During their seminary years the men 'conditioned themselves to abstinence', for the love of God and for the good of others, and as part of what was required of them to do God's work on earth. All of the narratives suggest that the men took on the celibate commitment willingly, and hoped that after ordination or profession they could take it for granted and get on with their lives. They found a similar expectation on the part of their superiors. The absence of open and honest dialogue in the seminaries combined with the silence from church leaders, mentors and other priests, on the struggle of celibate sexuality contributed to this perception. The men reflected on how little they understood about themselves and their emotional lives when taking on that commitment at that time.

The men who participated in my research had an intellectual understanding of the meaning and purpose of priestly celibacy and chastity at the time that they were ordained or professed. They accepted celibacy freely as a 'gift' or a 'sacrifice', and none of them believed the vow of celibacy was responsible for their sexual abusing. Celibacy as a 'loss' was not considered. In order to live as 'good clergymen' they tried to become sexless beings and avoid intimate or close relationships with adults. They believed this was the best way to do 'celibacy'. The men did not engage with the emotional aspect of such a loss until they were experiencing significant emotional and social conflicts.

The participants in my research believed that they were not adequately prepared emotionally and sexually for a celibate commitment, and they were unrealistic in thinking they could walk this path alone. Their experience in the seminary neither supported nor challenged them sufficiently to be honest with their emotional and sexual selves. Five of the nine men reflected that they had no way of knowing how difficult life-long abstinence from sexual relations would be when they accepted the vow. Eight of the nine men had no sexual experience in relationships whatsoever before entering the seminary or religious life. It is evident from the men's narratives that all of them had difficulty coping with celibacy and that it created significant intrapersonal conflicts for them. However, as much sexual abuse of minors (and sexual boundary violations) is perpetrated by adults who have adult sexual outlets available to them, one could reasonably suggest that there is no link to be made between the commitment to celibate living (and the lack of sexual outlet) and sexual abuse of minors. The narratives in my study suggest that whilst the discipline of celibacy itself may not be the main problem; the lack of preparation for living a celibate life and the lack of support in living the celibate commitment must be considered significant in the men's subsequent sexual offending mainly as the men tried to live without emotional intimacy as a way of protecting their celibate commitment. In such situations the problems of emotional loneliness and isolation were heightened and with this the risk of sexual boundary violations. Their understanding of the theology of sexuality that was devoid of the latest research on the biological and psychological aspects of human sexual development must also be considered significant in the subsequent sexual violations. This view supports other research in this area (Bennett *et al*, 2004).

The men who participated in my research, who entered the seminaries sexually immature or with significant sexual and emotional conflict (especially following sexually abusive experiences in childhood or struggles with sexual orientation), left the seminary further entrenched in their conflicts and with a deeper sense of emotional alienation and fear. None of the men had access to an honest and open fraternal life amongst classmates or superiors or church leaders as part of their seminary training, and none of the men had ease of access to elder mentors (not spiritual directors) who would provide a discursive space to support them as they learned to live and love within the context of their priestly and religious lives. It was not their spiritual relationship with God that the men believed to be in trouble, but their human relationship with 'man'. By avoiding discussions on the human aspects of the celibate life, an environment was created in the seminaries and subsequently in religious communities and dioceses where difficulties with sexuality and with celibacy were more likely to be seen as isolated problems, rather than as ones shared by many. Within this context of isolationism, in which there was lack of dialogue and relationship, it was then easy for the Catholic Church to perceive sexual abuse by clergy as individual cases of pathology or deviance with little organisational relevance. Ranson (2002a) suggests that the individualised unacknowledged struggle with celibacy is likely to find an unhealthy expression. The narratives of the men in my study indicate that this is exactly what happened for them.

Recidivism, Repeat Offending and Effectiveness of Treatment
Although media accounts of clergy abuse continue to flourish, many of the most publicised accounts portray clergy offenders as a homogeneous highly predatory group. My research and that presented by the John Jay Study (John Jay College, 2004,

2006) suggests that such constructions of the clerical child sexual offender do not bear a strong relationship with the reality. Current constructions of the clergy child sexual offender are influenced by power relations, vested interests and professional judgements. Rather than representing the 'objective' reality that they purport to be, professional discourses help construct the child sexual offender as fundamentally different from the rest of society and in doing so they unwittingly contribute to the situation where child sexual offenders are marginalised and demonised. Despite the heterogeneity of clergy men who have sexually abused minors, they are often portrayed singularly as 'monsters', 'beasts' 'predators' in the media, creating a moral panic that inflates the risk of sex offending by misrepresenting the recidivism rates and construing all sex offences as paedophilic in nature (Douard, 2007; Jenkins, 1998). Although there are certainly dangerous clergy offenders who recidivate at high rates, this is only a small minority, and further research is necessary to understand how those clergy who desist and stop their offending come to make such decisions and what factors distinguish those men who stop their offending from those clergy who continue to recidivate following treatment interventions. The data on recidivism following current sexual offender treatment is very heartening.

By far the strongest predictor of repeat sexual offending in a number of studies (Hanson and Bussière, 1998; Hanson and Morton-Bourgon, 2004, 2005, Hanson et al, 1993) is deviant results on phallometric testing and general criminal history, suggesting that men with deviant sexual arousal patterns, particularly sexual interest in children and with a general criminal history, are at a substantially increased risk for repeat offending. Since few priests with allegations of sexual abuse exhibited behaviour consistent with paraphilic activity and few if any clergy had non-sexual criminal convictions or even charges (Tallon and Terry 2008: 617) the suggestion is that the risk of reoffending for clerical sexual offenders is low. This finding fits with anecdotal research findings reported by treatment programmes for Catholic clergy (Rosetti, 2002; Hanson et al, 2004).

By far the most comprehensive review of psychological treatment for sexual offenders is that conducted by the Collaborative Outcome Data Project Committee in the United States (Hanson *et al*, 2002). This committee was formed in 1997 by a group of leading researchers with the goal of organising the existing outcome literature for sexual offenders and encouraging new evaluation projects to be conducted in a manner that will make for more comparable research and lead to cumulative knowledge. The project is ongoing but the first report concluded that current psychological treatments are associated with reductions in both sexual and general recidivism (Hanson *et al*, 2002: 169). In what is regarded as a highly robust study, the Committee reported that after an average of four to five years of follow up, 9.9% of the treated men had sexually reoffended compared to 17.4% of the untreated groups (p 187). The study reported conclusively that current treatment is effective in reducing sexual offending and in fact since 2002 even greater treatment effects have been reported by some treatment providers (Serran *et al*, 2006). The public misconception that treatment does not work for sexual offenders, which was propagated by earlier works that relied on outdated and unsatisfactory treatment approaches (Furby *et al*, 1989), needs revision in the light of current encouraging research outcomes. This trend is expected to continue as there have been considerable changes in treatment programmes since the 1970s and the studies of the newer forms of treatment are only recently becoming available (Hanson *et al*, 2002: 188). In addition, clerical men who have successfully completed treatment are reported to have an even lower recidivism rate than general child sexual offenders, with some treatment centres reporting recidivism rates for Catholic clergy of less than 3% (Rosetti, 2002; Hanson *et al*, 2004).

Church leaders have in many ways fallen into a trap of succumbing to the portrayal of clergy offenders as a homogenised and a highly recidivistic group and current regulation and management of clerical men who have sexually abused minors suggest that this is the case. There is also evidence to suggest that the church leadership is fearful of an angry public and an ever vigilant press and that fear is driving some of the decisions made. The church's zero tolerance policy that mandates the permanent removal of clergy with even a single substantiated allegation of historical sexual abuse against a minor, supports this analysis. The one-size-fits-all approach to managing clergy offenders adds further weight to the claim.

Control of Abuse – Abuse of Control

In many senses control of sexual abuse by Catholic clergy is fast becoming the abuse of control by some parts of the leadership of the Catholic Church. Mistakes are being made in the name of child protection, just as mistakes were made in the past in the name of church protection. At the very least current, policies for the handling of abuse complaints have contributed to endless pain and trauma for several priests against whom false allegations have been made, policies and processes that have without doubt violated their civil and human rights. Relationships between bishops and clergy are also being damaged by such policies and practices in ways that only the future will fully unfold. In addition, the one-size-fits-all approach to the management of clergy who have abused, and the policies that govern many of their highly regulated lives, suggest that some of the principles of reparation and forgiveness, on which the Catholic Church is built, are seldom to be found.

Balance needs to be brought into policies regarding the risk posed by accused priests, with more refined analysis undertaken in partnership with professional and lay advice. Although protecting future children from future sexual crime is laudable and important, taking care of all church members, including the erring clergy (and those church leaders who are identified as having failed in handling abuse complaints) is also important. The handing over of thousands of documents without regard to the rights of countless individuals, as happened in the case of the inquiry into the handling of abuse complaints in Diocese of Ferns and the Archdiocese of Dublin, although welcomed by many, in my opinion gives further testimony to a Catholic Church leadership so besieged by the popular discourse that good decisions are still not being made. The Ferns Inquiry team reported that they were given far more documents than they requireded and far more than any court could have compelled (*Ferns Report*, 2005).

Documents pertinent to the relevant inquiries should and could have been handed over to the various Commissions of Inquiries and Commissions of Investigation in a manner that would protect the rights of 'innocent' individuals, who did not ever want the details of their experiences put before any court, albeit a *quasi* one. Their experience now is one of betrayal. Many clergy and indeed church leaders might also have a right to feel betrayed at the manner in which the processes were handled – again processes that could be seen as oppressive and unjust in the name of 'justice'. Just as many child abuse inquiries in the United Kingdom found that blame and criticism always surrounded the public inquiries (Reader *et al*, 1993: 1) it appears that the very same processes are taking hold in relation to the inquiries into child sexual abuse by Catholic clergy in Ireland. The reports seem more intent on passing judgement and focusing on degrees of blameworthiness, rather than learning constructively from what went wrong in the past, including what were the emotional and context factors within the professional and religious networks which allowed the relevant church leaders and clerical perpetrators to be dislodged from making good judgements. The judgemental tone of many of these final reports suggests that, rather than providing constructive lessons from the past that can help with preventing similar tragedies from happening again in the future, many of these reports seem intent on public humiliation of individuals. Time will undoubtedly bring scholarly and critical analysis of the work and reports of the various Commissions of Inquiry and Commission of Investigation into sexual abuse by Catholic clergy and the handling of abuse complaints by the Catholic hierarchy.

Conclusion

Sipe (1995: 134) refers to the sexual abuse of minors by Roman Catholic clergy as 'the tip of the iceberg' when it comes to problems with sexuality for the Roman Catholic Church. Because illicit sexual activity may well be more likely when there is little openness about or value placed on sexual honesty and sexual maturity, the sexual abuse of minors by Catholic clergy may well serve to bring the general state of sexual health and maturity of Roman Catholic clergy into view. It could be argued that the sexual abuse problem by clergy has accelerated a simmering problem and represents a systemic push to bring the sexuality of clergy onto the church's agenda. My research on child sexual abuse by Catholic clergy suggests that child sexual abuse by Catholic clergy must be considered against the background of the literature on 'normal' clergy and clerical sexuality and not as an unrelated sphere of clerical activity. The need for compassionate leadership has never been more urgent.

My conclusion is that child sexual abuse by Catholic clergy represents a complex interplay of individual and systemic factors and no one cause can be seen to determine the problem's nature. Whilst some works on the subject tends to be about deviant or 'perverted' Catholic clergy, my research[15] shows how ordinary men walked their way into abusing children and minors and it points to the small, maybe understandable compromises that ordinary men made on the road to abusing (Keenan, (in press)). For many of us this can be more confronting than other accounts of sexual abuse by Catholic clergy, mainly because it can no longer be just about 'paedophile priests', but maybe about you and me. Much public commentary on the subject tends to be about 'perverted' clergy, psychological dysfunction or criminal danger. The search is for an overall character trait or personality type that explains it all. My conclusion is that this is a meaningless search. New thinking is urgently required. By truly examining child sexual abuse by Catholic clergy and its developmental and systemic pathways, we may be able to go some way towards preventing future offending. However, this is not enough. If we truly want to help children and create a safer society for all, then we need to get beyond a blaming stance and towards more preventative and rehabilitative/restorative perspectives. In this way we might also work towards healing the myriad of lives burdened by the legacy of child sexual abuse within the Catholic Church – victims, perpetrators and both sets of families, clerical men who have been falsely accused and their families, priests and religious and the Catholic laity and the many bishops and church leaders, some of whom live lives as frightened and broken men and women.

Bibliography

Abel, G.C., Becker, J.V., Mittelman, M., Cunningham-Rathner, J., Rouleau, J.L. and Murphy, W.D. (1987), 'Self-reported sex crimes of non-incarcerated paraphiliacs'. *Journal of Interpersonal Violence*, 2 (1), 3-25.

American Psychiatric Association (APA) (1994), *Diagnostic and Statistical Manual of Mental Disorders: IV*, Washington, DC: American Psychiatric Association.

Ariés, P. (1962), *Centuries of Childhood*, Harmondsworth: Penguin.

Arthurs, H., Ferguson, H., and Grace, E. (1995), 'Celibacy, secrecy and the lives of men', *Doctrine and Life*, 45 (7), 471-480.

Ashenden, S. (2002) 'Policing Perversion: The Contemporary Governance of Paedophilia', *Cultural Values*, 6: 197.

Balboni, S. (1998). 'Through the 'Lens' of the Organizational Culture Perspective: A Descriptive Study of American Catholic Bishops' Understanding of Clergy Sexual Molestation and Abuse of Children and Adolescents', Unpublished PhD, Northeastern University, Boston, Massachusetts. Available at HYPERLINK "http://www. bishops accountability.org/" www.BishopsAccountability.org accessed 10/1/07

Bell, V. (2002). 'The vigilant(e) parent and the paedophile: The *News of the World* campaign 2000 and the contemporary governmentality of child sexual abuse', *Feminist Theory*, 3 (1), 83-102.

Bennett R. and the staff of the National Review Board for the Protection of Children and Young People (2004), *A Report on the Crisis in the Catholic Church in the United States*, Washington DC: The United States Conference of Catholic Bishops.

Benyei, C.R. (1998), *Understanding Clergy Misconduct in Religious Systems. Scapegoating, Family Secrets and the Abuse of Power*, New York: The Hayworth Pastoral Press.

Berger, P. and Luckmann, T. (1966), *The Social Construction of Reality. A Treatise in the Sociology of Knowledge*, Harmondsworth: Penguin Books.

Berry, J. (1992), *Lead Us Not into Temptation, Catholic Priests and The Sexual Abuse of Children*, New York: Doubleday.

Best, J. (1995a), 'Typification and social problem construction', In J. Best (ed), *Images of Issues, Typifying Contemporary Social Problems* (pp 1-16) New York: Walter de Gruyter.

Best, J. (ed) (1995b), *Images of Issues, Typifying Contemporary Social Problems*. New York: Walter de Gruyter.

Blanchard, G.T. (1991), 'Sexually abusive clergymen: A conceptual framework for intervention and recovery', *Pastoral Psychology*, 39, 237-245.

Bleibtreu-Ehrenberg, G. (1990), 'Pederasty among primitives: Institutional initiation and cultic prostitution', *Journal of Homosexuality*, 20 (1-2), 13-30.

Bolen, R., and Scannapieco, M. (1999), 'Prevalence of child sexual abuse: A corrective meta-analysis', *Social Services Review*, 73, 281-313.

Boston Globe Investigative Staff (2002), *Betrayal: The Crisis in the Catholic Church*, Boston: Little Brown.

Boswell, J. (1990), *The Kindness of Strangers: The Abandonment of Children in Western Europe from Late Antiquity to the Renaissance*, New York: Vintage.

Breen, M. (2004a), 'Rethinking Power: An Analysis of Media Coverage of Sexual Abuse in Ireland, the UK and the USA.' Paper presented at the Kogakuin University/University of Limerick International Conference of Science and Humanities. Marsh. Unpublished paper.

Breen, M. (2004b), 'Depraved Paedos and Other Beasts: The Media Portrayal of child sexual abusers in Ireland and the UK', in Paul Yoder and Peter Mario Kreuter eds, *Monsters and the Monstrous: Myths and Metaphors of Enduring Evil.*

Brenneis, M. (2001), 'Personality characteristics of clergy and of psychologically impaired clergy: A review of the literature', *American Journal of Pastoral Counselling*, 4 (77), 7-13.

Bryant, C. (1999), 'Psychological treatment of priest sex offenders', in T. G. Plante (ed), *Bless Me Father For I Have Sinned: Perspectives on Sexual Abuse Committed by Roman Catholic Priests* (pp 87-110), Westport, CT: Praeger Publishers.

Buckley, H., Skehill, C. and O'Sullivan, E. (1997), *Child Protection Practices in Ireland. A Case Study*, Dublin: Oak Tree Press.

Camargo, R. J. and Loftus J. A. (1992), 'Child sexual abuse among troubled clergy: A descriptive study.' Paper presented at the 100th Annual Convention of the American Psychological Association, Washington DC (unpublished paper).

Camargo, R .J. and Loftus J. A. (1993), 'Clergy sexual involvement with young people.' Paper presented at the 101st Annual Convention of the American Psychological Association, Toronto, Canada (unpublished paper).

Catechism of the Catholic Church (1994), Dublin: Veritas Publications.

Celenza, A. (2004), 'Sexual misconduct in the Clergy. The Search for the Father', *Studies in Gender and Sexuality*, 5 (2), 213-232.

Code of Canon Law (1983) (English translation), Great Britain: Collins.

Commission on Child Abuse Report (2009), Dublin: Government Publications (Also referred to as the *Ryan Report*).

Corby, B. (2000), *Child Abuse: Towards a Knowledge Base*, Milton Keynes: Open University Press.

Cowburn, M. and Dominelli, L. (2001), 'Masking hegemonic masculinity: reconstructing the paedophile as the dangerous stranger', *British Journal of Social Work*, 31, 399-415.

Cozzens, D. (2000), *The Changing Face of Priesthood*, Collegeville, Minnesota: Liturgical Press.

Cozzens, D. (2004), *Sacred Silence. Denial and the Crisis in the Church*, Collegeville, Minnesota: Liturgical Press.

De Young, M. (1982), 'Innocent seducer or innocently seduced? The role of the child incest victim', *Journal of Clinical Psychology*, 11, 56-60.

Dokecki, P. (2004), *The Clergy Sexual Abuse Crisis*, Washington, DC: Georgetown University Press.

Doyle, T. P. (2003), 'Roman Catholic clericalism, religious duress and clergy abuse', *Pastoral Psychology*, 51, 189-231.

Doyle, T. P. (2004), 'Canon Law and the clergy sex abuse crisis: The failure from above', in T. G. Plante (ed) *Sin against the Innocents. Sexual Abuse by Priests and the Role of the Catholic Church* (pp 25-38), Westport, Connecticut, London: Praeger.

Doyle, T. P., Sipe, A.W.R. and Wall, P. J. (2006), *Sex, Priests and Secret Codes. The Catholic Church's 2000-year Paper Trail of Sexual Abuse*, Los Angeles: Volt Press.

Dublin Archdiocese Commission of Investigation (2006), March

Dunne, J. and Kelly, J. (2002), *Childhood and Its Discontents: The First Seamus Heaney Lectures*, Dublin: Liffey Press.

Flakenhain M. A. (1999), 'Cluster analysis of child sexual offenders: A validation with Roman Catholic priests and brothers", *Sexual Addiction and Compulsivity*, 6, 317-336.

Featherstone, B. and Lancaster, E. (1997), 'Contemplating the unthinkable: Men who sexually abuse children', *Critical Social Policy*, 17 (4), 51- 71.

Ferguson, H. (1995), 'The paedophile priest. A deconstruction', *Studies*, 84 (335), pp 247-256.

The Ferns Report (2005). Delivered to the Minister for Health and Children, Ireland.

Finkelhor, D. (1984), *Child Sexual Abuse: New Theory and Research*, New York: Free Press.

Finkelhor, D. (1994), 'The international epidemiology of child sexual abuse', *Child Abuse and Neglect*, 18, 409-417.

Fones, C. S. L., Levine, S. B., Althof, S. E. and Risen, C. B. (1999), 'The sexual struggles of 23 clergymen: A follow-up study', *Journal of Sex and Marital Therapy*, 25, 183-195.

Fortune, M. (1994), 'Is nothing sacred? The betrayal of the ministerial or teaching relationship', *Journal of Feminist Studies in Religion*, 10 (1), 17-24.

Foucault, M. (1988), 'The Dangerous Individual', in L Kritzman (ed), *Politics, Philosophy, Culture: Interviews and Other Writings 1977-1984*, (pp 125-51), New York: Routledge.

Foucault, M. (1990), *The Care of Self. The History of Sexuality: 3*, trs Robert Hurley, London: Penguin.

Foucault, M. (1992), *The Use of Pleasure. The History of Sexuality: 2*, trs Robert Hurley, London: Penguin.

Foucault, M. (1998), *The Will to Knowledge. The History of Sexuality: 1*, trs Robert Hurley, London: Penguin.

Foucault, M. (2004), *The Archaeology of Knowledge*, trs A. M. Sheridan Smith, (First published in 1969; first published in English 1972), (Sixth edition), London: Routledge Classics.

Francis, P. C. and Turner, N. R. (1995), 'Sexual misconduct within the Christian Church: Who are the perpetrators and those they victimize?' *Counselling and Values*, 39, 218-228.

Frawley-O'Dea, M. (2004), 'Psychosocial Anatomy of the Catholic Sexual Abuse Scandal', *Studies in Gender and Sexuality*, 5 (2), 121-137.

Freeman-Longo R. E. and Blanchard, G. T. (1998), *Sexual Abuse in America: Epidemic of the 21st century*, Vermont: The Safer Society Press.

Goldner, V. (2004), 'Introduction – The Sexual-Abuse Crisis and the Catholic Church. Gender, Sexuality, Power and Discourse', *Studies in Gender and Sexuality*, 5 (1), 1-9.

Goodstein, L. (2003), 'Decades of damage: Trail of pain in Church crisis leads to nearly every diocese', *New York Times* (January 12th).

Gordon, M. (2004), 'The Priestly Phallus. A Study in Iconography', *Studies in Gender and Sexuality*, 5 (1), 103-111.

Greeley, A. M. (1972a), *Priests in the United States: Reflections on a Survey*, Garden City, New York: Doubleday.

Greeley, A. M. (1972b), *The Catholic Priest in the United States: Sociological Investigations*, Washington DC: United States Catholic Conference.

Greeley, A. M. (1993), 'How serious is the problem of sexual abuse by clergy?' *America*, 168 (10), 6-10.

Greeley, A. M. (2000), 'How Prevalent is Clerical Sexual Abuse?' *Doctrine and Life*, 50 (2), 66-71.

Greer, C. (2003), *Sex Crime and the Media: Sex Offending and the Press in a Divided Society*, Devon: Willan.

Hacking, I. (1999), *The Social Construction of What?*, Cambridge, MA, and London: Harvard University Press.

Hanson, R. K. (1998), 'What do we know about sex offender risk assessment?', *Psychology, Public Policy and Law*, 4 (3), 50-72.

Hanson, R. K. (2003), Personal Communication during Annual Research and Treatment Conference of the Association for the Treatment of Sexual Abusers, St Louis, Missouri, October.

Hanson, R. K. and Bussière, M. T. (1998), 'Predicting relapse: A meta-analysis of sexual offender recidivism studies', *Journal of Counselling and Clinical Psychology*, 66 (2), 348-362.

Hanson, R. K., Morton, K. E. and Harris, A. J. R. (2003), 'Sexual Offender Recidivism Risk. What We Know and What We Need to Know', *Annals New York Academy of Sciences*, 989, 154-166.

Hanson, R. K. and Morton-Bourgon, K. E. (2004), *Predictors of Sexual Recidivism: An Updated Meta-Analysis* (Research Report, No 2004-02) Ottawa, Canada: Public Safety and Emergency Preparedness Canada.

Hanson, R. K. and Morton-Bourgon, K. E. (2005), 'The Characteristics of Persistent Sexual Offenders: A Meta-Analysis of Recidivism Studies', *Journal of Consulting and Clinical Psychology*, 73, 1154-1163.

Hanson, R. K., Pfafflin, F. and Lutz, M. (2004), (eds) *Sexual Abuse In the Catholic Church. Scientific and Legal Perspectives*, Vatican City: Libreria Editrice Vaticana.

Hanson, R. K., Gordon, A., Harris, A. J. R., Marques, J. K., Murphy, W., Quinsey, V. L. and Seto, M. C. (2002), 'First Report of the Collaborative Outcome Data Project on the Effectiveness of Psychological Treatment for Sex Offenders', *Sexual Abuse: A Journal of Research and Treatment*, 14, 2, 169-194.

Haug, F. (2001), 'Sexual deregulation or the child abuser as hero in neo-liberalism', *Feminist Theory*, 2 (1), pp 55-78.

Haywood, T. W., Kravitz, H. M., Grossman, L. S., Wasyliw, O. E., and Hardy, D. W. (1996), 'Psychological aspects of sexual functioning among cleric and noncleric alleged sex offenders', *Child Abuse and Neglect*, 20, 527-536.

Haywood, T. W., Kravitz, H. M., Wasyliw, O. E., Goldberg, J. and Cavanaugh, J. L. (1996), 'Cycles of abuse and psychopathology in cleric and noncleric molesters of children and adolescents', *Child Abuse and Neglect*, 20, 1233-1243.

Hoge, D. (2002), *The First Five Years: A Study of Newly Ordained Catholic Priests*, Collegeville, Minnesota: Liturgical Press.

Hudson, K. (2005), *Offending Identities. Sex offenders' perspectives on their treatment and management*, Devon: Willan Publishing.

Inglis, T. (198, 2nd ed), *Moral Monopoly. The Rise and Fall of the Catholic Church in Modern Ireland*, Dublin: University College Dublin Press.

Inglis, T. (2005), 'Origins and Legacies of Irish Prudery: Sexuality and Social Control in Modern Ireland', *Eire-Ireland: An Interdisciplinary Journal of Irish Studies*, 40, 3-4, (Fall-Winter), 9-37.

Jenkins, P. (1995), 'Clergy sexual abuse: The symbolic politics of a social problem', in J. Best (ed) *Images of Issues, Typifying Contemporary Social Problems*, (pp 105-130). New York: Aldine De Gruyter.

Jenkins, P. (1996), *Paedophiles and Priests. Anatomy of a Contemporary Crisis*, New York: Oxford University Press.

Jenkins, P. (1998), *Moral Panic. Changing Concepts of the Child Molester in Modern America*, New Haven and London: Yale University Press.

John Jay College (2004), *The Nature and Scope of Sexual Abuse of Minors by Catholic Priests and Deacons in the United States, 1950-2002*, Washington DC: United States Conference of Catholic Bishops.

John Jay College (2006), *Supplementary Report. The Nature and Scope of Sexual Abuse of Minors by Catholic Priests and Deacons in the United States, 1950-2002*, Washington DC: United States Conference of Catholic Bishops.

Johnson, J. M. (1995), 'Horror stories and the construction of child abuse', in J. Best (ed) *Images of Issues. Typifying Contemporary Social Problems*, New York: Aldine De Gruyter.

Kafka, M. (2004), 'Sexual molesters of adolescents, ephebophilia and Catholic clergy: A review and synthesis', in R. K. Hanson, F. Pfäfflin and M. Lütz (eds) *Sexual Abuse in the Catholic Church: Scientific and Legal Perspectives* (pp.51-59), Vatican City: Libreria Editrice Vaticana.

Keenan, M. (2006), 'The Institution and the Individual – Child Sexual Abuse by Clergy', *The Furrow*, 57 (1) 3-8.

Kennedy, E. (1971), *The Catholic Priest in the United States: Psychological Investigations*, Washington DC: United States Catholic Conference.

Kennedy, E. (2001), *The Unhealed Wound. The Church and Human Sexuality*, New York: St Martin's Press.

Kincaid, J. R. (1998), *Erotic innocence. The Culture of Child Molesting*, Durham and London: Duke University Press.

Kitzinger, J. (1999), 'The ultimate neighbour from hell: Media framing of paedophiles', in B. Franklin (ed), *Social Policy, the Media and Misrepresentation*, London: Routledge.

Kitzinger, J. (2000), 'Media Templates: Patterns of Association and the (Re) Construction of Meaning Over Time', *Media, Culture and Society*, 22 (1), 61.

Kung, H. (2003) (second edition), *The Catholic Church. A Short History*, trs John Bowden, New York: Modern Library.

Lane, D. (ed) (1997), *Reading the Signs of the Times. A Survey of Priests in Dublin*, Dublin: Veritas.

Langevin, R. (2004), 'Who engages in sexual behaviour with children? Are clergy who commit sexual offences different from other sex offenders?' in R. K. Hanson, F. Pfäfflin and M. Lütz (eds), *Sexual Abuse in the Catholic Church: Scientific and Legal Perspectives* (pp 24-43), Vatican City: Libreria Editrice Vaticana.

Langevin, R., Curnoe, S. and Bain, J. (2000), 'A study of clerics who commit sexual offences: Are they different from other sexual offenders?', *Child Abuse and Neglect*, 24, 535-545.

Loftus, J. A. (1999), 'Sexuality in priesthood: Noli me tangere', in T. G. Plante (ed), *Bless Me Father for I Have Sinned* (pp 7-19), Westport, Connecticut, London: Praeger.

Loftus, J. A. (2004), 'What have we learned? Implications for future research and formation', in T. G. Plante (ed), *Sin against the Innocents. Sexual Abuse by Priests and the Role of the Catholic Church* (pp 85-96), Westport, Connecticut, London: Praeger.

Loftus, J. A. and Camargo, R. J. (1993) 'Treating the clergy', *Annals of Sex Research*, 6, 287-303.

Lukes, S. (2005), *Power: A radical view*, London: Palgrave Macmillan.

McGee, H., Garavan, R., de Barra, M., Byrne, J. and Conroy, R. (2002), *The SAVI Report: Sexual Abuse and Violence in Ireland. A National Study of Irish Experiences, Beliefs and Attitudes Concerning Sexual Violence*, Dublin: The Liffey Press.

McGlone, G. J. (2001), 'Sexually offending and non-offending Roman Catholic priests: Characterization and analysis', unpublished PhD thesis. California School of Professional Psychology, San Diego.

McGlone, G. J., Viglione, D. J. and Geary, B. (2002), 'Data from one treatment centre in USA (N=150) who have sexually offended.' Presented at the Annual Research and Treatment Conference of the Association for the Treatment of Sexual Abusers. Montreal, Ontario: Canada. October. Unpublished paper.

McGuinness, C. (1993), *Report of the Kilkenny Incest Investigation*, Dublin: Stationery Office.

Marshall, W. L. (1996), 'The sexual offender: monster, victim or everyman?', *Sexual Abuse: A Journal of Research and Treatment*, 8 (4), 317-335.

Marshall, W. L. (2002), 'Historical Foundations and Current Conceptualisations of Empathy', in Y. Fernandez (ed), *In their Shoes: Examining the Issue of Empathy and Its Place in the Treatment of Offenders* (pp 36-52), Oklahoma: Wood 'N' Barnes Publishing.

Marshall, W. L. (2003) 'Consulting at the Vatican.' Keynote Address given at the Annual Research and Treatment Conference of the Association for the Treatment of Sexual Abusers, St Louis, Missouri, October. Unpublished paper.

Marshall, W. L. (2004), 'Cognitive Behavioural Treatment of Child Molesters', inn R. K., Hanson, F. Pfafflin, and M. Lutz (eds), (2004), *Sexual Abuse In the Catholic Church. Scientific and Legal Perspectives*, (pp 97-114), Vatican City: Libreria Editrice Vaticana.

Mercado, C., Tallon, J. and Terry, K. (2008), 'Persistent Sexual Abusers in the Catholic Church. An Examination of Characteristics and Offence Patterns', *Criminal Justice and Behaviour*, 35, 5, 629-642.

Mercer, D., and Simmonds T. (2001), 'The mentally disordered offender. Looking-glass monsters: reflections of the paedophile in popular culture', in T. Mason, C. Carisle, C. Walkins and E. Whitehead (eds), *Stigma and Social Exclusion in Healthcare* (pp 170-181), London and New York: Routledge.

Moore, C. (1995), *Betrayal of Trust, the Father Brendan Smyth Affair and the Catholic Church*, Dublin: Marino Books.

Nelson-Rowe, S. (1995), 'The Moral Drama of Multicultural Education', in J. Best (ed) (1995), *Images of Issues, Typifying Contemporary Social Problems*, New York: Walter de Gruyter.

Nines, J. (2006), 'Sexuality Attitudes and the Priesthood.' Unpublished PhD thesis, School of Human Service Profession, Widener University.

Noyes, T. (1997), 'Broken Vows, Broken Trust: Understanding Clergy Sexual Misconduct.' Unpublished PhD thesis, The Union Institute.

Oakley, F. and Russett, B. (eds) (2004), *Governance, Accountability and the Future of the Catholic Church*, London and New York: Continuum.

O'Brien, C. (2009a), 'Twenty Dead and 6500 at Risk of Abuse: The State]s Children Today', *Irish Times*, .

O'Brien, C. (2009b), 'Lack of Inspections Leaves Thousands in Care Vulnerable to Abuse – Groups', *Irish Times*, 23 May, 7.

O'Brien, C. (2009c), 'HSE to Review Child Deaths in Care over Decade', *Irish Times*, 6 July, 5.

O'Brien, C. (2009d), 'Childre still at risk, says Ombudsman', *Irish Times*, 1 July, 6.

O'Brien, C. (2009e), 'State's Aftercare 'Responsibility' for Young', *Irish Times*, 4 June, 8.

O'Mahony, P. (1996), *Criminal Chaos. Seven Crises in Irish Criminal Justice*, Dublin: Round Hall, Sweet and Maxwell.

O'Malley, T. (1998), Opening Remarks, Conference on Treatment of Sex Offenders, Irish Penal Reform Trust, Dublin: 14 November. Unpublished paper.

Papesh, M. (2004), *Clerical Culture, Contradiction and Transformation*, Collegeville, Minnesota: Liturgical Press.

Perillo, A., Mercado, C. and Terry, K. (2008), 'Repeat Offending, Victim Gender and Extent of Victim Relationship in Catholic Church Sexual Abusers. Implications for Risk Assessment', *Criminal Justice and Behaviour*, 35, 5, 600-614.

Plante, T. G. (1996). 'Catholic priests who sexually abuse minors: Why do we hear so much yet know so little?', *Pastoral Psychology*, 44 (5), 305-310.

Plante, T. G. (ed) (1999), *Bless Me Father for I Have Sinned*, Westport, Connecticut, London: Praeger.

Plante. T. G. (e.) (2004), *Sin Against The Innocents. Sexual Abuse by Priests and the Role of the Catholic Church*, Westport, Connecticut, London: Praeger.

Plante, T. G. and Boccaccini, M. T. (1997), 'Personality expectations and perceptions of Roman Catholic clergy members', *Pastoral Psychology*, 45 (4), 301-315.

Plante, T. G., Manuel, G. and Bryant, C. (1994), 'Catholic priests who sexually abuse minors: Intervention, assessment and treatment.' Paper presented at the 13th annual conference of the Association for the Treatment of Sexual Abusers, San Francisco, CA.

Plante, T. G., Manuel, G. and Bryant, C. (1996), 'Personality and cognitive functioning among hospitalised sexual offending Roman Catholic priests', *Pastoral Psychology*, 45 (2), 129-139.

Plante, T. G., Manuel, G. and Tandez, J. (1996), 'Personality characteristics of successful applicants to the priesthood', *Pastoral Psychology*, 45 (1), 29-40.

Piquero, A., Piquero, N., Terry, K. Youstin, T., and Nobles, M. (2008), 'Uncollaring the Criminal. Understanding the Criminal Careers of Criminal Clerics', *Criminal Justice and Behaviour*, 35, 5, 583-599.

Pollock, L. (1983), *Forgotten Children: Parent-Child Relations from 1500 to 1900*, Cambridge: CUP.

Quinn, D. (2005), '241 clerics accused of sex abuse over four decades', *Irish Independent*, pp 26-27, 28 October.

Ranson, D. (2002a), 'The climate of sexual abuse', *The Furrow*, 53 (7/8), 387-397.

Ranson, D. (2002b), 'Priest: Public, personal and private', *The Furrow*, 53 (4), 219-227.

Reder, P., Duncan, S. and Gray, M. (1993), *Beyond Blame. Child Abuse Tragedies Revisited*, London: Routledge.

Robinson, G. (2007), *Confronting Power and Sex in the Church. Reclaiming the Spirit of Jesus*, Dublin: The Columba Press.

Robinson, E. A., (1994). 'Shadows of the Lantern Bearers: A Study of Sexually Troubled Clergy.' Unpublished Doctoral Thesis, Loyola College, Maryland, USA.

Rossetti, S. J. (ed) (1990), *Slayer of the Soul: Child Sexual Abuse and the Catholic Church*, Mystic, CT: Twenty-Third Publications.

Rossetti, S. J. (1997), Personal communication.

Rossetti, S. J. (2002), Few Priests Molesters, CNN.com, 11 April. Accessed 16.05.2009.

Rossetti, S. J. (2004), Remarks made during Conference Sexual Abuse In the Catholic Church, Scientific and Legal Perspectives, Vatican City.

Russell, D. E. H. (1983), 'The incidence and prevalence of intra-familial sexual abuse of female children', *Child Abuse and Neglect*, 7, 133-146.

Seran, G. (2006) Preliminary Recidivism Data from Rockwood Psychological Services, Kingston, Ontario, Canada, presented during Conference, Dublin, to mark 10th anniversary of Granada Institute.

Sipe, A. W. R. (1995), *Sex, Priests, and Power: Anatomy of a Crisis*, London: Cassell.

Smith, M., Rengifo, A. and Vollman, B. (2008), 'Trajectories of Abuse and Disclosure. Child Sexual Abuse by Catholic Priests', *Criminal Justice and Behaviour*, 35, 5, 570-582.

Stone, L. (1977), *The Family, Sex and Marriage in England 1500-1800*, London: Weidenfeld and Nicolson.

Tallon, J. and Terrry, K. (2008) 'Analyzing Paraphilic Activity, Specializations and Generalizations in Priests who Sexually Abused Minors', *Criminal Justice and Behaviour*, 35, 5, 615-628.

Terry, K. (2008), 'Stained Glass: The Nature and Scope of Child Sexual Abuse in the Catholic Church', *Criminal Justice and Behaviour*, 35, 5, 549-569.

Valcour, F. (1990), 'The treatment of Child Sex Abusers in the Church', in S. J. Rossetti (ed), *Slayer of the Soul: Child Sexual Abuse and the Catholic Church* (pp 45-66), Mystic, Connecticut: Twenty-Third Publications.

White, M. And Terry, K. (2008), 'Child Sexual Abuse in the Catholic Church. Revisiting the Rotten Apple Explanation', *Criminal Justice and Behaviour*, 35, 5, 658-678

Wilson, S. (1984), 'The Myth of Motherhood a Myth: The Historical View of European Child Rearing', *Social History*, 9, 181-198.

Notes:

1. The Bishop of Ferns, Bishop Brendan Comiskey, resigned for his part in the alleged inadequate response to abuse cases in his Wexford diocese.

2. Bishop John Magee, Bishop of Cloyne, stepped aside following allegations that he mishandled abuse complaints in his diocese, in order to prepare for a commission of investigation to be held by the state in his diocese into the handling of abuse complaints.

3. The Ferns Inquiry into the handling of abuse complaints in the diocese of Ferns reported in 2005. The commission of investigation into the handling of abuse complaints in the Archdiocese of Dublin is due to report in the autumn of 2009.

4. The Commission to Inquire into Child Abuse in the Industrial and Reformatory Schools, run by the religious orders on behalf of the state, presented its five volume report in May 2009.

5. Child sexual abuse by Catholic clergy has been reported in Argentina, Australia, Austria, Belgium, Brazil, Canada, Chile, China, Colombia, France, Germany, Ireland, Mexico, New Zealand, Nigeria, the Philippines, Poland, Scotland, South Africa, Spain, Tanzania, the United Kingdom and the United States of America.

6. Foucault (2004: 49, 50) conceptualised discourse as 'a group of relations established between institutions, economic and social processes, behavioural patterns, systems of norms, techniques, types of classification and modes of characterisation'.

7. My research was conducted in a treatment centre in Ireland with clerical men who had perpetrated sexual abuse against minors. Grateful acknowledgement is made of the financial contribution made towards the cost of the research project by the Irish Episcopal Conference, The Franciscan Order and the Irish Jesuits. My clinical experience in working as a psychotherapist with individual adults and adolescents who

had experienced sexual abuse in childhood and with men who have perpetrated sexual offences spans a period of twenty five years. The results of this research form part of a book currently in press.

8. For a fuller discussion of these issues see Haug (2001) and Foucault (1990, 1992, 1998).

9. See Foucault (1990, 1992,1998).

10. For a fuller discussion of the history of the concept see Jenkins (1998) and institutional practices of pederasty see Bleibtreu-Ehrenberg (1990).

11. A full treatise of this literature is beyond the scope of this article.

12. Repeat offending is seen as similar to recidivism in the John Jay study, although I would argue that it is different. Most research on repeat sexual offending focuses on recidivism – a form of repeat offending in which additional acts of sexual abuse occur after some form of correctional intervention, such as incarceration or participation in a treatment programme. Some studies define recidivism as a new charge whilst others define it as a new conviction. Whatever the case, the idea of recidivism is that an offender has reoffended following an intervention. The John Jay team interpret the reporting of the allegation as an intervention for the purposes of their analysis of repeat offending whereas my understanding of recidivism is that the intervention must be of a significant magnitude involving apprehension or treatment.

13. I wish to acknowledge the helpful comments on this subject of an anonymous reviewer of my book.

14. These issues are fully explored in Keenan (in press).

15. I successfully took a case through the Broadcasting Complaints Commission in 2002 against the Gerry Ryan Show on RTÉ 2 in which Gerry Ryan Show was found guilty of incitement to hatred and of being unfair and unbalanced in the manner in which they dealt with the issues involved in the release from prison of a Catholic priest who had served a sentence for the sexual abuse of minors.

List of Contributors

Seán Fagan is a Marist priest in Dublin, with more than fifty years experience teaching, counselling and writing in twelve countries in Europe, America, Africa and Asia, with a special ministry to gay and lesbian people for over 30 years. He is the author of Has Sin Changed? (1977), Does Morality Change? (1997) and What Happened to Sin? (2008) and was the subject of a special book published in his honour Quench not the Spirit (2005). For many years he was a frequent speaker on radio and television. He has published more than a hundred articles on theology, spirituality and religious life. He was Secretary General of the Society of Mary in Rome from 1983 to 1995.

A native of Belfast, **Brendan McConvery** is a member of the Irish Redemptorist Province. He studied scripture in Rome and Jerusalem and is currently teaching in St Patrick's College, Maynooth. He is a member of the editorial team of Scripture in Church and has served as reviews editor of the Irish Theological Quarterly.

Margaret Lee, a native of Ballingarry, Co. Limerick is a retired Social Worker who holds an MSc in Social Work Studies from the London School of Economics. She now lives in Newport, Co Tipperary.

Dáire Keogh is a member of the History Department at St Patrick's College, Drumcondra. In 2008, he was awarded an IRCHSS Government of Ireland Senior Research Fellowship to pursue a history of the Irish Christian Brothers, from their foundation up to 1968. The first volume of this appeared as *Edmund Rice and the First Christian Brothers* (Dublin, 2009).

Terry Prone is a communications consultant, broadcaster and writer. She is author of dozens of books including practical guides, short stories and bestselling fiction.

Tom O'Malley is a Barrister and Senior Lecturer in Law at NUI Galway. Publications include *Sexual Offences: Law, policy and Punishment* (1996), *Sentencing Law and Practice* (2nd edition, 2006), *The Criminal Process* (2009).

Donal Dorr is an Irish Kiltegan missionary priest and a former consultor to the Pontifical Commission on Justice and Peace. Donal has spent many years providing training and support for community activists and offering workshops on spirituality. He is the author of ten books dealing with various aspects of spirituality. His most recent book is *Spirituality our Deepest Heart's Desire*, Columba Press, 2008.

John Littleton, a priest of the Diocese of Cashel and Emly, is Head of Distance Education at The Priory Institute, Tallaght, Dublin. He was President of the National Conference of Priests of Ireland for six years (2001-2007), and is a weekly columnist with *The Catholic Times*. He co-edited *Irish and Catholic? Towards an Understanding of Identity* (2006), *Contemporary Catholicism in Ireland: A Critical Appraisal* (2008) and *What Being Catholic Means to Me* (2009).

Eamon Maher is Director of the National Centre for Franco-Irish Studies at the Institute of Technology, Tallaght, and editor of the *Reimagining Ireland* book series with Peter Lang, Oxford. He is a regular contributor of articles on the current state of Irish Catholicism and has recently co-edited a book with John Littleton titled *What Being Catholic Means to Me* (The Columba Press). He is currently working on a monograph on McGahern, *'The Church and its Spire': John McGahern and the Catholic Question*.

Dr Fainche Ryan, a Kerrywoman, is a lecturer in theology at the Mater Dei Institute, Dublin. She also works occasionally with the Redemptorist Mission and Novena Team.

Tony Flannery is a Redemptorist priest and well-known writer. He is a native of Attymon, Co Galway.

Joe O'Riordan is a primary school teacher based in county Galway. Since finishing his Bachelor of Education degree in 2003 he has taught in both multidenominational and Catholic run schools. In 2008 he completed a research Masters in Philosophy.

Dr Marie Keenan lectures at the School of Applied Social Science, UCD. She is a Registered Psychotherapist who has worked extensively with victims and perpetrators of sexual crime. Her forthcoming book, to be pubished in 2010, is on clerical men who have perpetrated sexual offences against minors.